THE UNIVERSITY OF MICHIGAN

CENTER FOR SOUTH AND SOUTHEAST ASIAN STUDIES

MICHIGAN PAPERS ON SOUTH AND SOUTHEAST ASIA

Ann Arbor, Michigan
USA

Men to Bombay Women at Home

Urban Influence on Sugao Village, Deccan Maharashtra, India,

1942-1982

Hemalata C. Dandekar

MICHIGAN PAPERS ON SOUTH AND SOUTHEAST ASIA
CENTER FOR SOUTH AND SOUTHEAST ASIAN STUDIES
THE UNIVERSITY OF MICHIGAN   MICHIGAN 28

Library of Congress Number: 85-48240

ISBN 0-89148-035-8 (cloth)
ISBN 0-89148-036-6 (paper)

Photographs courtesy of Hemalata C. Dandekar

Printed in the United States of America

To the memory of my father,
Chintaman Damodar Dandekar.
He faced with integrity the paradoxes
that beset the modern Indian man.

CONTENTS

Contents

FIGURES

TABLES

PREFACE

Luxurious five-star hotels belonging to multinational chains and bustling with elegantly clad men and women exist in Bombay, Delhi, and Calcutta. As in other cities in developing countries, these modern palaces are located in areas thickly populated with street hawkers, pavement dwellers, and beggars, who possess little more than what they carry with them. These two kinds of people occupy the same cities without living in the same worlds, and the dichotomy between them has become a problematic, structural characteristic of all developing countries.

This dualism is one of the results of the last three or four decades of planning for development in India. Of all the countries to gain independence following the Second World War, India was the first to embark on national planning efforts to achieve rapid socioeconomic change. Although it was a predominantly rural country, in these early efforts most investments were concentrated in industrialization at chosen metropolitan centers. The assumption was that the benefits, although initially concentrated in core cities, would in time spread to peripheral areas. Rural development would follow.

Today, almost forty years after Indian independence, a long list of material improvements in village life can be cited: more miles of better roads; more schools and increased literacy; electricity; piped water systems providing clean drinking water; primary health centers; post offices; cooperative credit societies; and so on. Relevant figures are often quoted to prove that rural areas are developing. These statistics, and the literature that accompanies them, though satisfying to development planners, rarely give a sense of what it is like to live in a village in India today or how life there has been changing.

This book is meant to fill this gap in the literature. It attempts to portray the fine-grained impacts of industrialization and the availability of work in a major city on a single village, called Sugao in this book, located some 150 miles from Bombay. It describes some of the effects of macro-level, "top-down," development planning on a village microcosm as observed from the vantage point of the village itself. As far as it is possible for an outsider to do so, I have attempted to understand and convey the perceptions of some of the people I got to know well in Sugao. It is my belief that, contrary to the conventional wisdom prevalent in the field of development, particularly economic development, such micro case-study, worm's-eye views *are* important to our understanding of rural development in countries such as India, and that this "bottom-up" vantage point yields insights seldom obtained when macro-level, aggregate statistics are scanned for indications of "progress" in Third World nations. Micro case-studies can improve our understanding of social systems and can help capture descriptively the mechanisms and processes at play.

With people and place a priority, rather than numbers and statistics, Sugao is described in a regional context. The village's evolving relationship to local market centers and the increasing linkages and flows of people, money, and goods between it and the city of Bombay are examined. Also described are the impact on the village and its families of changes in living and working conditions in the city and of cash and kind remittances sent home. The psychological and social toll of prolonged family separations is elaborated from a societal as well as an individual perspective. Thus, this book deals both with the worker in the urban industrial milieu and with the family "at home" in the rural, agrarian hinterland over four critical decades of planned, induced change.

The importance of attempting to maintain the fullest possible understanding of the social and cultural forces at work and in conflict in Indian development needs no explication. Such efforts pertain not only to scholarly inquiry but to questions of policies involving investments, international assistance programs, political alignments, and the like. Decisions about such matters will continue to be made, with consequences affecting millions. It thus seems vital to try to provide information about and perspectives on the way village society truly works, perspectives that may furnish the grounding in reality too often absent in theoretical discussions or quantified analysis of planned social change.

An earlier version of this book was described by an editor who was impressed by it, but could not get it approved by his discipline-rooted reviewers, as a mermaid book: "not enough fish to fry and not enough woman to love." Interdisciplinary writing is particularly vulnerable to such criticism, for it rarely tests directly the established theoretical models embedded in a discipline. The methods used to collect information are at worst suspect by "mainstream" disciplinary scholars and at best discounted as "merely descriptive." It has been difficult, in the face of such attitudes, to persist in a belief that the understanding of development is enhanced by such work, which may allow to surface certain relationships and forces not recognized in the ruling paradigms of traditional, discipline-based research. My hope is that this book will not only interest the nonexpert who is curious about development processes and India, but also will serve to broaden the understanding of planners and other specialists. India is, and for some years will continue to be, a country where people live predominantly in the countryside. With this documentation of life at the grassroots, village level, and by the amplification of voices heard in Sugao, I have attempted to enhance such an understanding.

ACKNOWLEDGMENTS

The years of research that culminated in the writing of this book have left me with a rich legacy of friendships. John Friedmann started me on this journey and guided me through the transition from architect to planner during my student days in the School of Urban Planning at UCLA. Without him this work would not have been started. Peter Marris has consistently encouraged me to write and rewrite, and provided a valuable perspective about earlier versions of this book.

In Poona, India, affiliation with the Gokhale Institute of Politics and Economics was crucial. V. M. Dandekar (no relation to myself), director of the Gokhale Institute when I began my fieldwork in India, suggested Sugao as a possible study site and generously made available not only the surveys of the village completed by the institute in 1942 and 1958 but his own research notes and unpublished writings on the village. My Sugao and Bombay fieldwork builds upon that of M. B. Jagtap, a man of village Maharashtra. His endorsement of my work gave me credibility with Sugao people, and his knowledge of them and insights into rural life in general have been invaluable. I shall always treasure the memories of our hikes together through the Deccan countryside. Sulabha Brahme guided me through the intricacies of field research methods in India. The views expressed in this book have been strongly influenced by her perspective. I have enjoyed many hours of discussion of a wide range of issues, some of which led to our collaborative papers on women and rural industries. In her I discovered a new, particularly Indian, facet of feminist awareness.

Acknowledgments

It is impossible to thank adequately the people of Sugao who gave generously and good-naturedly of their time. The names of villagers mentioned in this book, and of the village itself, have been changed in an attempt to protect them from any repercussions that might arise from this documentation of their confidences. I am particularly indebted to three Sugao women, Bharatibai, Priya, and Suma, who lovingly accepted me as a member of their family. When Suma died in a household accident in 1982, I lost a young sister. Rani, our neighbor, was another close friend and confidant. Sharing daily events with these women gave me an intimate insight into village living, especially as it determines a woman's sphere. My field assistant, Vilas, cheerfully hiked with me to outlying fields, even in adverse weather, to corner some of the more recalcitrant respondents to my questionnaires.

Understanding the reality of daily life in Sugao changed my world view. Living there provided me an opportunity to return to my native land and rediscover it along with my own "Indianness." I shall always remember village faces and conditions, recollections of which have compelled me to complete this book.

A Fulbright-Hays Dissertation Award funded the first two years of fieldwork in India in 1976–77 and a travel grant from the American Institute of Indian Studies allowed a return visit in the summer of 1979. A Postdoctoral Fellowship and teaching position at the Massachusetts Institute of Technology in 1979–80 provided time for reflection. A Rackham Faculty Grant from The University of Michigan supported a return visit in 1982 and a Rackham Publication Fund award from the university helped bring this volume to print. The university's College of Architecture and Urban Planning helped meet some of the final costs of preparing this document.

I am grateful to my parents, Mrinalini and Chintaman Dandekar, and to David Weisblat, for their faith in me as I proceeded through the fieldwork in typical headstrong fashion. Although my father's life ended before this book was completed, his years of encouragement of my independence have sustained me. Rudolf Schmerl has provided encouragement as well as critical editorial and organizational help. I am indebted to Nancy Nishikawa for her heroic efforts in preparing earlier versions of this manuscript. Finally I would like to express gratitude to the Center for South and Southeast Asian Studies at The University of Michigan for publishing this book and to its editor Janet Opdyke for her meticulous care and dedication beyond the call of duty.

Hemalata Dandekar
Ann Arbor, September 1986

INTRODUCTION

My first glimpse of village Sugao was at twilight. It had been a hot and dry October day, one of many I had spent walking through dusty fields and riding in rattling buses in various districts of Maharashtra State, searching for a suitable village for a study of the impacts of planned socioeconomic development on rural areas of independent India. This quest for a "typical" village had lasted so long that my friends in Poona teased me that I was being more selective than someone searching for a suitable mate in an arranged marriage.

This journey through the Deccan countryside was an eye-opening one for me, a city-bred Maharashtrian fresh from the School of Urban Planning at UCLA in the United States. I arrived with an intellectual baggage of development theories and a romanticized picture of Indian rural life gleaned largely from novels and short childhood vacations in the countryside. These villages, so foreign and alien, fit none of my preconceptions. They seemed undifferentiated, all equally inscrutable to an outsider like me. The closed, stone-walled houses, huddled together on a bleak landscape, presented, as did their inhabitants, a uniformly hostile face to the stranger. I realized with a shock to my liberal, urban understanding that families did not randomly occupy houses in a village. Caste and family status, powerful determinants in village India, influenced location. Inevitably the formerly untouchable and "depressed" castes such as the Mahars lived segregated on the village outskirts.

1

Sugao is nestled in the foothills of low, flat-topped spurs of the Mahadev hills in the *mawal* (sufficient rainfall) area of Satara District, Maharashtra. Its picturesque setting and patches of cool, green, irrigated land made it appear more inviting than villages to the east, in the drought-prone region I had visited earlier. My reception by its inhabitants was warmer too. My guide, M. B. Jagtap, a man from rural Maharashtra who was to become a good friend, had lived in Sugao and was respected by its people. In fact, I later discovered that some Sugao people addressed him as "uncle," a strong affirmation of acceptance and kinship. As we walked the three miles of dirt road that led from the highway to the village, we were greeted often and affectionately. One farmer even greeted me effusively, thinking I was a Canadian woman who had lived in Sugao some years before. I am somewhat taller and lighter skinned than most Maharashtrian women, and this may partly explain his confusion, but his mistake illustrated the fact that to the villager anyone from the urban, outside world, whether from Bombay or Toronto, is foreign.

We entered the village from the southeast, skirting Mahar housing, and came to our destination, the house of Bharatibai Jadhav. Climbing the generous stone steps on which I was destined to spend countless hours talking to Sugao residents, observing their goings-on and they mine, I had a sense of having arrived home. In the entry room were three or four women dressed, as peasant women usually are in this part of the country, in traditional nine-yard *saris* of dark hue. They were sorting through heaps of peanut plants, plucking off the mature nuts and setting the foliage aside for fodder. My city eyes would not have recognized the plant but for the mature nuts. Little did I realize that before I finished my study I would be able to distinguish different varieties of peanuts from a hundred yards away when they were only tiny plants.

We were received with a flurry of welcomes. Bharatibai was apparently in the fields supervising the peanut harvest. Widowed and owning one of the larger farms in Sugao, she had sole responsibility for managing its cultivation. Her granddaughter, Priya, came bustling out of an inner room to greet us. She was a beautiful young woman, eighteen or so years old, dressed startlingly in a contemporary six-yard *sari* of the kind city women typically wear. Bright-eyed, dark-hued, earrings sparkling and two braids reaching to her waist, she reminded me of former school friends in Bombay. Priya was in fact a third-year college student, working toward a degree in commerce, who commuted to the nearby market town of Wai for her classes. In the months to come, I realized that the modernity she projected was deceptive, but on this first day I could only wonder at the urbanity of this village woman, in stark contrast to the others in the room, clad in somber earth-toned *saris* decorously draped over their heads upon our arrival.

When Priya learned the reason for my visit she exclaimed that Sugao would be a perfect village for my study and that I must stay with them while I did the work—comforting words to my tired mind and body. She made us tea, brought out in dingy, cracked cups. A characteristic of Indian rural life, this cracked and grimy teacup. When there is little running water and soap is too expensive even for washing oneself, the traditional cleansing agent, mud, is used to scour the pottery, with predictable results. Cooking and eating utensils made of brass, copper, or cast iron take kindly to this method of cleaning, but the ceramics and cheap aluminum ware that are now pervasive in the village do not, and the results are far from desirable, aesthetically or hygienically.

After drinking the welcome cup of tea, we walked through the intricate maze of village alleys trying to get a sense of the community before darkness set in. The pleasant aroma of millet bread, baked for the evening meal on wood-burning, terra cotta stoves, wafted from each household. Cattle and goats, bells tinkling, returned with their masters from the fields. Loaded bullock carts creaked along the boulder-strewn lanes in the dusk. It was a pastoral, somewhat feudal scene.

Invited into the home of an old friend of my guide, we sat in the dark on the dung-plastered floor, huddled around a fire. Our host roasted freshly harvested peanuts and insisted we drink cups of warm milk, an especially hospitable gesture as I learned later, while he regaled us with stories of his continuing litigation with his two brothers over division of the family lands. As far as I could gather, the two brothers had worked in the textile mills of Bombay, an important occupation for men who migrate from Sugao. They invested their savings in small businesses, which were profitable, allowing them to purchase additional lands in Sugao. Our host had remained in the village, cultivating these and the family's ancestral lands, which were jointly owned. Now the city-bred brothers were ready to retire from their work in the mills, and, as is customary, were planning to return to the village. However, contrary to tradition, at least until recently, they were asking for a division of the family holdings, claiming major portions of the newly acquired land on the grounds that they had earned the money for its purchase.

"But," our host said, jabbing his finger at us for emphasis, "they would never even have smelled that this land was available if my ear hadn't been close to the ground to catch rumors of possible sales. You know how it is. No one advertises such intentions here in the country. They think this is Bombay where they can look in the newspaper for announcements when they are ready to buy. I had to rub the seller's back, talk sweetly to him, while my brothers were going to the movies in Bombay." Slapping his right hand in the palm of his left, he said, "Not only that, if I hadn't been watching out for our family lands and cultivating them, the lands themselves might have been lost to the sharecropper under this new land-to-the-tiller legislation! I am going to file a countersuit against my brothers tomorrow at the district courthouse in Wai." How incongruous this talk of legal writs, affidavits, and court appearances seemed in a setting which reminded one of medieval times. It was not long before I realized that such dichotomies are now a characteristic of Indian village life, which has been in the throes of change since independence in 1947.

The following days confirmed my first impression that life in Sugao was generally rudimentary, archaic, and stagnant, yet in transition. Most farmers cultivated their crops with primitive wooden implements and animal power. Village lanes and alleys were mere dirt pathways, the larger ones rutted by bullock carts and dotted with boulders and stones. Open drains on the sides of main alleys were lined with rough stone and in general disrepair,

A main alley in the Jadhav ward. Afternoon is women and children's time to frequent public spaces.

Bullock cart near a village dwelling.

clogging up and becoming dysfunctional when the rains came. In the monsoons one inevitably had to traverse the mud, ankle-deep in places, to get from house to house. In the summer the road got progressively drier and dustier and at the peak of the hot weather every passing vehicle, animal, or human kicked up a cloud of dust that coated the throat and left one coughing.

Most of the pushing, pulling, and hauling of agricultural implements and products was done by animals or people. Although the village had two or three tractors and a couple of motorcycles, these were used largely for such purposes as transport to the market town of Wai. What went to and from the fields was carried, except for the occasional bullock cart, on the heads of men, women, and children.

Housing, too, though picturesque to the urban eye, was primitive, lacking water and sanitary facilities. Families collected water from common taps and stored it in the house for use during the day. People went to designated fields on the outskirts of the village to relieve themselves. Only a third or so of the houses had electrical connections for domestic use, and families with electricity used it for lighting or for powering the radio that was often tuned, at peak volume, to a station transmitting the latest pop songs from Hindi movies.

But just as clearly the village was caught up in modern times and was changing. For economic reasons almost half of Sugao's men live and work in the city of Bombay, more than 150 miles and an uncomfortable ten-hour bus ride from Sugao. The city plays a crucial role not only in Sugao's economy but in that of most villages in Satara District. This relationship between villages on the Deccan Plateau and cities on the Konkan, or western coastal strip, is not new. Sugao is a nucleated village with clustered houses spreading out on the slope of a small foothill of the Mahadev Range on the eastern banks of a stream called the Chandraganga. Village lands fan out around the settlement, which has been inhabited for several centuries, probably due to its proximity to a year-round source of water.[1] In the village the major axis lane runs east-west downhill (see figure 1). At its eastern end, on top of the hill, is a temple

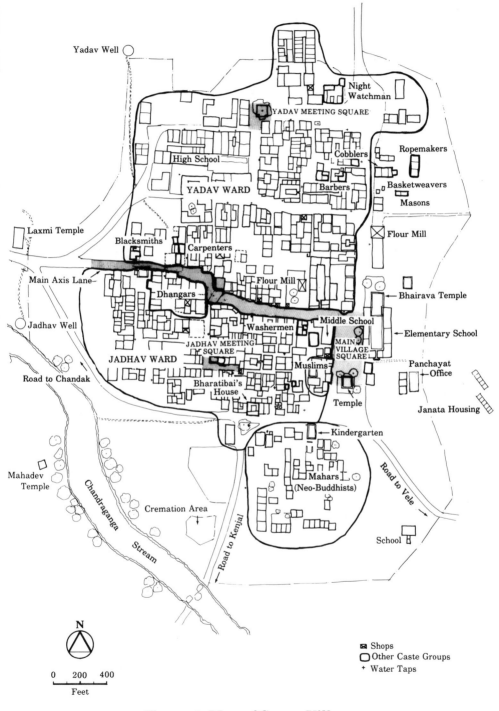

Figure 1: Map of Sugao Village

dedicated to the god Bhairava. To the west, at the bottom of the hill, is another dedicated to the goddess Laxmi. Bhairava and Laxmi, brother and sister, are the most important deities in the village, around whom its religious and ceremonial life revolves. Folklore has it that the gods were brought to this site by a group of nomadic traders called the Pandharas. Apparently Sugao was a place where the Pandharas camped on their journey west over the Sahayadri Mountains to trade Deccan grain for rice grown on the coastal plain of the Konkan. This connection to the coast was sustained for centuries, because until recently Sugao weavers sold all their blankets to the rice farmers of the Konkan.

The establishment of a textile industry in Bombay in the 1860s, its subsequent expansion in the 1930s, and its continued prominence in the urban and regional economy in the 1980s have changed the lives and work of people in the Deccan. This influence has been particularly strong in Satara District, from which a steadily increasing stream of men have migrated to Bombay to work as mill hands.

The cotton textile industry in India has always been headquartered in the city of Bombay, and its labor drawn primarily from the Konkan and Deccan regions of Maharashtra State. Although now in decline, the textile industry continues to be a major force in the lives of these rural people.[2] A trickle of Sugao men migrated to Bombay at the turn of the century, drawn to newly available jobs as dock workers in the port. Most were from higher-caste Maratha families (see table 1) who migrated to the city seasonally at the time of the *rabi* (second, dry-season) crop while their women remained in Sugao, working within the joint or extended family, primarily in agriculture (see table 2).[3] By 1942, as can be seen in table 3, the main occupation of the Sugao male migrant to Bombay was that of textile worker. By then migration was no longer seasonal, as jobs in the mills had become more difficult to obtain. Men migrated year-long for all their productive work years, returning to their families once or twice a year for vacations.

Over the years, men from the village have become better educated, have developed more contacts in Bombay, and have been able to find better, more diversified work in the city. Thus jobs in the textile industry have been an avenue for upward mobility for village men. Nevertheless, mill work has remained a mainstay occupation for Sugao migrants, despite having dropped from 67 percent of all migrants to Bombay in 1942 to 41 percent in 1977. In real numbers there were more men from Sugao in the textile industry in 1977 (195) than in 1942 (135).

Industrial growth in Bombay and the continuous departure of village men for jobs in the city also have changed the lives and work of those remaining in Sugao. By 1977 almost half of the adult males (468 out of 965) had left for work in Bombay, leaving their families behind. Since 1942 the percentage of families with no resident adult male has ranged from 23 to 26 percent (see table 2). An increasing proportion of the population that remains in the village is female, and women do more of the work involved in farming. This, however, has resulted in few fundamental changes in the way Sugao society is organized or in the relative status and power of the men and women who remain behind.

In early 1982 I visited some of the Sugao mill workers in the city. One of the longest strikes in the history of the Bombay textile industry was brewing. In the middle of a long discussion about Sugao with a group of leaders from the village who are active in the labor unions we heard sounds of glass shattering and crowds shouting. It was late at night and I was quickly provided with a taxi driven by one of "our men"—a man, that is, who was related to a Sugao family through marriage. I was ceremoniously but firmly told to get safely home. The strike that ensued some months later continued in one form or another for almost two years. While informal and formal resolutions have occurred, the long-term effects of that strike on the people of Sugao and villages like it remain unknown in the detail. This book does not address the fate of the Bombay textile industry, still in flux and under stress, nor the outcome of the strike.[4] No doubt there will be profound implications for the viability of the village economy and, in particular, for the livelihood of farmers with too little land to subsist on. Documented in this book is only what was known, on the eve of this major upheaval, about Sugao people, their lives, and the effect of the outmigration of men to Bombay.

As my guide and I continued our tour, I realized that Sugao was an ideal village for me. Mr. Jagtap was an old and trusted friend of Bharatibai Jadhav's deceased husband and of the remaining male members of the family. With his introduction—he told Bharatibai that I was the "last deposit" he was going to make on her doorstep—I was invited to live in the household, an unusual one in that it consisted only of three women: Bharatibai, who was childless, and her two step-granddaughters. Since the family was relatively affluent and somewhat enlightened, the two girls were getting more than the normal education. Priya, the elder, was in her last year of college at Wai, and Suma was in her final year of high school.

When Mr. Jagtap and I returned to Bharatibai's house, we found it bustling with activity. With quiet dignity Bharatibai, a slight, fair-skinned woman, welcomed us and made us feel at home. In our absence Suma had returned from school. More reserved than Priya, she expressed her pleasure at our presence through various gestures of hospitality—making tea, sweeping the floor before she would allow us to sit, and smiling shyly. In the following days Mr. Jagtap and I visited other local villages and hamlets to see if one of them might be more suitable for my study, but after one particularly glorious hike over the mountain range that separates Sugao from Wai, I beheld again the beauty of this village at dusk. Basking in the familial welcome of Bharatibai, Suma, and Priya, I knew that I must do my work in Sugao. Gratefully I accepted their invitation and thus found a loving and secure home, as well as a base from which to conduct my investigations. I left the next day to make the necessary preparations for my fieldwork.

Study Design

Planners and politicians who evaluate the results of development efforts in India cite various "improvements" in today's lifestyle as indicative of "development." When speaking of rural areas, they list the existence of more miles of better roads, more schools, increased literacy, electricity, piped drinking water, primary health centers, post offices, cooperative credit societies, and so on as the tangible manifestations of progress, implying that such easily quantifiable changes, isolated phenomena that they are, add up to development. Some of these changes have resulted directly from efforts by the government to bring about planned socioeconomic change. Of the various programs implemented under the national five-year plans, some were specifically aimed at rural areas. In addition, life in Sugao and villages like it has been affected by post-independence economic changes in the nation and in the region. The desire to study these direct and indirect effects of planning and to assess the implications for rural areas (given that India in 1975 was still 80 percent rural) suggested a study of a village such as Sugao.

As noted above, when planners and politicians talk about change they usually quote statistics to prove that rural areas are developing, tending to consider each instance of induced change in isolation. They rarely ask how these separate, sectoral changes affect a village's economic and social relationships with the region around it or whether these changes result in net gains in the long as well as the short term. To obtain a total picture, additional questions should be asked: How are these changes affecting the day-to-day lives of the different groups of inhabitants within the social and economic hierarchy of the village? Have there been substantive improvements in the villagers' ability to meet the basic needs of food, shelter, and clothing in all strata? Have these occurred in relative terms? In absolute terms? Do villagers from all strata have access to the new improvements in village life? Has the distribution of productive assets become more equitable?

What is rarely analyzed, in short, is how these changes have affected the various groups within the village society and modified the village's relationship with its region. Even when a more comprehensive viewpoint is taken, change is not considered within a dynamic context wherein transformations are considered over time and analyzed in terms of their implications for the future. A more holistic look at a village community in the process of transition is critical if one is to gain some understanding of how development feels to those who are the targets of the planned change. The experience of a few decades of planning has shown that without participation by the residents of a community in creating a better life for themselves, self-sustaining development and progress become impossible. The quality of people's existence is enhanced as they become more secure and gain control of their futures. In a village such as Sugao an increased sense of security and control for everyone would be as good an indication of development, and perhaps a better one, than statistics of growth or change.

My goal in the study was to examine the transformations in rural life then occurring in India from a more holistic point of view. I decided to explore socioeconomic and spatial relationships within one village and document their impact on its people. I hoped to elicit the meaning of the changes occurring in village life in terms of some organizing principle or framework. Finally, I wanted to discover whether the economic structure was changing faster than the social, and if social relationships were changing faster than the values in which they were embedded, and the consequences of such uneven shifts for overall "societal development" as well as for subgroups and individuals within that society.

Of Indian origin and from a Marathi-speaking family, I had little hesitation in choosing Maharashtra State as the site for my study. With a 1981 population of almost 63 million, Maharashtra is India's most urbanized state. At the same time it is still predominantly rural: some 68 percent of its population continues to live or be based in the countryside. If urbanization is regarded as a major indicator of modernization and development, then Maharashtra should provide a prime example of the changes that occur when the "benefits" of industrial development in the cities diffuse into the rural hinterland. Thus, the choice of Sugao, on the Deccan Plateau and within the hinterland of the city of Bombay, was by no means arbitrary.

To perform this study to my satisfaction, I first lived in Sugao for more than a year and a half (1976–77) and then spent an

Mr. Jagtap, Bharatibai, and Suma on our doorstep.

Suma and Priya in our kitchen.

additional three months in Bombay finding and interviewing migrants from the village. My time in the village was spent in making friends, sharing routines, administering household and small business questionnaires, and experiencing the day-to-day reality of the villagers' lives. Slowly a multidimensional picture emerged. The shifting balance between rural and urban, traditional and modern, which I had observed the first day was reinforced by aggregate numbers produced from the surveys, by anecdotes and descriptions offered by the people themselves, and by my first-hand observations of village life and relationships. I have attempted to convey this picture in the belief that only through such wider, contextual perspectives can the effects of development be assessed. For this reason Sugao is described in a regional context. Its evolving relationship to local market centers is examined, as well as the increasing linkages and flows of people, money, and goods between it and the city of Bombay. Changes in living and working conditions in the city over forty years and the impact of cash-and-kind remittances sent home to the village and its families are described in order to hint at the psychological and social toll of prolonged family separations from a societal as well as an individual perspective. The goal is to deal both with the family "at home" in the rural, agrarian hinterland and with the worker in the urban industrial milieu over forty critical years of planned, induced change.

The story is a simple one, for Sugao is an ordinary "typical" village. The changes that have occurred there, however, demonstrate in microcosm the ways in which national planning and its subcategory, rural development planning, have affected the connections within and between traditional villages, and between villages and cities in India. The picture of Sugao that emerges permits some insights into trends that can be logically expected if the present direction of development continues.

Village Selection and Field Methods

When I first conceived of this village study, I discussed the idea with several eminent academics in Poona and Bombay. One particularly well-established sociology professor informed me that his female students did not work on village problems: village life was difficult for the middle-class urban student, particularly with the lack of good sanitary facilities, and especially difficult for the single female researcher concerned about personal safety. Trepidation resulting from this conversation and similar warnings from well-meaning friends and relatives, as well as an urbanite's inherited fears of the countryside and its alien social structure, troubled my search for a village base. The professor's attitude was not an isolated one. The fact that village living is intimidating to the Indian urban intellectual, male or female, is evident from the paucity of good analytic writing and research based on in-depth work at the village level.

As a result, while selecting a village for the type of detailed participant-observer study that I had in mind, other criteria became important beyond the village's representativeness in terms of size, location in and connection to transport and communications networks, range of amenities, and public services provided by the state. One of the major considerations for me was whether there was a person who could introduce me to a particular village in such a way that I could justify my presence there, execute the surveys, and ask necessary questions without causing undue anxiety and suspicion.

One quickly discovers that, in this part of Maharashtra (accounts of researchers who have worked in other regions indicate that this is typical in most Indian villages), the inhabitants live within a closed social system in which any outsider is regarded with suspicion. To gain acceptance it is necessary to be introduced to the villagers by someone they know and trust. To execute a study successfully, one must be accepted by important village leaders such as the *patil* (village headman), *sarpanch* (chairman of the elected village governing body), police *patil*, and the chairman of the cooperative credit society. The leaders are usually drawn from the wealthier and more powerful elements in the village, and convincing them that your study will not threaten their long-range interests or their present status is important. They exert a great deal of influence, and many villagers consult them before agreeing to be interviewed. It is helpful if one can convince the leaders to be at least indifferent to one's study and presence in the village. If, in fact, a leader becomes enthusiastic about a project, as happened with friends doing research at a nearby site, he is quite capable of rounding up recalcitrant respondents and locking them up in the village office with the investigator until the questionnaire is completed. Although these situations are rare, in many villages the headman does have the moral authority to do such things.

It is also important to introduce oneself to the block-level administrative officials. For this a letter of introduction from some authority or institute, such as the one I was given by the Gokhale Institute, is invaluable. With it I introduced myself to the *mamlatdar* at Wai (the *taluka,* or subdistrict-level, revenue official) and to the block development officer (the chief administrative officer in the area). These officials issued directions to their subordinate, village-level, office holders, the *talathi* for revenue and the *gram-sevak,* or village-level worker, that I should be given full access to government records and documents. Such sanction and acceptance, besides making access to data easier, validates one's existence in the eyes of the villagers.

Vacant housing is scarce in the countryside, and, as the sociology professor in Poona pointed out, it is unusual for a female researcher to live alone in a village. Thus another consideration in selecting a village was the availability of suitable living accommodations. In rural areas, the joint family system is prevalent and few women live alone. Those who do, such as a widow or a woman who belongs to a nuclear family but whose husband has recently migrated for work, are still part of a family or clan group and are protected by this in subtle ways. To be sure, in some villages there are government employees such as a nurse, medical officer, or schoolteacher who are women and who sometimes live alone. However, such women are rare and to some extent protected by their official status in the village. In most cases, they prevail upon some relative, such as a mother or aunt, to live with them, since a woman living alone can become the target of a variety of harassments or unwanted attention. Therefore, unless one is going to move into a village as part of a research team, in

Vilas and Mr. Jagtap at work on a survey.

Rani and I in the fields.

which case setting up a separate establishment is feasible, it is better for a single person, particularly a female, to live with a family as their guest, even though there will be practically no privacy in the living arrangement.

Sugao is fairly representative of villages in Satara District. It is not too far from major transport and road facilities, and is in fact connected by a dirt road to a state highway. At the same time it is not on any major road or rail line. It does not have a strong political leader who can channel state funds and programs to his home village.[5] As is typical of most villages, the people of Sugao are fairly apathetic about government programs. The leaders rarely approach development agencies on behalf of the village as a whole, and the officials in charge seldom visit Sugao.

India now has a well-developed tradition of research in the social sciences and an internationally recognized body of scholars. I knew this when I returned to Maharashtra, and, as I believed it was important to build upon existing work in the country and to collaborate with resident scholars if at all possible, I was happy to accept an affiliation with the Gokhale Institute of Politics and Economics. The institute, which has been deeply involved in the study and analysis of rural, and particularly agricultural, development, is located in the city of Poona in Maharashtra State. Much of its fieldwork and data collection have centered on the Marathi-speaking region of Maharashtra, and access to this information, as well as to the institute's experienced research and field staff, was extremely useful.

The institute provided me with raw data, in the form of completed questionnaires collected in Sugao during surveys executed in 1942–43 and 1957–58. In both surveys every household in the village had been interviewed. These materials provided very complete base-line data for demographic characteristics and assets distribution, as well as additional anecdotal information about a variety of subjects useful in assessing changes since 1942. Thus, I was able to draw upon quantitative and qualitative information obtained in the village in 1942 (before the inception of planned development in India) and again in 1957. This latter survey was replicated by me in 1976–77 in order to sketch the major measurable parameters of change that occurred during the planning decades.[6] This outline was supplemented by detailed first-hand observations and case studies aimed at capturing the qualitative nature of induced change and its impact on rural people. Subsequent trips were made to Sugao and Bombay for three months in 1979, a week in 1980, two months in 1981–82, and a month (in Bombay) in 1984–85.

My guide to Sugao, Mr. M. B. Jagtap, was principal field investigator during the earlier surveys and had lived in the village for more than five years. He was still employed by the Gokhale Institute in 1976–77, and the institute made him available for some assistance with my study. In addition, there were available at the Gokhale Institute both published and unpublished books and papers in Marathi and English on various facets of life in Sugao, including such subjects such as agricultural development, village and family politics, history, land-reform legislation and its impact on the village, and education. Dr. V. M. Dandekar, director of the institute, and well known for his work on agricultural development in Maharashtra, was familiar with Sugao and provided written notes and published material on the subject. Several unpublished manuscripts by individuals affiliated with the institute, and publications on this and similar villages, also were extremely useful.[7]

Rural Development Planning in India

India's early national-planning efforts to achieve rapid socioeconomic change were concentrated in industrialization at chosen metropolitan centers, on the assumption that the benefits would "trickle down" through the economy (Myrdal 1968; Hirschman 1958; Rodwin 1963). Indian planners believed that the initial benefits would be concentrated in the core cities, but that they would in time spread to rural, peripheral areas; rural development would follow as a corollary to urban development. The assumption was that countries like India, newly emerging from colonialism, would replicate the process of economic growth of the developed countries, whether capitalist or socialist (Rostow 1960).

The plan was to promote rapid industrialization by systematically adopting advanced technology from the industrialized countries, making judicious investments of public funds through the instruments of central planning. From the beginning, centralized planning was accepted in India, and the principle that it is the business of government to be the planner, energizer, promoter, and director of accelerated development was little disputed (Waterston 1965; Lewis 1962). When India attained independence in 1947, Prime Minister Nehru was already one of the strongest proponents of this type of planning for national development.

Although fundamentally conforming to the model of development through industrialization, nearly all the Indian national plans recognized that it was also important to promote complementary rural development and reduce urban-rural disparities in wealth. However, the impact of industrial development on rural areas was not addressed, and most investments made in the countryside were in agriculture. Increases in agricultural production were stimulated through major and minor irrigation projects; promotion of cash-crop production; consolidation of landholdings; provision of better seeds, equipment, and fertilizer; and credit for agricultural investments. A system of extension services was established to introduce scientific farming techniques. Regulated markets were established, investments were made in roads and communications, and cooperatives were founded to buy and sell agricultural products and facilitate the marketing of goods in rural areas.

The consequence of investing in industry and in commercialization of agriculture was that, in both urban and rural areas, the gap between persons involved in the corporate formal sectors and in the informal, traditional, subsistence sectors began to widen. The rural landless and land poor found themselves squeezed out of their traditional positions in village society and began to migrate to the city, resulting in overcrowding and the proliferation of slums in urban areas. City services and infrastructure such as housing were unable to meet the needs of the burgeoning population.

Gradually stemming migration to the city by improving rural life and by diversifying the rural economy became a planning objective. Planners designed programs to keep people in the villages by making the countryside more and the city less attractive, by, for example, the provision of postal service, health-care facilities, clean drinking water, and electricity in the countryside. A large body of literature on growth centers, and in particular the works on India by E. A. J. Johnson (Moseley 1974; Johnson 1970, 1972), sparked attempts to create nodes of growth at small, interlinked, market towns; these, it was hoped, would stimulate decentralized and integrated development of rural areas.

Under this approach, in Maharashtra and other parts of the country, the power and wealth of the rural elites have become increasingly obvious. The privileged have profited from such programs as tax-exempt status for agricultural income, government subsidies, and extension services. In Sugao they were the ones best able to make the switch to cash cropping, also encouraged by the government. They have used their growing wealth and power to consolidate their traditional hold on village life and have begun to flex their muscles in the district, regional, and state political arenas.

Increasingly the growing disparity between rural and urban and poor and affluent people, disillusionment with the industries-led model of development, and problems resulting from an unexpectedly large migration to major cities compelled Indian leaders to rethink development strategies. Improvement of the conditions in the countryside was still a major concern, and a variety of new programs, replete with administrative and political institutions, were implemented in different phases of rural development planning.

One greatly publicized and widespread institution was the Panchayat Raj system of local elected government, introduced in 1959. It was meant to encourage local decision making and facilitate planning from below, so that programs could be designed to reflect local priorities and concerns. This, it was thought, would create a true democracy based on adult franchise and introduce some measure of egalitarianism through the concept of one person/ one vote.

The Panchayat Raj is a three-tiered structure of elected officials at the village, block, and district levels. A block is an administrative division which has varied in size but now consists of about one hundred villages with a total population of one hundred thousand people. At the village level the elected body is called a Gram (village) Panchayat. The word *"panchayat"* is taken from the unofficial bodies of *panch* (five) village elders that traditionally arbitrated and mediated intravillage matters. At the block level, there is a block *panchayat*, consisting of officials elected by the members of the various village *panchayats*. These work with the block development officer (BDO), the administrator responsible for development programs. A similar relationship exists between the Zilla Parishad, or district-level *panchayat*, and the development administration. Thus, the various administrators implementing rural development programs parallel the democratically elected, local government bodies. The expectation was that with such a structure the planning process would be more responsive to, and better informed about, the needs of local people. Unfortunately the lack of democratic traditions, the pervasiveness of caste, and the entrenchment of rural elites in the politics of villages like Sugao have worked against the realization of this goal.

The objective of increasing equity and distributing the benefits of development to the poor inspired such actions as land-ceiling legislation (restricting the amount of land any one individual can own) and tenancy reform (enhancing the rights to the land of those who cultivate it), both intended to get land into the hands of the tillers. However, in the case of villages such as Sugao, the impact on landownership was not dramatic. Programs were designed to support traditional village artisans with better tools, credit, and marketing networks, to help them compete with industry or at least sustain them until alternative jobs were created. Free, mandatory education was introduced and extended to improve skills the poor would require to compete for development benefits. These programs, and others like them, were implemented during different phases of the rural development effort in India. As priority was given to one objective or another, the emphasis would shift, but once initiated most programs were carried along with varying degrees of intensity. Thus, in a typical village like Sugao, one finds the residuum of numerous development programs with diverse objectives and target populations, the most recent programs receiving most of the institutional attention. Clarity and integration in a comprehensive development effort have not been achieved.

To date, rural development efforts have gone through three major phases, distinguishable by their explicitly stated central concerns and their allocation of funds for certain types of programs. It is becoming clear that if there is to be more successful rural-based development in India the national government's policies must be redesigned. The government must successfully involve and mobilize all strata of rural society and its policies must reflect the concerns and goals delineated in phase four (see figure 2) if a broad-based rural development strategy is to be achieved. The four phases of Indian development are briefly described below.

Phase I (1947–1960)

The first phase, which began prior to Indian independence in 1947 and continued until about 1960, drew on the philosophies of Mahatma Gandhi and Rabindranath Tagore. These leaders saw caste relationships and communal loyalties as standing in the path of social and economic reforms and set about changing them. Tagore started a model village-development program in Shriniketan, and Gandhi launched a rural development movement which reflected his concern with the improvement of the inner man. For Gandhi, self-help was the first step to moral advancement. Material advancement he saw merely as the means for solving the social and economic problems of the village. He was more interested in creating a vital spiritual fabric for rural life than in its economic transformation. About this time, rural development projects were initiated by American missionaries in India, notably by Dr. Spencer Hatch, an agriculturalist, and by William and

Charlotte Wiser, authors of *Behind Mud Walls,* who developed the India Village Service (Wiser and Wiser 1963).

Mosher, who has worked extensively in the field of international agricultural development, describes these various efforts as having three characteristics in common (Mosher 1976). First, they were concerned that rural people develop in health and breadth of vision, and that they derive increased satisfaction from their lives. Second, they saw that the existing pattern was an important conditioning factor in rural perceptions. Third, although they recognized the importance of economic development, it was not considered an essential precondition to the ultimate objective of social transformation.

The Etawah Project, inaugurated in the state of Uttar Pradesh in 1948 (Mayer 1958), was the first large-scale, government-financed, rural development effort that emphasized increasing agricultural production along with health care, rural industries, and the physical improvement of villages. It led to the National Community Development Program, launched in 1952, which in theory was to be a comprehensive program affecting every aspect of rural life. Under the first three five-year plans (1951–65), approximately 3 percent of total public outlays were devoted to this program, but this dropped to only 1 percent in the fourth plan (Ministry of Information and Broadcasting 1975, 1985). While funds also were allocated to sectoral ministries such as agriculture, health, and education, the low level of public outlays reflected the lack of emphasis on rural development. The Community Development and Cooperation Programs included an impressive list of projects such as the Village and Small Industries Program, Health and Family Planning, and Drought-prone Areas Program, but all were funded from this small allocation, as was the Panchayat Raj system of elected, local, government bodies.

Phase II (1960–1980)

Mosher identifies two factors as instrumental in revising the approach to rural development internationally: a technical

	1947–1960	1960–1985		1985 +
	PHASE I	PHASE II	PHASE III	PHASE IV
INSPIRATION	• Gandhi • Tagore	• Problems of industries-led development	• Widening disparities in income	• Failure to overcome dualistic development • Transformation of rural living
CONCERNS	• Elimination of caste and class • National integration • Village-focused development	• Diversify and strengthen rural economy	• Equity in development	
MAJOR GOALS	• Create egalitarian national society	• Increase agricultural production • Stimulate rural industries	• Reduce skewness in income and asset distribution	• Provide basic needs • Improve quality of rural life • Participation and mobilization of rural people
TYPICAL PROGRAMS	• Social development and physical welfare	• Agricultural extension • Green Revolution technology • Rural industries	• Credit and extension programs for small farmers • Aid to landless	• Build up societal structures that evoke commitment to development

Figure 2: Phases of Rural Development in India

revolution that drastically reduced the manufacturing cost of fertilizer in the mid-1950s, and the development of plant breeding and associated practices which produced high-yield varieties of cereals and increased expectations of a "Green Revolution." In India these changes, coupled with the implementation experience of the fifties, led to disillusionment with the industries-led approach to development and a conviction that agricultural growth was at least as important and now much more easily attainable.

This is not to say that there was a decisive shift to rural development or even to agricultural production as the central focus of development strategy. Budget allocations to agriculture during this period show that it continued to be secondary to urban-based industrial development. Agricultural programs stressed not just boosting food-grain production but increasing commercial cropping and monoculture, the production of commodities for which there was a demand in the international market. The plan was to meet local demand for food with increased cereal production; to export other commodities such as sugar, tobacco, and cotton; and to subsidize urban industrial expansion with the foreign exchange earned.

The impact of these shifts in cropping patterns on agricultural employment, on the distribution of assets within and among different strata of society, and on the nutritional levels of the rural population, was not given much consideration. Nor was the differing access of various strata of rural society to the benefits of agricultural programs considered. One well-known example of this approach is the introduction of high-yield varieties of wheat in the Punjab. Production and supply of improved seeds (particularly high-yield varieties), agricultural extension programs aimed at teaching scientific methods to the farmer, investments in minor irrigation projects, soil and water conservation, and fertilizer promotion were the characteristic programs initiated in this phase. But, because the reactions of and impact on the various societal groups directly and indirectly affected by the programs were not considered, inequities in asset distribution grew (Lo, Salih, and Douglass 1978). This state of affairs was reflected in Sugao, where the shift to cash crops such as sugarcane was made only by the large, landowning farmers. In reaction to this, and reflecting an increased emphasis by international institutions on equity in the distribution of development benefits, a third phase of rural development planning began in India.

Phase III (1970–1985)

Programs for rural development introduced during this phase reflected a concern for the poorer groups in rural society. Planners agreed that economic growth should be accompanied by income and asset redistribution leading toward greater equity. The priority given to this concept in India has varied with the political changes that have shaken the country.[8]

Phase IV (1985 and on)

Growing international recognition has been given to a self-reliant participatory model of development in which there is concern about the quality of life resulting from planned change, maintaining ecological balance, emphasizing cooperation, communal effort, social reorganization, and a focus on equity, distribution, mobilization of rural people, and rural development (Korten 1980). These concerns have yet to manifest themselves strongly in India, although arguments for such a self-reliant model can be heard. Some aspects of this approach are to be found in the integrated rural-development approach described in the fifth and sixth plans, but this effort is not aimed at introducing basic structural changes essential to a model of self-reliant development.

Barriers to Self-reliant Participatory Development in India

One structural reform essential for deep-seated change in rural India is the loosening of caste bonds. That caste loyalties stand in the way of group effort was recognized by Mahatma Gandhi, but despite his efforts Gandhian social workers were largely unsuccessful in trying to eradicate caste barriers. The Indian government, in recognition of this problem, has tried to downplay caste by secularizing education; the national plans are sprinkled with statements regarding the urgent need to remove caste and communal barriers and to reduce the disparity between rich and poor. However, such radical changes do not occur through the mere articulation of slogans nor through persuasion alone, as demonstrated by the ineffectiveness of the Gandhian voluntary workers.

In point of fact, most Indian leaders are not personally committed to removing social stratification and eradicating poverty if this must be at the cost of gains that can be made, under the current order, by the dominant class. This is not surprising, considering that most of the powerful themselves belong to the upper class. Given the lack of political commitment to this cause, few measures have been introduced to dramatically change asset distribution to the advantage of the poor.

At independence, attained after decades of colonial rule, a spirit of nationalism and self-reliance prevailed in India. There existed at that time an opportunity to introduce sweeping changes that would have established the grassroots involvement necessary to improve the condition of the masses. But even then planning was strongly centralized, incorporating principles largely based on ideology borrowed from the West. A new political system was conceived, democratic socialism, which had the goal of improving the welfare not just of Indian society but of the individuals who constituted it. Thus, at its inception the new order incorporated notions of egalitarianism at odds with the prevailing traditions in Indian society, which for centuries had maintained itself in equilibrium on the two hierarchical structures of caste and the joint or extended family. Today it is clear that, while gains are being made in overall development, the hierarchies of caste and family, both of which mediate against equity, will not be easily altered by democratic processes.

Notes

1. A small temple dedicated to the god Shiva (Mahadev) stands on the southern bank of the Chandraganga facing the village. The temple is constructed in the Chalukyan architectural style, which flourished from 550 to 750 A.D. This particular temple, however, could have been constructed much later; a more detailed study would be needed to precisely date it. The earliest references to the size and composition of the Sugao settlement that I was able to find in the Poona Archives came from some papers in the section known as the Inam Daftar. These papers are documents from the time of Mogul rule in the Deccan and consist largely of fragments of records of the taxes levied by rulers on the various villages in their domain. In the Inam Daftar, Satara District, section 44 contains papers relating to Sugao village. The oldest paper on Sugao is dated 1690 and indicates that at that time there were forty-three houses in the village subject to a tax. It also mentions taxes on five wool-weaving and six cotton-weaving looms. This implies that early record keeping for the village on the part of the state was quite detailed. Presumably Sugao was at this time a stable and permanent settlement.

2. By 1879, of the fifty-six spinning and weaving mills in India, three-quarters were in Bombay Presidency and more than half on Bombay Island itself; see Gadgil (1971, 54–56, 75–77, 104–8, 254–61, 327). This labor force was largely drawn from Bombay's hinterland. A 1957 survey of the textile labor force in Bombay shows that 45 percent came from the Konkan and almost 30 percent from the Deccan; see Patel (1963, 4–8). Harris (1978, 81) says that modern Bombay incorporates elements of two economic periods, nineteenth-century textiles and twentieth-century petrochemicals. The textile industry, employing 23 percent of the capital and 48 percent of the labor force in greater Bombay's industry, is still of decisive importance for the city. It indirectly continues to attract a sustained flow of new workers into certain heavily populated districts (Harris 1978, 81).

3. This caste selection seems to have been typical for textile
   labor recruitment in Bombay. Patel (1963, 43) notes in her
   survey of five hundred workers from the Konkan that almost
   63 percent were Maratha. Caste remains an important
   factor affecting an individual's life in village India. Its
   influence permeates most interactions and affects people's
   opportunities and decisions. Sugao is dominated by the
   Maratha caste (70 percent in 1977). The caste composition of
   the village, for 1942, 1958, and 1977 is given in table 1,
   listed by the locally accepted status hierarchy; it shows that
   caste composition has remained fairly constant over the
   years. The major caste groups in the village are the
   Marathas, Dhangars (weavers), Neo-Buddhists (formerly
   Mahars and considered untouchable), and a mixture of
   artisan castes.

The data on Sugao used in this book are drawn from several
surveys executed by the Gokhale Institute of Politics and
Economics, Poona, since 1936, particularly from two
comprehensive, socioeconomic, full-census surveys conducted
in 1942–43 and 1958–59. I repeated some components of
these in a full-census survey of village residents in 1976–77
during an eighteen-month residence and field investigation of
the village. A purposive sample of Bombay migrants was
intensively interviewed during the following three-month
period. The study was augmented by observations and
information collected during subsequent visits both to the
village and to Bombay in the summer of 1979, in December
and January of 1981–82, and in December and January of
1984–85. I also drew upon anecdotal information about
families who had some members living in Bombay during the
early 1900s, which had been collected by Gokhale Institute
fieldworkers in the thirties. Case studies indicate that some
of the families that are now well-to-do gained an economic
edge as a result of this early migration. The data also reveal
that the joint or extended family, in which married sons live
with their wives and children in the same household as their
parents, is still the prevailing family structure in Sugao, as

illustrated in table 2, which shows that in 1977 more than 52 percent of Sugao families were joint.

4. In 1978 the textile and clothing industry was the third largest in India, sharing that rank with the food and tobacco industry, each producing 19.3 percent of the country's gross output. In 1967 it was ranked second (see *World Tables* 1983). Although the textile industry was the second-largest employer in Indian industry in 1978, providing jobs for 27 percent of the work force, this too was a decline in importance from 1970 when it employed 32.6 percent. In 1956 cloth production in India was at its highest point, having increased by about 20 percent over pre-World War II levels. Since 1956 there has been a continuous decline in production. For an analysis of the Indian textile industry, see Mazumdar (1984). Mazumdar points out that production of cotton textiles grew in 1984–85, rising by 14 percent following the settlement of the strike. During the strike, small hand- and power-loom operations filled the gap in production. It is estimated that these now account for 70 percent of cloth production.

5. One of the leaders of Kawthe, a nearby village, has become influential in district-level politics and is currently the director of a development bank in Satara, the district headquarters. He has seen to it that the village of Kawthe has applied for, and implemented, a number of innovative projects. One was the planting of tamarind trees on the strip of land along the main access road to the village. The fruit is harvested and sold commercially, and the proceeds are invested in other village development projects.

6. The full-census survey of 1976–77 was personally administered and served as a vehicle for collecting anecdotal material and case studies as well as documenting living conditions for each family. Observations were made using techniques such as participant observation. An additional three months were spent surveying and interviewing village migrants in Bombay. Copies of the household, migrant, and

small-industries surveys are reproduced in H. Dandekar
(1978).

7. In their book *Gaon Rahati* [Village life] (1966), V. M.
Dandekar and M. B. Jagtap describe one year in Sugao, the
climate, the agricultural seasons, and the ways in which
people's lives are entwined with them. I drew extensively on
V. M. Dandekar's notes for the chapters on land-man
relationships and the settlement. Some material dealt solely
with Sugao, and some treated it as one of several villages in a
sample. The most readily available materials are in Jagtap
(1970), in which Sugao is one of the three villages studied to
determine changes in methods of agricultural production. V.
M. Dandekar and Jagtap (1959) deals with physical infrastructure, employment, business, and social stratification of
villages. Sugao is one of the villages drawn upon for
quantified illustrations. In addition there are two unpublished
monographs written by M. B. Jagtap, one on the Neo-
Buddhists, "Notes on the Mahars of 'Sugao'" (1974); and one
on the community of Dhangars, "Notes on the Dhangars
(Weavers) of 'Sugao'" (1975). I also found notes and rough
drafts of papers by V. M. Dandekar on land legislation,
history, and population changes in Sugao. Information on the
school system is included in *Progress of Education in Rural
Maharashtra* by A. R. Kamat (1968).

8. For example, during the state of emergency proclaimed by
Prime Minister Indira Gandhi in June 1975, a twenty-point
development program was announced, including projects
designed to improve the condition of the poor. Some of these
provided for credit extension to landless laborers and rural
artisans, and the building of *janata* (people's) housing. It
created administrative units like the Small Farmers
Development Agency to provide a variety of services to
farmers with holdings of less than five acres. This emphasis
on distribution and equity was echoed by international lending
agencies such as the World Bank and is reflected in the titles
of some of their publications, for example, *Balancing Trickle
Down and Basic Needs Strategies: Income Distribution Issues*

in Large Middle-Income Countries with Special Reference to Latin America, by Marcel Selowsky (1979). See also Streeton et al. (1981) and the International Labor Organisation (1982).

PART I

LIFE IN SUGAO

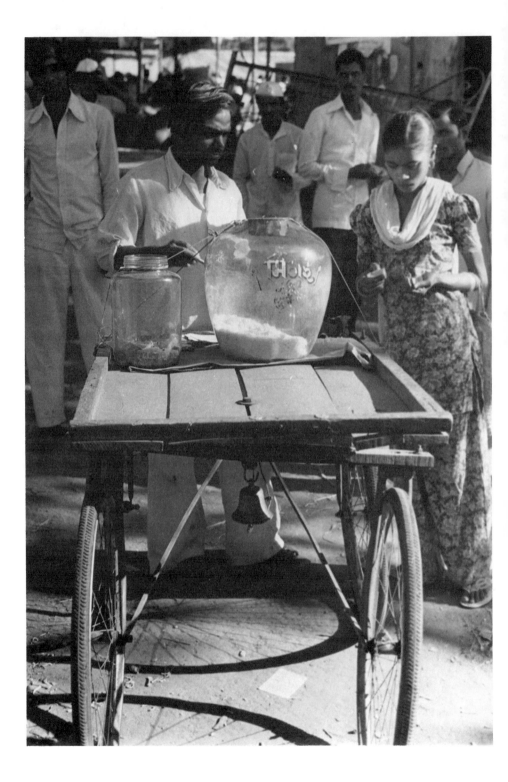

CHAPTER 1

REGIONAL CONNECTIONS

On my second trip to Sugao I was accompanied only by a cheap, blue vinyl suitcase, one I hoped did not glare of urban affluence. Packed in it were a couple of my cheapest *saris*, camera equipment, masses of writing paper, and two sets of printed questionnaires. I had delayed returning, ostensibly to do background reading and prepare the questionnaires, but also because I was afraid. A stranger to village ways, I might unknowingly break some social code and not be accepted by the people of Sugao. End of research.

The bus deposited me at the village of Vele on the Poona-Bangalore highway. Two and a half miles of dirt road led west to Sugao. I dragged my suitcase to one of the two tea shops beside the bus stop, the one where I had been told I could find Bhikku, a man from the Mahar community in Sugao. He could be prevailed upon to carry my luggage to Sugao. When Bhikku appeared from the rear of the shop, he refused to negotiate his fee. "You are our guest in Sugao," he said. "I am poor, you decide." And with that we were off, my suitcase perched precariously on his head, the preferred way of carrying things in the village. Later I was to have my Sugao women friends convulsed in mirth when I ineptly tried walking and balancing various containers on my head, as village women do with such ease.

To reach Sugao from Vele, one walks. The connecting road is no better than an all-weather cart track which can be negotiated by tractors, jeeps, and other heavy transport, but not by light motor cars. Reportedly even this road was not laid out until 1933–34, when the British governor of the Bombay Presidency visited Sugao. Since then no comparable dignitary has visited the village, and the road has not been maintained. In 1942 it was noted that the road had deteriorated to a cart track, which is what it is today.[1]

Since 1975 Sugao villagers have voluntarily maintained a road connecting Sugao to the neighboring village of Kenjal. That year an all-weather road was built by the government to connect Kenjal to Wai, the market town. A daily bus service started between Kenjal and Wai, and now goes on to Sugao during the six months or so each year that the Sugao-Kenjal road is passable. Following the monsoons the villagers rally to repair the damage caused by the rains and heavily loaded tractors transporting cane to the sugar factory. It usually takes some time to mobilize Sugao men to repair the road. In 1977, when I lived in the village, the bus did not start operating to Sugao until January, almost three months after the end of the rains, and ran until June when the monsoons began. It made one round trip between Wai and Sugao in the morning and another at dusk. This bus was particularly convenient for the handful of students who commuted to Wai for college and for those two or three individuals who had jobs there.

Since Sugao is located three miles from a major highway with no year-round motorable road connecting it, it receives fewer services from those government agencies implementing development programs than the better-linked villages. Most of these agencies, especially those that require field visits, lack adequate staff and vehicles to accomplish their work. So villages like Sugao, which are physically difficult to reach, are the last to hear about new government programs and subsidies and are often too late to apply for available funds.

Sugao is not far from urban centers. Vele, two and a half miles away by dirt road, is seventy-five kilometers south of Poona on the highway and forty-two kilometers north of Satara, the district headquarters (see figure 3). Three kilometers south of Vele, and also on the highway, is Sirur, the weekly market town, where a

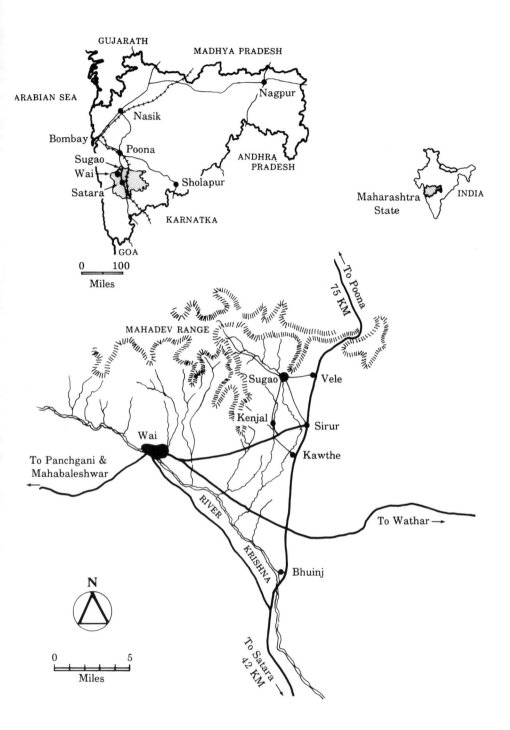

Figure 3: Location of Sugao

road branches westward to Wai. The most convenient way to reach Sugao is still by road, despite its poor condition; the nearest railway station is at Wathar, thirty-two kilometers east of Wai, on the Poona-Bangalore meter-gauge railway.

Highways, generally two-lane, tar-surfaced, macadamized roads, are a ribbon of the developed world slicing through a rural order whose tempo is older, slower, and more routinized. Trucks, buses, and motorcycles go careening down the highway, horns blasting, while in adjacent fields a farmer slowly tills his land with bullocks and a wooden plough. Accidents are frequent, and the road from Poona to Vele is dotted with the rusting carcasses of trucks and the occasional bus that flew off the road in this mad rush. Village women and men walking back and forth along the road are often injured by vehicles; neither the drivers nor the pedestrians fully understand the difference in their relative speeds. This is not merely a traffic problem to be solved with the latest transportation planning techniques, but a deep philosophical gap, an incomplete internalization of the transition to a new order and of the new demands of their physical world.

Roads, although channels to the outside, only connect nodes of the more developed world without transforming the interstices: villages fifty yards off the highway can lack even a year-round supply of clean drinking water. Some nodes achieve dominance as a result of a new improved road. Sugao people once walked on a track through the fields to Sirur, the nearby weekly market center, for their shopping. Now Wai, though further away, seems closer because of the bus, and most people from Sugao do their weekly shopping there.

Although the distances to urban centers may seem short, the condition of the roads can make even the shortest trip an ordeal, especially in bad weather. Once I traveled to Sugao on my Vespa scooter, just before the monsoons were to begin. While visiting friends in the village I scanned the skies for fear the rains would start, rendering the mud road to Vele impassable. In fact, my fears were well founded and I barely made it to the highway. It started to sprinkle the day I was to depart, and the last mile was a nightmare, as I trotted beside the running scooter, holding on to prevent it and myself from sliding away on the mud.

During the monsoons the students who commute to Wai slog through mud and rain and wade through the stream, normally a trickle over the road but by then at least calf-deep. The year I lived in Sugao, Priya was a student in the college at Wai. Many days she would rise early and wade through the mud and rain to Vele, only to find that the buses to Wai were full of passengers and she could not squeeze on. The bus conductors have been instructed to give preference to students trying to get to Wai for classes, but there is a limit to the number of bodies that can cling to a vehicle. For a young woman like Priya, from a respectable family of the Maratha caste, propriety demanded a certain amount of modesty in her contact with men. Often she would return home because she had missed several buses and was too late for many of her classes. There was no point in going all the way to town just for one or two. Students are allowed to buy season passes for the bus at a reduced rate, but by village standards the cost is still high. The social and economic costs of the commute and other aspects of education prevent children from poorer families, and women from the more affluent ones, from obtaining a college education. As a result, the annual resumption of bus service to Wai after the monsoons is eagerly awaited by the village residents. The commuting college students, and those in their final year of high school, are then spared the walk from Sugao to Vele and the hustle to get on overcrowded buses en route from Poona or Khandala to Wai.

On Mondays, the main market day at Wai, the bus is packed with men and women seizing this opportunity to visit the town and escape the monotony of village life. On these Mondays one or two tractors from Sugao also go to Wai, dragging trailers loaded with sacks of seasonal agricultural products to be sold at the government-regulated market or to private traders in the town. Any remaining space in the trailers is filled with villagers who pay one *rupee* for the ride into town. So lucrative is this passenger business that one of the tractors makes a regular run on Mondays carrying some forty or fifty people. In fact, tractors in Sugao are used as much, if not more, for transporting human beings and products as they are for agricultural cultivation. The tractor owners are well-to-do farmers who have enough land to justify their use. A contract business by tractor owners who might till other farmers' land is limited by the smallness of the individual holdings in Sugao, which makes use of a tractor inefficient. Owning a tractor confers status on the owner and allows him to earn some income transporting people, although it is clearly not the most efficient vehicle for such use.

Bicycles, on the other hand, are an important and efficient means of transport in rural areas. Several people own bicycles in Sugao and three shops rent them on an hourly or daily basis. A couple of students commute to Wai on bicycles, and the shopkeepers use them to get supplies from surrounding towns. However, you never see women or even young girls on bicycles in the village. Even in Wai, urban and less traditional, a woman riding a bicycle is a rare sight. I remember a conversation with my neighbor, Rani, who had learned to ride in her home village. "I was the first girl to learn in my village," she proudly told me, but she went on to add that she would not dare rent and ride a bicycle in Sugao. If she did, her in-laws and the village as a whole would be scandalized. And if some man were to accost her on the road she would lose face and the villagers would blame her for putting herself in a vulnerable position. Priya and Suma, too, felt constrained by Sugao norms and never thought they would be allowed to learn to ride. In later years, when Priya became engaged to a medical student in Poona, she confided that she had sat behind him on his motorcycle, sedately side-saddle and draped in her *sari*, as they had driven around in town. This in itself was risque; driving the vehicle herself was out of the question. In the village, riding bicycles, driving tractors, and ploughing with a bullock team are not considered socially appropriate activities for women.

Although bicycles are an important means of transport, few improvements have been made to adapt them to rural conditions. There are few three-speed bicycles in Sugao and hardly any ten-speed machines in the entire state, even in the cities. Given the rutted country roads and the difficulty of maintaining equipment in the village, this is perhaps just as well.

The Wai vegetable market.

A specialty shop in Wai.

Some of the more affluent families in Sugao own motorcycles, which are used by the men for trips to Wai, Poona, or Satara. The motorcycle provides the mobility needed to establish and maintain contacts with local officials and politicians. In this way cycle owners hear about new legislation or government programs that may affect their position in the village. They can monitor any litigation they may have on hand and circumvent programs or policies that may adversely affect their power base in the village, as well as capitalizing on those that can enhance it. In short, they can take care of the political aspects of agricultural business. Ownership of a motorcycle or a tractor is a symbol of power in Sugao, and rightly so.

Farmers who own bullock carts use them for transport, for travel to adjacent villages, or for an occasional trip to Wai to sell produce. The ride is bumpy, and, if the bullocks are spirited, can be quite rambunctious. Some Sugao farmers took particular pleasure in offering me a ride in their carts and then spurring their teams to make the ride as eventful as possible.

Since Sugao is a nuclear village, in which all the year-round residences are closely packed on a central village site, the daily trip to outlying fields can be more than three miles. The bullock cart is still the most important means of transport between the home and the field. Owning a pair of bullocks and a cart is not only a sign of status but greatly facilitates transport of seeds, manure, and pesticides to the field and the hauling of crops home for storage. Those who cannot afford to maintain a bullock team and whose fields are at a distance hire the services of someone with a cart to transport these materials. The design of the bullock cart is traditional: a two-wheeled vehicle with metal-rimmed, wooden wheels, and a wooden platform, most of which is constructed in Sugao by village carpenters. The design of the cart has been criticized by urban engineers bent on improving rural technology. They claim that it places too much stress on the animal and that high friction losses are sustained by the hard wooden wheels. Still, it is the sturdiest vehicle available for the rutted paths and dirt roads of rural India, wearing better than any of the improved versions that have been offered so far.

Plastic shoes for sale at the Sirur market.

Aluminum ware, trinkets, and cosmetics displayed at Sirur.

Although specialized markets are held at different villages in the region, such as the cattle-trading market held once a month at the nearby village of Kikli, Wai has become the main market town for Sugao people. A trip to Wai is recreation and a welcome change from the closely watched life in the village itself. Couples involved in illicit liaisons, generally well known to everyone since little can be kept private in Sugao, will surreptitiously steal away to see a movie or have a snack in Wai. The banks, the Panchayat Samiti, the extension offices, and the courthouse are in Wai, as is the nearest post office with telephone and telegraph facilities.

For the past seven years, Sugao has had its own post office, which is open half a day. Villagers receive mail, buy local stamps, and receive money orders there, but have to go to Wai to buy postage for foreign letters or aerograms. The village grapevine is an extremely good means of communication within the village itself, aided and abetted by Vilas, the part-time postman, who was also my field assistant in Sugao. Vilas often gave me a summary of what to expect in my mail when he handed it to me in the afternoon, and I expect that others were kept as informed of the contents of my mail as I was of theirs. One way I verified the amount of money people claimed they received from family members working in the city was by asking Vilas about the money orders he received every month.

Sugao men keep in touch with the larger world by reading the newspapers every day. The village has a small, makeshift library housed in a tiny cupboard in the village office. A part-time librarian, a Sugao man retired from a Bombay textile mill, takes care of the books for a nominal salary. In 1976 it was Rs. 10 per month, at that time equal to about U.S. $1.10. The library subscribes to three or four vernacular newspapers. A steady stream of men drop in, morning or evening, to look at the headlines and comment on the news. Women do not come to the library to read the newspapers. Such socializing between men and women is not acceptable. As a result women are denied direct access to a major channel of information. A few of the better educated girls in the village are library members and borrow books to take home, but they do not linger in the building and certainly never sit on one of the hard wooden benches and scan the day's news.

When electricity came to Sugao in 1964 a number of families bought radios. Television sets, which are becoming quite common in the cities, have yet to reach the village. There is a government scheme to provide every village with a communal television to be housed in the village office, but in Sugao the surrounding hills interfere with reception and villagers have not bothered to erect an antenna. The prevailing sentiment is "Eventually the government will come and do it, so why should we bother now?" Some matters are apparently felt to be real village concerns, such as repairing the road to Kenjal so that the bus can run between Sugao and Wai. Others are perceived as government concerns that result in programs for which there is little spontaneous support in the village.

In general, the existence of daily mail service, increased numbers of radios, the newspapers in Marathi (the vernacular language), bus service to Wai for at least part of the year, more student commuters to Wai, more bicycles, and the presence of a motorcycle or two in Sugao are all gradually helping to integrate the village into the larger region. This stronger communications network is changing daily life in the village in various ways, some obvious, some hidden. However, the most important link to the outside world is that established by the continued, cyclical migration of Sugao people to the city of Bombay.

Historically, this region has always been oriented westward toward the Arabian Sea. Maritime commerce flourished and the area is known to have had commercial contacts with Egypt, Arabia, Greece, and Rome. During the fifteenth and sixteenth centuries, in the Hindu and Muslim periods, this area was split politically and under the control of several kings. Political unity was attained only during the days of the Maratha Empire, beginning with Shivaji in the seventeenth century. Only recently, with the formation of Maharashtra State in 1960, has the region emerged as a cohesive political and administrative unit.

The westward orientation of the state increased dramatically during the British period, when Bombay became a major port for exporting raw materials like cotton to England and importing finished goods. As the hub of a rail and road network, the city was a center of communications and commerce. When England allowed industries to be established in India, many of them, particularly the textile mills, based themselves in the city. Eventually Bombay came to dominate all of western India, and its influence has persisted. Road and rail networks remain focused on the city (see figure 3). Despite government efforts to decentralize industrial activity, the concentration of transport and other networks in the city continues to make it the most attractive place for industry.

The western orientation of the region also results from its geography and natural resources. Maharashtra, the third largest state in the Indian Union (308,000 square kilometers), covers a major portion of western peninsular India. Geologically, nine-tenths of the state is a basaltic formation, some seventy million years old, known as the Deccan lavas. These consist of plateaus sloping gently to the east and southeast, rimmed on the west by a mountain range, the Western Ghats or Sahyadris. The Western Ghats run almost continuously for 650 kilometers from the northern limits of the state to the south. Rising quickly in elevation from the west coast and reaching their peak (750 to 1,200 meters) within 6 or 8 kilometers, they are the main watershed of the peninsular rivers and separate the swift westward-flowing streams from the long, winding eastern ones. The eastern slopes of the Ghats, as they are commonly known, descend gently to form the Deccan Plateau, which has an average elevation of 300 to 400 meters. Satara District is on this plateau. A series of transverse spurs extend eastward from the main ridge of the Ghats. Sugao nestles on the foothills of the Mahadev hills, which is one of these spurs.

Satara District is climatically in the *mawal* zone of Maharashtra. This is a belt about twenty to thirty kilometers wide immediately to the east of the Ghats. Rainfall is moderate (averaging 28 inches per annum) but well distributed over the year, allowing reliable, rainfed cultivation of diverse crops. Sugao is located in this *mawal* zone, which allows for reliable and diverse agricultural production with the potential of making the village self-sufficient in food production. In the drought-prone areas further east, large investments in irrigation will be needed before development efforts can begin.

Aside from sporadic planning efforts to decentralize industry, such as the establishment of a Vespa scooter assembly plant in the city of Satara, Satara District's economy is based predominantly on agriculture. About 70 percent of the district's land is cultivated and another 14 percent is forest. Most agriculture depends on rainfall; only 11 percent of the cultivated land is irrigated. Well irrigation is common in the central and eastern parts of the district, and canal irrigation projects are underway on the Neera and Krishna, the two major rivers of the area. The Krishna Left Bank Canal misses Sugao but provides water for villages in its vicinity further downstream. The limiting factor for irrigation in the Deccan is the total amount of surface and ground water available. Much of the area's irrigated land is used to grow cash crops, primarily sugarcane, a crop that farmers with large landholdings can best profit from.

Satara District is fairly representative of Maharashtra State in population density. The state had a population of almost 63 million in 1981 (9 percent of the country's population) with a density of 204 people per square kilometer, slightly lower than the national average of 216. Seventy percent of Maharashtra's population depends on agriculture, but only 12.2 percent of the total cropped area is irrigated (Ministry of Information and Broadcasting 1983, 9, 494, 496). Satara District has an area of over ten thousand square kilometers, a population of over 2 million, and a density of 195 people per square kilometer, close to the average for the state.

The population of Satara's rural areas is increasing. Sugao lands support only 25 percent of its population in comfort. This, combined with the availability of jobs in the cities, particularly in Bombay where Satara District villagers have ties dating from the turn of the century, has resulted in mass migration of men to Bombay for work and increasing integration of the Sugao economy with that of the region. Sugao men living in Bombay send packages home containing consumer goods such as clothing, tea, sugar, cosmetics, and toys. In 1977, 7 percent of families in the village claimed that they received all their consumer goods from Bombay, an additional 13 percent said they received about half, and another 7 percent received from one-tenth to one quarter. Thus, more than 25 percent of the village families were getting at least one-tenth of their consumer goods from the city. The Bombay world has become tangibly closer for the Sugao resident.

When I hiked in the countryside around Sugao, I found that some hamlets in the less fertile, unirrigated, hilly areas were completely bereft of men, all of whom were away working, largely in Bombay. A strong linkage to Bombay and the rest of the region is thus a significant characteristic of Sugao and of the Satara District as a whole.

Notes

1. The national and state governments in India have made
   considerable investments in road building since independence.
   Kilometers of paved roads in the country have increased from
   963,000 in 1970 (35 percent of all roads) to 1,534,000 in
   1980 (43 percent of all roads). In 1980, 2 percent of these
   were national highways, 33 percent were secondary roads,
   and the remaining 65 percent were lesser roads including the
   type that services villages like Sugao. Since 1970 most
   paving has occurred in the secondary road system, which
   increased from 17 percent of all paved roads to 33 percent in
   1980. These figures include the gradual upgrading of lesser
   roads to secondary roads. See Jain (1983, 208).

CHAPTER 2

THE SETTLEMENT AND POWER

Understanding power and resource distribution in Indian village society is impossible without looking at social relationships as codified in the Hindu caste system. These have been institutionalized in the village over hundreds of years and continue to exert a great influence. A look at the history of settlement in Sugao illustrates the paucity of change that has occurred in the traditionally stable socioeconomic and spatial organization of ancient villages in India. Historically such a village society was characterized by rigid stratification along caste[1] and communal lines, which determined distribution of land, the major economic asset in the village. Land was distributed between groups in such a way that a stable balance of occupations sustainable by the village economy was maintained and protected.

Traditional village society in Deccan Maharashtra was hierarchical and consisted of three major groups: (1) a dominant class of cultivating landowners who usually belonged to upper castes such as Brahmins or Marathas; (2) a subordinate class of individuals belonging to the lowest castes (considered untouchable) who acted as village servants, performing the menial and ritually polluting tasks essential to the community, and were paid by revenue-exempt tenure on village lands; and (3) a group of artisans who provided services to the village as a whole for which they were also paid by revenue-exempt tenancy on village lands.[2] These artisans also rendered services to families and individuals in the

village for which they received payments in kind under a system
known in Maharashtra as *baluta*.

Historically, most of Sugao's land has been divided between
two dominant Maratha families, the Yadavs and Jadhavs. Each
family owned an equitable share of prime, medium, and inferior
village land. Some 10 percent of village land was earmarked for
artisan families providing supportive services. The unequal distribution of agricultural land between groups and the arrangement of
housing in the village (segregated by caste and family) explicitly
manifested the hierarchy in the village community. It remains so
today. The fact that, despite planning interventions, the layout and
distribution of housing and land in Sugao have not appreciably
changed is physical proof that traditional economic relationships and
status have been perpetuated in the village.

Sugao people today are mostly peasant farmers of the
Maratha caste, of whom the patrilineal Yadav and Jadhav families
are the most important. Although villagers are not certain where
these families originated, they believe the Yadavs are from Devagiri
(today's Daulatabad) near Aurangabad; the Jadhavs are from Verul
(today's Ellora) in the same area. If this is true, the Yadavs may
be descendants of the Yadav dynasty which ruled Devagiri in the
thirteenth century. This dynasty was the last of the early Hindu
kingdoms in the south, which around the middle of the thirteenth
century extended to the west coast. The Yadavs may have come to
Sugao during this time of expansion or stayed behind after the fall
of the Yadav dynasty in the fourteenth century. In any case, the
Jadhavs apparently accompanied the Yadavs and may have been
part of the original family.[3] Today the Sugao Yadavs and Jadhavs
regard each other as relatives, and marriage between them is
neither condoned nor practiced.

The Yadav and Jadhav houses are in two clearly separated
wards to the north and south of the village's main axis lane, which
runs east-west down the hill (see "Introduction," figure 1). This
separation of a village into distinct zones belonging to two dominant
families is a characteristic of many settlements in Satara District.
At the top of the lane separating the two wards in Sugao is a

clearing, in front of the temple of Bhairava, which is the main village square. This is used for activities in which the whole village participates. The Jadhav and Yadav wards each have meeting areas where the men congregate of an evening to chat. Each ward has a *talim*, or exercise building, where the men once gathered for recreation. The buildings are now in disrepair and exercise at the *talim* is no longer part of a man's daily routine. Attached to the Bhairava temple in the main square is a large colonnaded courtyard surrounded by rooms that house the elementary school. This addition to the temple structure was communally built to house the school in the hope that Bhairava would inspire the generally vocal Sugao youth to pursue knowledge diligently.

In the middle of the residences of the high-caste Yadavs and Jadhavs, on the main axis lane, is a cluster of houses belonging to the Dhangar caste. Dhangars traditionally are sheep and goat herders and the caste is considered lower than the Maratha. The Sugao Dhangars are a subcaste, known as Khutekar Dhangars, who traditionally weave sheep's wool blankets. This central group of Dhangar houses is owned by families who claim to be descendants of the original settlers of the village. This claim is substantiated by the fact that their houses are large, solidly constructed, and located in the middle of the Yadav and Jadhav enclaves. It is unlikely that this group could have obtained such strategic home sites in a village first settled by the higher-caste Marathas. It is much more probable that, as their descendants now claim, some Dhangar families were already settled on the present village site when the Yadavs and Jadhavs arrived.

Village people say, and there is evidence to suggest, that when the Yadavs and Jadhavs came to Sugao, they lived in two separate settlements not far from the peasant village. These locations (see figure 4) are referred to today as *pahndhri*, meaning white soil, a term usually applied to house sites, as opposed to *kali*, or black soil, the word used to denote agricultural land. The old Yadav house site was on the western bank of the Chandraganga and that of the Jadhavs was located upstream.

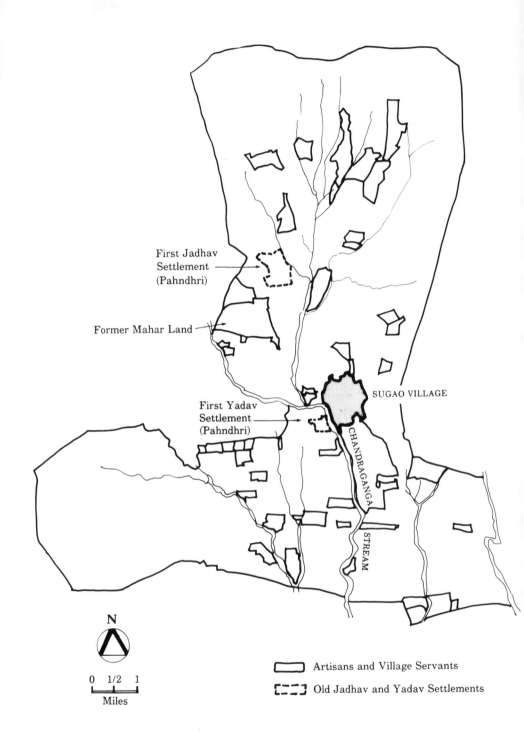

First Jadhav
Settlement
(Pahndhri)

Former Mahar Land

First Yadav
Settlement
(Pahndhri)

SUGAO VILLAGE

CHANDRAGANGA STREAM

N

0   1/2   1

Miles

▭ Artisans and Village Servants

⊏⎯⎯⊐ Old Jadhav and Yadav Settlements

Figure 4: Sugao Village Lands Reserved for Artisans and Village Servants

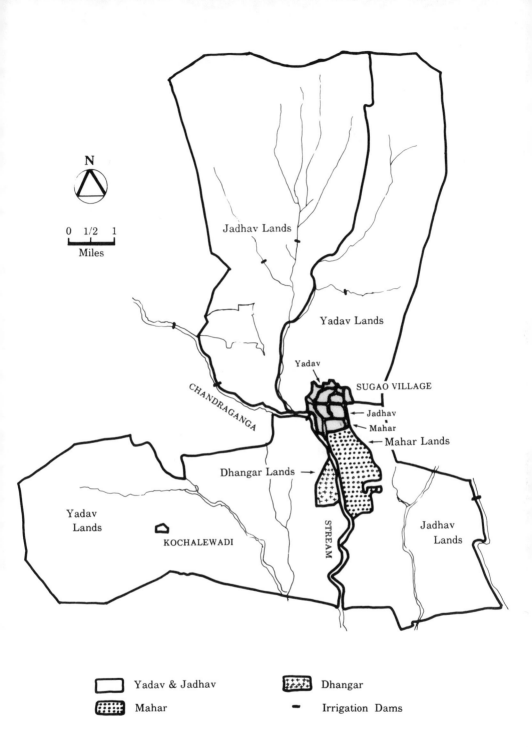

N

0   1/2   1
Miles

Jadhav Lands

Yadav Lands

Yadav

SUGAO VILLAGE

CHANDRAGANGA

←— Jadhav

←— Mahar

←— Mahar Lands

Dhangar Lands →

Yadav
Lands

KOCHALEWADI

STREAM

Jadhav
Lands

	Yadav & Jadhav		Dhangar
	Mahar	—	Irrigation Dams

Figure 5: Settlement of Sugao Lands Between Major Groups

The two families eventually moved from these locations to their present settlement around the Dhangars. The move made sense for many reasons. This new site, on a hill slope, was better drained and therefore healthier. The hill was rocky, suitable for house construction, and useless for farming, whereas the old sites had occupied good agricultural land. These former sites were brought under the plough and are still cultivated by the Yadav and Jadhav families. Farmers say that occasionally while ploughing they have turned up potsherds and utensils that may have belonged to these early settlers. Ancestry and history are only casually acknowledged but they do provide a framework for the villager's view of reality.

Another important group in the village, as old as the Yadavs and the Jadhavs, is the Mahar, now known as the Neo-Buddhists. The Mahar is an untouchable caste; until recently, when its members converted to Buddhism under the leadership of Dr. Ambekdar, a social reformer who was a Mahar, they functioned as village servants performing such distasteful but essential services as disposing of dead cattle and cleaning. In return, the Mahars were given specific village lands, generally inferior ones, to cultivate (see figure 5). Since the Mahar caste is the most widespread in Maharashtra, scholars have theorized that its members are the original inhabitants of the area (Zelliot 1970). Some of their traditional village duties, such as arbitrating boundary disputes, suggest that they originally may have owned all the village lands.

Soon after they settled in Sugao, the Yadavs and the Jadhavs divided the village lands between them, each receiving a more or less equal share of the irrigable and nonirrigable acreage. An acute sense of the balance of power between the two groups is indicated by this careful distribution of land. The Chandraganga turns sharply south as it flows to the village from the west and divides the southerly village lands. The Yadavs took the land to the west and the Jadhavs the land to the east. Lands to the north are similarly divided by a small, north-south stream that joins the Chandraganga near the village. In this area the Yadavs have the land to the east, the Jadhavs the land to the west. The land northwest and southwest of the village is irrigated (and probably has been since the families settled there in the thirteenth and fourteenth centuries) by small earthen dams built across the Chandraganga, allowing water to be channeled to the adjacent fields.

The Dhangars traditionally occupied a small area of prime irrigable land opposite the village site. They retain possession of it to this day. Even though the Dhangars preceded the Marathas, they may not have occupied all the village land, especially since their main occupation was weaving and trading wool blankets. Sizable areas were available for the Yadavs and Jadhavs. The two families were of the ruling class, and, even when they first arrived, probably outnumbered the Dhangars. The latter thus would have had more than one reason to acquiesce to the status and claims of the Yadavs and Jadhavs. The Marathas, in turn, did not displace the Dhangars, but recognized their traditional proprietary rights.

In the middle of the seventeenth century a family named Kochale came to Sugao seeking political asylum. They were probably part of an aristocratic family, the More, of Javali, who were defeated by Shivaji, the famous Maratha warrior king. They migrated to Sugao to escape persecution. The Yadavs gave them land to the west where they established a hamlet named Kochalewadi (see figure 5). The Kochales are Marathas, and, although they came defeated to Sugao, their social status was on a par with, if not superior to, that of the Yadavs and Jadhavs. They were probably also too few in number to pose a threat to the dominant families in Sugao, or to strain the village's resources. When the Yadavs gave them a part of their land, they conferred on them not only proprietary tenure but the status accompanying it. The Kochales thus enjoy the same social standing in Sugao as the Yadavs and Jadhavs. Status in village India is inherited with family and caste, not simply assumed through possession of land and resources.

Since the Kochales came to Sugao, no other major group has settled there. Most of the Maratha and Dhangar families that later settled in the village were related to the Yadavs, Jadhavs, or Dhangars. They acquired their land from these Sugao families through inheritance or purchase but they were not admitted to the main proprietary body and did not enjoy its status in village affairs. Even today, after many generations in Sugao, the descendants of these families are referred to as *pahune* (guests) of the families they married into.

Besides these landowning groups, Sugao society is comprised of artisans and servants of whom the Mahars are the most stable and numerous. Traditionally, proprietary farmers were served by these Mahars and service artisans, as they are today. The social hierarchy is clear: landowning proprietors are at the top, artisans below, and the untouchable castes and village servants at the bottom.

Traditionally, the artisans have provided services needed by individual farmers and the community at large. Services rendered to the whole village were paid for with use of village lands for as long as the service-caste families satisfactorily performed the needed work. In Sugao such land-tenure grants were made to the *koli* (water carrier), *ramoshi* (watchman), *gurav* (priest), *gondhali* (minstrel), *kalabantin* (songstress), *chambhar* (cobbler), and others. Lands also were reserved for those maintaining the village temples and mosques. In fact, most of the services required by the community were connected with religious and ritualistic activity. For example, the cobbler's main duty was to hold the oil lamp in the annual village festivals honoring Bhairava. For this task he was allowed to till a designated piece of village land, the income from which augmented his other earnings. Although these relationships have now changed, they are worth noting for the stability and continuity they gave to the traditional village society.

These allocations of land for specific services and functions were made years ago, probably long before the village came under the Maratha Empire. Thus, a sophisticated system has evolved of setting aside land to pay for public services considered essential for the proper functioning of a traditional village society in the Deccan. Land allocated in this fashion amounted to about two hundred acres or one-tenth of the total village acreage (see figure 4). Since the Jadhavs and Yadavs considered themselves two distinct groups in

A *sutar* (carpenter) making a bullock cart.

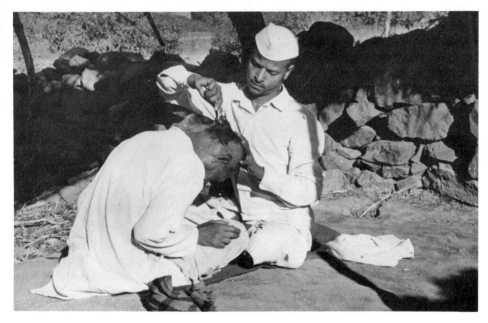

Another *balutedar* is the village *navi* (barber).

the village, each allocated land in their section of the village for the various functionaries. Even today, one *gurav* (priest) family ministers to the Yadavs and another tends to the Jadhavs.

Thus, historically in Sugao, a major portion of the prime land was owned by the dominant Maratha groups. A small portion was retained by the lower-status Dhangars by virtue of their earlier tenure, and a fraction was reserved to secure the services of artisans essential to the community. Land, the most valuable productive asset of the village, was distributed so that the higher castes had the most and best while some was set aside to support lower-caste artisans who provided necessary services. The system was structured to maintain stability in occupation mix, asset distribution, and social status.

In addition to public functions, families in Sugao required personal services and maintenance and repair of agricultural equipment. Traditionally, these services were obtained through a system of barter prevalent in many parts of India and known in Maharashtra as *baluta*. In this, the artisan, in return for providing year-round services, received a certain quantity of all crops the cultivator harvested throughout the year. Some of these *balutedars* still reside and practice in Sugao, for example, the *sutar* (carpenter), *lohar* (blacksmith), *mang* (rope maker), *chambhar* (cobbler), *navi* (barber), and *parith* (washerman).

At any one time the farmers of Sugao might employ only one or two households providing a particular service, usually performed by the male head of the artisan family. If anything happened to him, another family of that service caste was brought in and the first family was required to leave. Thus, continuity in lineage has not always been maintained and some service families now residing in Sugao are recent arrivals. In contrast, the family of village *ramoshi* (watchmen) have lived in Sugao for as many generations as people can remember. Most other artisans have been in the village for three or four generations. The artisans rendering personal services were not given village land to cultivate as payment for their services but were allowed to buy occupancy rights if land became available. There are therefore families belonging to the carpenter, barber, or other service castes who are not *balutedars*. They own land in the village and their main occupation is farming.

Thus, traditionally, stability of occupation mix and social hierarchy was maintained through a system that limited access to landownership. There was little room in this order for "new money" to destabilize old power and status relationships.

The social hierarchy in Sugao is made explicitly manifest by the segregation of housing by castes or communal groups (see "Introduction," figure 1). As noted above, the Yadavs, Jadhavs, and Dhangars occupy the main village. The higher-caste artisans such as the carpenters, blacksmiths, and to some extent the barbers and washermen, who are a part of the old order of *baluta* relationships, live in the main village, own their houses, and are an integrated, if subservient, part of village society. The Mahars are segregated in a distinct area outside the main village, and other untouchable lower castes such as cobblers and rope makers cluster in small groups on the periphery.

A number of Muslim families have also lived in Sugao for several decades and are well established socially. The Muslims are of course a religious group, not a Hindu caste, but in Sugao they are treated as yet another caste. Most of the women have adopted Hindu dress, and as a group they are indistinguishable, at first glance, from the rest of the population. Their housing is modest and clustered in two areas. One surrounds a tiny village mosque, in the courtyard of which the goats for the Sunday "mutton" meal are slaughtered. The other is a small concentration in the Jadhav section of the village.

There is great stability in this physical arrangement of land and housing, and the established villagers tacitly acknowledge their satisfaction with the system. Even in the face of strong economic pressures, most will resist selling houses or land except under extreme duress. Even when forced to sell, they will give priority to their family and clan groups, Yadavs to Yadavs and Jadhavs to Jadhavs, preferably those on adjacent branches of the family tree.

Population growth and the slow break up of the joint family system (in which two or three generations, related through the males, live together) has resulted in subdivision of residential and agricultural land, but this has not changed the major asset distribution within the groups. Divided families set up households in individual rooms of former joint households and farm side-by-side in the subdivided fields. Few sell these rights, and, if they do, it is usually back to their kin. There is little room for encroachment by the outsider.

The fate of the outsider, especially a poor one, is not enviable. Looking at Sugao, it is quite clear why a poor person forced out of his village would choose to seek refuge in a strange city rather than another village. One can live in the cracks and crevices that are "no man's land" in the city: the pavements, the railroad, or the bridge embankments. There is no "no man's land" in the village — every nook and cranny, every physical asset, is jealously guarded and possessed.

In Sugao one can see basket weavers and masons who have been in the village for only one or two generations living very much on the fringe of the community in precarious and makeshift housing that usually consists of only a dilapidated hut (see H. Dandekar 1986). Their houses are built on land that belongs to one or another Maratha farmer, and they have no security of tenure. They are afraid to invest in their houses, even if they could afford it, or improve their living conditions; they fear that the landowner, worried that they may claim tenure, will evict them. Those who enjoy such "squatter's rights" in the village pay their rent in a variety of in-kind, and relatively substantial, ways. If rent is paid in the form of cash, no receipt is given for it, for the landlord fears that the tenants may claim tenure through occupancy rights, just as they do in the cities. In addition, the "squatter family" is required to show its gratitude by fetching and carrying throughout the year for the owner's family and being available to provide day labor when there is a high demand for hired hands.

On one of my trips to Sugao, I was invited into the house of a very poor family of the goldsmith caste. While plying me with tea they could ill afford, and that I had trouble drinking so inferior was its quality, the man told me with shining eyes of a new program by the central government under which they were to be given tiny plots for house sites on the barren upper slopes of village-owned grazing land. Just tiny sites, no services, and a symbolic cotton blanket—a very basic and simple development program. Successfully implemented, it would significantly improve the quality of life of this "have not" family, for even a small share of the village resources would reinforce its sense of security and belonging in Sugao. But this scheme and others like it are opposed covertly and overtly by the village landed, none of whom want that particular piece of wretched land for grazing cattle or anything else. The tradition that power must be conserved and kept concentrated is an old one in Sugao, and those who are in control will struggle to keep others out for as long as they can. On a subsequent visit to Sugao I found that not only had sites been given but a *Janata* (people's) Housing Scheme had been implemented under Indira Gandhi's twenty-point program to eradicate poverty. The dwellings had been built, but the recipients complained of bad workmanship by the contractor. They claimed that adulterated and inferior cement was used and that the houses were crumbling under the pressure of the monsoon rains. Later I found that the walls of three or four of these houses had in fact collapsed and the inhabitants had returned to their old quarters in the village. The contractor had disappeared and the owners had no recourse. Other owners, who had some savings, had repaired their homes.

This inability of development agencies to efficiently and effectively implement programs for the rural poor is typical. It is a characteristic of advocacy planning for the poor in developed as well as developing countries. Programs such as the Sugao housing scheme, carefully conceived by the outside planner to "give" to the rural poor without "taking away" from the rural rich, constantly founder in the thick mesh of complex, traditional, power relationships that have been refined over the centuries. The existence of such relationships is only dimly and incompletely understood by the would-be intervenor, and the planner's efforts and programs are emasculated by the village elite.

Of the men who remain in Sugao, those from well-to-do families control the village. The position of *gaon patil* (village headman) rotates between the Jadhavs and the Yadavs. So do the three other socially powerful positions in the village. The police *patil*, the sole representative of the legal system residing in Sugao, is a part-time position currently held by the son of a former *gaon patil* from the Jadhavs. The chairman of the elected village governing body, the Gram Panchayat, and the secretary of the agricultural cooperative are from branches of the same Yadav family.

This new institution of government, which drew on the notion of equality, assumed the name of an organization in traditional village society that had never operated in an egalitarian manner. The old *panchayat* elders were all males, representative of the dominant class and family interests in the village. Their decisions were grounded on an acute sense of and adherence to the history of the given village order. Village society, in their eyes, consisted of a group of families and individuals that had coexisted in a social hierarchy for centuries, and the elders made decisions that would facilitate that pattern's continuity. Obviously, maintaining the status quo was important.

In *Gaon Rahati*, V. M. Dandekar and M. B. Jagtap (1966) describe an incident in Sugao in which the *panchayat* heard a dispute about cultivation rights to a particular piece of village land dedicated to the temple. The protagonist, who clearly had no substantial claim to the land, clinched his argument by asking, "Are you going to believe me, Ganpat Tukaram Yadav, your kinsman, or this low-caste, no-account *teli*?" (*Telis* are oil pressers by occupation and much lower in the caste hierarchy than the Yadavs.) The case was decided in his favor.

It was easy to perceive the traditional village *panchayats* as fine institutions if you were male and of high caste. They were to be approached with caution if you were female or a lower-caste male. The new Gram Panchayat system was designed with some recognition of this. The Gram Panchayat is a group of representatives, elected by all the villagers exercising adult franchise.

This *kaikadi* (basket weaver) has only "squatter's rights" to the land on which he lives.

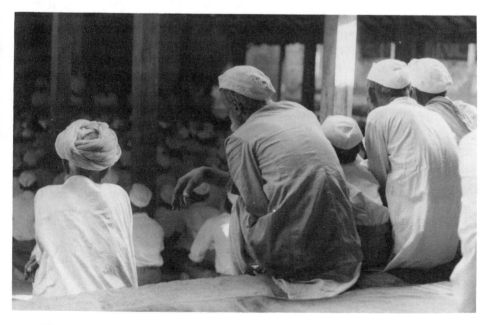

Village meetings are seldom attended by women or Mahars.

Two seats are specially reserved, one for a woman and one for a representative of those lower castes classified as "backward."

Despite this, the lack of active participation in the social and political affairs of the village by women is almost total. Women do vote but there too they are largely guided by the men in their family. They do not show much active interest in the cooperative society or other village-level institutions, or in political or economic affairs. Although there is a structural provision of a seat for one female on the village *panchayat*, Laxmibai, who was the member when I was in Sugao, was not actively involved. She did not attend the meetings, and papers that needed her signature were taken to her home. Usually her husband or sons made the necessary decisions and used her position to assert themselves in village politics. Women are taught from childhood to confine themselves to household tasks and help men in the family occupation, and their horizons are hardly broadened through formal education or laws such as this one reserving a place for them in the village *panchayat*.

When I attended the Gram Panchayat meetings in Sugao, and only a few were called while I lived there, I saw very few men from the Mahar community and no women at all. The seat reserved for the backward castes might just as well not exist because it does not bring with it any real power in the village. Eight representatives are elected for four-year terms, two from each of the four wards. With the one woman and the representative of the backward castes, the Gram Panchayat has ten members.

Theoretically, the Gram Panchayat was designed to be responsible in the village for agricultural production, rural industries, medical relief, village-owned common grazing grounds, village roads, tanks and wells, and the maintenance of sanitation. It was given the power to levy taxes on houses, fairs, festivals, and the sale of goods, and to control *octroi*, a tax on goods entering the village. However, taxation powers are seldom exercised when they might cost the well-to-do more than the poor. For example, as I was making a survey of the new houses and their increasing construction costs, I discovered that none of this housing was being taxed. Reassessment of housing would not be popular in Sugao since most of the richer families have added to their homes and would have to pay more. The house tax therefore continued to be levied on the basis of an assessment made in the 1950s.

Given this reduced property tax, when money is needed for repair and improvement of public facilities such as schools, roads, street lighting, and the water system, special "equal" fees are levied on each family in the village, some of whom sell their kitchen utensils or other belongings to make the payments. People cannot refuse to pay or plead poverty in Sugao. Village leaders can walk into any house, pick up some article of value, and sell it to obtain the required fees. The new decentralized form of the *panchayat* system has not decentralized local power.

The first time I met the block development officer (BDO) for Sugao, at his office in Wai, he was busy listening to the commentary on a cricket match in Bombay. He was a bit uneasy with me, insecure about his command of English but unwilling to talk only in Marathi. The BDO is an important person in rural areas, but the man I met in Wai was not particularly interested in rural problems; the cricket match was much more his style. His job is the first rung of the ladder to higher administrative positions. The fact that the technical development and extension service at the *taluka* (subdistrict) level reported to him did not seem to weigh heavily in his concerns. He was an administrator, and the technicians took care of the extension service without much involvement on his part.

For the villagers the BDO is a person of status. In Sugao the BDO conferred instant prestige on me when, during his only visit to the village, he requested that I be invited to the meeting he was to hold with Sugao leaders. The meeting concerned the percolation tank for the village and the building of a new direct road to Wai. The negotiations between Sugao's leaders and this representative of government were illuminating. The leaders were articulate in presenting their case and making their requests, all of which would especially benefit their group. There was no mention of the various existing programs for the rural poor. It would never have occurred to any of these men to invite me to the meeting because I am a woman; these things would not, in their view, be of concern to me. An outside authority was needed for them to see me differently. After this incident, I was invited to all the Gram Panchayat meetings in Sugao.

There are supposed to be two representatives of outside government at the village level: the village-level worker (VLW), who represents the development component of the national government and keeps the farmer informed of new technology and programs; and the village *talathi* or revenue collector. I saw the latter only once in Sugao. He is a Brahmin by caste. (Brahmins have traditionally monopolized revenue positions and are often accused by villagers of using their position to exploit the poor and ill-informed.) A resident of Wai, he dislikes even occasional visits to the villages and makes anyone who wants to consult his land records go to Wai and pay him a small gift under the table before he makes copies of the documents they need. If the gift is not paid, a villager might have to make several trips to Wai before he can find the *talathi*. I had to ask a higher-level official to exert authority upon the Sugao *talathi* before I got access to the land records of the village.

The VLW for Sugao lives in the village. He is not a Sugao man and often leaves to spend a few days in his own village, where his family lives. He is not given high status in the village, since he is neither a high-caste person nor very well paid by the government. He therefore treads gingerly and tries not to displease the village leaders. When I requested the housing tax log, he knew he must provide it because he had a written directive from Wai to give me all the documentation I wanted. He did not, however, want to worry the Sugao leaders. The log was delivered to me one evening, wrapped in white cloth, and I had to quickly copy the information I needed and return it to him as inconspicuously as possible.

When power relations do not change, it is wishful thinking to expect that the VLW can act as a catalyst to transform village life. Even when the VLW is aware of major programs or changes initiated by the government that could benefit the poor in Sugao, he is not aggressive about disseminating the information unless this is sanctioned by the leadership. Once, when Bharatibai was concerned that records pertaining to her land had been tampered with, she had to invite the VLW to dinner just to learn where and how she should go about getting more information. As everywhere, information is power and not easily obtained in Sugao.

I attended that dinner and noticed that the VLW was not particularly informative; Bharatibai paid many *rupees* to the *talathi* before she got copies of her land records. Even to an educated outsider like me, intervening on her behalf seemed a complex and difficult undertaking because information on authority and its sources was difficult to obtain. How much more intimidating it must be to the illiterate.

A new system of recording land rights was introduced under the British government. As a result the legal system became increasingly able to control and affect property relationships in the village. This undermined the traditional system of arbitration of village disputes by the old village *panchayat* consisting of village elders. As a result, one finds today an increased tendency toward litigation through the formal court system to settle disputes over land rights and other issues. People in Sugao claim that the number of court cases in the village has increased. Some also note, ruefully, that Sugao is known for being a particularly cantankerous village in this respect, appearing to resolve more than its share of problems in the courts. But increasing use of the courts seems to be a fact of rural life these days. It is therefore important for a farmer to be able to read and write and keep abreast of the new laws that govern property and landownership or affect his life in other ways.

As is true everywhere, those well versed in legal matters and better able to afford the costs are the ones who benefit most from litigation. They tend to be the better educated or the wealthier farmers in the village. Thus one finds that one reason they continue to prosper in Sugao today is that they are able to mount the legal battles necessary to preserve and extend their control.

Police protection at the village level is minimal. The village police *patil* is paid a very small stipend for his work, so only men with other sources of income can afford to take the job. Since it is a power position, only the families in control aspire to it, and the concept of justice is based upon what the elite will accept. In the election of 1977 that first pitted a viable opposition party against the dominant Congress party in Sugao, the son of a farmer in the village who was an opposition leader was murdered. Sugao is a staunchly Congress village and this was a warning. The murder was made to look like a motorcycle accident but everyone in the village knows which local leaders engineered it and why. The father was shattered and spent scarce resources in taking the case to court. He got nowhere with the case. No one in Sugao dared to testify. His experience serves to reinforce the poor Sugao residents' conviction that it is useless to try to buck the village elite.

This is not a new situation. In Mr. Jagtap's field notes[4] I read a poignant story of a family of Sugao Mahars who tried to assert their traditional claim to some village land, a parcel the leadership wanted to acquire for construction of a school. The family was blackballed by the village. No one would rent them bullocks to plough their fields. The four brothers yoked themselves to the plough and managed to cultivate the land, but before they could harvest the crop they lost their litigation. The crops were destroyed by the Sugao leaders. Still not satisfied, the village ostracized them for years. In one drought year they had to walk the two and a half miles to Vele just to get drinking water. No one in the village would help them, not even the other Mahar families, for they feared retribution by the other villagers. Some twenty years later, when I met the descendants of this family, they were still scarred and broken by this experience. The village's memory is long, and the new political structure has not changed old power relationships. On the contrary, the new structure and its economic development programs appear in some cases to have strengthened and revitalized the old order.

Notes

1. The word "caste," originally from Portuguese, has been used to describe the prevailing social order in India as well as the component groups within that order. It would be impossible to describe here the intricacies of the caste system as it evolved and still exists in India today. There is a vast literature on the subject. Dumont (1970) gives a theoretical analysis of the stratified caste system in India. Mandelbaum (1972) takes a comprehensive look at Indian society; an especially good description of family and kinship ties as major components of the social order is given in volume one. It is perhaps sufficient to point out here that in a typical village the family is the basic unit of the social system. Karve (1965) deals with various kinship and family forms in different regions including Maharashtra. Families maintain endogamous groups called *jatis*. These *jati* names were originally occupational categories. All the members of a *jati* are required to conform to its rules and strictures and they share in the *jati*'s status in the social hierarchy. Because the word "caste" is more familiar than *jati*, I shall use it in this study.

2. A detailed description of social life in village communities in Maharashtra under the eighteenth-century Peshwas is provided in Desai (1980). In this book the author corroborates the fact that village society was land oriented and that status depended on an individual's access to land (p. 3).

3. This information was taken from unpublished notes and rough drafts of papers on land legislation, history, and population changes in Sugao by V. M. Dandekar of the Gokhale Institute of Politics and Economics.

4. Mr. Jagtap has written two unpublished monographs on the Neo-Buddhists (Jagtap 1974) and Dhangars (Jagtap 1975).

CHAPTER 3

AMENITIES AND SERVICES

Sugao is picturesque when the sky is blue, the breeze cool, and the surrounding fields and hills a soothing green after the monsoon rains. Closer observation reveals that this idyllic first impression is misleading. In fact, the amenities and services available in Sugao are rudimentary. This helps explain why Sugao's single woman doctor, Vidya, will not consider returning home to practice, why better-educated teachers dislike village life, and why trained medical practitioners from elsewhere do not settle there. The lack of basic amenities, the paucity of appropriate playmates for children or kindred spirits for friends, the oppressive village politics, and the problems of collecting outstanding bills all mitigate against this. Few medical services or personnel are available.[1] Health care is provided by an unschooled midwife and one "doctor," who is in fact only a self-taught compounder of medicine. He comes from a caste group known as *vaidu* (medicine man), which was originally a nomadic tribe, and has lived in Sugao since 1967. He was not trained in any rigorous medical system, having learned his skills from his father and from working for six months as a compounder with a doctor in the town of Miraz. But his practice in Sugao has been successful, for he fills the important need for medical services. As a result, in 1977 he was able to earn the comfortable village income of ten *rupees* per day.

Practicing medicine is never just a business in any society; the profession requires many interpersonal skills. This is particularly true in villages like Sugao. The present "doctor" understands this and knows how to operate in the village in a way that a degree-holding, urbanized, medical practitioner could not. The secret of his success is that he knows how to manage village folk, and when to press for payment and when not. I experienced the doctor's finesse one day when he came to attend me. I was exhausted from a long night of vomiting and diarrhea induced, as it turned out, by some contaminated fish curry and not, as I then feared, by the cholera then reaching epidemic proportions in Maharashtra. He encouraged me, quite eclectically, to take tetracycline or any other antibiotic I owned, gave me some pills that he claimed would reduce nausea, and suggested that I suck on a lemon filled with honey and warmed in ashes (a household remedy also prescribed by Bharatibai). He assured me that a vehicle capable of getting me to Poona would be requisitioned in short order if my condition did not improve, and he refused to accept payment for his visit, medicine, or advice, claiming I was a village guest.

I did not take all the suggested pills, preferring to stick with the lemon and honey, but I was impressed by his manner. Upon my recovery I presented him with all the medications in my possession, substances he no doubt used to good profit at a later date. This sensitivity has earned the doctor a good reputation in Sugao. The villagers in turn demonstrate a reciprocal tolerance of his idiosyncracies. They know that he is usually inebriated at night, and whenever possible patronize him only during the day.

In an effort to make modern medicine and health care available to villagers, the government has established a system of rural health centers. The primary health center closest to Sugao is at Sirur, a good six miles away. Sugao people seldom use its facilities because it is a two-hour walk; there is often a long wait; the staff is comprised mostly of young interns; and medicine, when available (frequently it is not because some doctors use it for illegal private practice on the side), is prescribed for only a few days at a time. Few villagers can afford the time to fetch fresh medicine at frequent intervals, even if it is dispensed at subsidized prices. Minor ailments are treated with home remedies or are ignored. If the condition persists, the village "doctor" is called in. As a last resort the villager consults a degree-holding private practitioner in Wai.

Private doctors and clinics are favored by most Sugao people, for they believe the treatment given there is more efficacious. There is a deeply ingrained belief that an "injection" is the best medicine for any problem, and rural doctors who acknowledge this do very well. Most trained doctors find it difficult to adjust to the lack of amenities and facilities even in a town like Wai. Adjusting to a village like Sugao, even if there were sufficient demand for medical services, would be even more difficult. Doctors from the outside are also isolated from the closely connected social system of the village.

While private health care is preferred, it is also expensive. Many villagers have to borrow when a major illness occurs in the family, and these loans sometimes take a lifetime to repay. On one of my return visits to Sugao, I discovered that my field assistant, Vilas, had been hospitalized in Wai. I visited him there and found that, although he was fit to be discharged, he lacked the money to pay his bill. The hospital would not release him until he paid, and his family was using all its contacts to raise a loan, while every additional day in the hospital meant a larger bill. Although I was able to rescue him from this situation, I realized, as we got final instructions from the medical staff and bought the tonics and medicines they suggested, that he could not afford enough medication to insure a full recovery. Due to situations like this, modern medicine and health care are beyond the reach of most of the rural poor. One group particularly affected is women of childbearing age.

Childbearing and Family Planning in Sugao

In Sugao the most effective means for a bride to consolidate her position in her new family is to produce a male child who will carry on the family name, run the family farm, and care for the aged. The process of conception and childbearing, however, is fraught with difficulties for such young women. Since marriages are arranged, young Sugao couples generally do not know each other beforehand. The woman is usually from another village. Once married, the couple lives under the control of the elder members of their family. Social interaction between men and women, even within the family, is fairly restricted in Hindu society. For example, in a traditional family it is expected that a young bride will draw the end of her *sari* over her head to screen most of her face when a man walks into a room. She is not encouraged to address the men in the family directly too often. Older family members often criticize a new couple for talking or displaying too much interest in, or affection for, each other. As other authors have pointed out, perpetuating this distance between husband and wife is a traditional operating principle for the extended, joint, Hindu family (Roy 1972; Desai 1957). Under these circumstances it is difficult for a husband and wife to establish a relationship based on companionship. The situation is naturally aggravated when the man spends most of the year working in Bombay or other places far from Sugao. His visits home elicit pressure on the couple to produce sons.

Compounding the difficulties of such unions, couples in rural households rarely have any privacy. Contrary to popular perceptions, housing in rural areas is crowded. Even the few big houses are divided into only a few large rooms.[2] Men and women generally sleep in separate rooms. Women reported that in the early days of their marriages their mothers-in-law arbitrarily decided on which days to make special provisions so that the young couples could sleep together in some corner of the house. If a couple rebelled at these arrangements or was found to be meeting surreptitiously, the mother-in-law was liable to loudly describe to all, in unflattering terms, their unbecoming itch for sex and need to sleep "leg in leg"![3]

Family elders assume the right to advise couples in matters of childbearing. Whether a couple should have children is not considered a personal choice but one in which the father-in-law and mother-in-law have a strong say. If they do not want the young to restrict their families, it is difficult for couples to go against their wishes.

Generally there is a fair knowledge of family-planning methods in Sugao, but their adoption and practice are hindered by the lack of privacy or even a place to store contraceptive devices or pills. Because of these social and spatial restrictions, sexual activity occurs at erratic and unpredictable times, whenever a couple can seize a few moments of privacy. It is difficult for them, even if they wish to prevent conception, to arrange to have contraceptive devices at hand. None of the households in Sugao has running water and very few have a screened bathroom area where a woman can cleanse herself or maintain the minimum personal hygiene required for using contraceptive devices.[4] Oral contraceptives are expensive and some women complain of side effects. The intrauterine device, which requires little care, has fallen into disfavor because of a reported high rate of infections and related problems stemming from poor follow-up treatment.

Only a few of the young, better-educated women said that they were practicing family planning. One woman had restricted her family to two sons by getting herself sterilized. Another intended to stop after one child but noted that she had been eager to produce a son to cement her place in her new family. Almost invariably, women are too restricted by the social and family environment to make unilateral, independent decisions about whether to get pregnant or when and where to have sex. Vidya, the woman doctor from Sugao who I met in Bombay, confided to me that some villagers know secret methods for terminating unwanted pregnancies. She knows who these people are, and that village women sometimes avail themselves of their services, but she has never been able to ascertain the content of their remedies. Such secrets are closely guarded and handed down only from parent to child.

Childbearing is still hazardous in the village. During my one-year stay, two women from Sugao died in childbirth. One was in transit to the hospital at Wai, in the back of a tractor-trailer hired for the purpose, when it became obvious that complications were arising. Since this was her third delivery, her family had assumed that she could safely give birth at home, saving them the cost of hospitalization. The other woman died delivering her first child because her family felt they could not afford even the nominal fees of the municipal hospital.

In 1977 the village "doctor" estimated that about 60 percent of Sugao women give birth in town hospitals. This cost about sixty *rupees* at the time. Another 10 percent were attended by the midwife. The remaining 30 percent had childbirth "naturally"; in other words, no one trained was around to help. There is one sixty-year-old woman in Sugao who acts as a *sueene* (midwife). She tends to the mother at childbirth, and massages and bathes the mother and child for the next twelve days. Her fee in 1977 was sixty *rupees* plus a traditional offering of a blouse piece and a coconut. These are presented at the end of the twelve days. Richer farmers also give a *sari*, which costs at least thirty *rupees*. The midwife is not trained in any formal medical sense and all her skills are derived from experience. Whenever I tried to question her about her methods she denied that she ever performed such services. Nevertheless, I often encountered her at houses where a new birth had occurred, and, embarrassed and somewhat frightened, she would acknowledge my presence. I think she believed I was a government official who wanted to meddle in her business.

Clean Drinking Water and Sanitation

In 1967 a system was installed to provide clean, treated, drinking water for the entire village population.[5] This has had a demonstrable positive effect on the residents' health. The system pumps water from a clean new well near the Chandraganga to a storage tank above the town, where it is treated and distributed for about three hours in the morning and a shorter time in the evening to thirty-three common taps scattered throughout the village (see "Introduction," figure 1). It has led to a great reduction in certain parasitic maladies, including the virtual elimination of a particularly horrible infection caused by a large tapeworm known as *naroo*. The incidence of water-borne diseases such as cholera also has been reduced.[6]

Women now fill their water pots early in the morning at the tap nearest their houses. There are queues to get the water and to store it for use during the day. Villagers prefer the morning time to the evening one since they are often working in their fields late in the day. While a pecking order has developed at each tap, conflicts arise about who should get water and when. Many mornings I was awakened by graphic curses and obscenities at the tap outside my house, arguments over whose turn it was to fill her pot. But these altercations are a minor problem, perhaps even an entertainment. The fact is that the new piped water system has considerably lightened the daily tasks of drawing and storing water. Formerly, women went to the bottom of the hill to fetch water from one of the two main wells, one for the Jadhav side of the village, the other for the Yadav. These wells had steps leading down so that people could reach the changing water level. This caused the water to become infected by feces and other organic matter carried on their feet, which led to infestations of intestinal parasites such as roundworms and hookworms. To combat this the government also introduced a well-upgrading program, in which at least one well in designated villages was to have such steps removed and a pulley system installed. These measures, coupled with better access to modern medicine, especially antibiotics, have raised life expectancy in Sugao.

Upgrading the supply and quality of water in a village is only a first step in the provision of safe drinking water to all inhabitants. In some villages, in spite of the laws against it, upper castes will not allow Mahars (untouchables) to use the common well. In dry summers, when other wells run low, Mahars may have to walk two or three miles to obtain drinking water. At such times, of course, there is no water to spare for bathing, and scabies and other skin diseases flourish. I once saw a whole Mahar community so infected, living in a village only a hundred yards from the major Bombay-Poona highway. Living near one of the most modern communications and transport networks in India was not enough to bring this depressed group into the twentieth century.

In spite of laws banning untouchability, many de facto examples of it persist in Sugao. Housing continues to be segregated into wards; the Mahars, cobblers, basket weavers, and rope makers remain confined in their segregated sectors on the periphery of the village. The laws forbidding discrimination in access to water from common wells have been circumvented by providing the Mahars with two taps for their exclusive use.

New Technology

One technical introduction that made possible the establishment of a piped water supply in Sugao was the extension of the electrical grid to the village in 1964.[7] One of the goals of this program was to provide power for agricultural equipment. Electricity is also used to power two of the three *gur*-making units and both of the flour and oil-pressing mills in Sugao. Before the flour mills were introduced, women had to grind the cereals and pulses that constitute their staple diet at home almost daily on hand-turned stone mills, a back-breaking task which has now, thankfully, been eliminated.

Use of electricity for house lighting is not widespread. In 1977 only about 35 percent of Sugao households had invested in electrical connections for the home. Many other families have chosen not to invest in domestic lighting as they feel they cannot afford the installation or the monthly charges. Many households with electricity own radios, but only rarely did I hear them tuned to the daily broadcasts of news or farm-related information such as market prices. This is partly due to the fact that small, marginal farmers have little control over when they sell their products. By the time crops are harvested many are in debt and must sell immediately, even if the market price is low. Only the large farmers can bide their time and sell in the off-season when prices are higher. During my stay in Sugao I heard most village radios tuned by younger villagers at maximum volume to stations that play modern, romantic, film music. There are few sources of entertainment in the village, and the radio has helped to fill this gap. From my perspective the effect was often less than desirable.

Electricity is used for street lighting in Sugao. The lights are a feeble yellow, and very sparse, but they do allow a fair amount of activity. When the moon is small or hidden by clouds the night can be menacing in the village, and the working day is all too short. Electric lighting has lengthened the day to some extent. A tax is assessed on all families to pay for the street lighting. This is resented by some who claim that they have no need to be "up and about at night."

The technology of producing methane gas from cow dung or other wastes, including human excreta, and using it as fuel for such purposes as cooking and lighting, received considerable attention in India in the 1970s. Bio-gas facilities (or *gobar*-gas plants, as they are called in India) were expected to deliver numerous benefits including better health. This was to occur as a result of more sanitary disposal of human and animal wastes, with an accompanying reduction in insects and parasites, and through the introduction of cleaner cooking fuel. I have discussed elsewhere (H. Dandekar 1980, 887–93) the reasons why *gobar*-gas plants have not been adopted in Sugao. My major finding was that the scarcity of cattle, the shortage of water, and a lack of land on which to build plants, as well as the dubious gains from an individual farmer's perspective, made the plants unattractive.

New technology in health care, agricultural cultivation, and other areas has made an appearance in Sugao. Its "fit" with respect to social and cultural forces in the village is at times poor. Its adoption often depends on who will benefit from it most—men versus women, upper versus lower castes, educated versus noneducated persons, and residents versus migrants. Each group has its respective social roles and mores and differing capabilities for technological absorption. These have to be well understood when planners develop technologies appropriate to rural needs. One way to achieve this is to develop methods to involve targeted populations in program design and implementation. Only then will truly appropriate technologies be developed.[8]

Notes

1. The number of health personnel in India has been steadily increasing. For example, the number of doctors per *lakh* (10,000) of population grew from sixteen in 1950 to thirty-three in 1975; the number of hospital beds per *lakh* of population also increased from thirty in 1950 to seventy-six in 1976 (Jain 1983). However, most medical personnel prefer to practice in urban centers, where most of the advanced medical facilities are located.

2. In 1977 in Sugao, 77 percent of the families were living in one- or two-room houses. Thirty-three percent of the families, which ranged in size from one to fourteen people, lived in one-room homes. Another 44 percent, ranging in size from one to eighteen people, lived in two-room houses. The size of these rooms varies from two to eight *khan* (a *khan* is a unit of measure approximately five by ten feet, depending upon the distance between two spanning joists). A large joint family can be accommodated in a room of six to eight *khan*.

3. For a description of Sugao women's position in matters of control over their bodies, see H. Dandekar (1981).

4. In 1977 only 14 percent of Sugao households had a *mori*—an area about three by two feet with a trap to drain water, used for washing. None of the houses has a private water tap, although since 1964 the village has had a piped water supply system with common outdoor taps. Water for personal hygiene and cleanliness is therefore restricted.

5. A national water supply and sanitation program was launched in 1954 under which new drinking-water wells were bored and old wells restored.

6. When an illness does strike (for example, one Sugao people call *mothi bai* "big woman," which causes swelling of lymph glands that eventually burst, leaving the patient completely debilitated), I observed villagers making offerings to the

goddess Laxmi rather than seeking medical treatment in Wai. Appeasing Laxmi can be as expensive as obtaining antibiotics in the city, but for certain ailments many villagers seem to place more faith in her.

7. Village electrification in Maharashtra has been extensive. By 1981 almost 72 percent of villages in Maharashtra (some 27,914 of them) had been electrified, up from only 564 in 1958. In 1968, some years after Sugao was electrified, only 19 percent of Maharashtra's villages had the service (Bureau of Economics and Statistics 1960, 84–88; 1974, 52; 1977, 53). Thus Sugao had some "head start" in the modernization of its agriculture. The electrification figures for Maharashtra contrast favorably with those for all of India. In 1980, only 48 percent of Indian villages were electrified (Jain 1983, 94, 145).

8. For a discussion of an application of one tool intended to involve rural people in planning, see H. Dandekar and Feldt (1984).

CHAPTER 4

EDUCATION

Increased public investment in education has brought schools within reach of even rural people. A common experience for a visitor to a Deccan village today is to pass some undistinguished little structure and overhear the refrain of children's voices chanting in unison the multiplication tables or some other basic of education in India. The value of education is acknowledged in Sugao. However, its importance for a particular individual is tempered by considerations of gender, landownership, social status, and the general economic position of the family. Completion of high school is becoming a prerequisite for Sugao men who aspire to jobs in the formal, wage-paying sector of Bombay industry, or in that of the country at large.

The educational system in India has expanded considerably during the last four development decades. Statistics for 1981 place the overall literacy of the Indian population at more than 36 percent, up from 29 percent in 1971, and 17 percent in 1951 (Ministry of Information and Broadcasting 1983, 48). Sugao's literate population has increased dramatically, from 20 percent in 1942 to 62 percent in 1977 (see table 4B). These national, aggregate, or micro-level statistics do not, however, give much indication of the content of this education, except that more people now know how to read and write. What this education does for the individual and society remains a hotly debated topic.[1] The fact remains, however, that unlike developing countries that have not

enjoyed relative stability and constant investments in education,
India has become more literate.

Historically the country has esteemed education, and its
leaders have seen it as a means of transforming Indian society.
Even before independence, social reformers considered education the
most powerful means available to change discrimination rooted in
rigid social and economic stratification. After independence,
planners hoped to pull the depressed and untouchable groups up the
social ladder and loosen the bonds of caste by enhancing their skills,
widening their horizons, and enabling them to obtain better
employment. The lot of women was meant to improve as well,
through increased freedom from ignorance and dependency.[2]
Educated people, the proponents of increasing investments in
education claimed, would be enlightened people, and the oppressions
existing in society would be reduced. In short, education was seen
as the key program for needed social change.

The first records of a primary school in Sugao date from 1887,
making the current village school almost a hundred years old.[3]
There may have been some earlier indigenous schools as well. The
primary school system in the Bombay Presidency in 1901 consisted
of a class for infants and standards one through seven, making a
full primary course of eight years. The Sugao school's enrollment is
unknown until the year 1899, at which time there were seventy-two
pupils in six classes and one teacher. Of these only forty-six
appeared for the annual examination, which gives an idea of actual
attendance. In 1887 the school met in the large house of a Brahmin
and then moved to the house of a Maratha *pahuna* (guest). After a
few years it was moved again to the Maruti temple. By 1918 the
Sugao school was at least thirty years old and some of its earlier
graduates had children of school age. But this did not seem to make
the acquisition of an education and school attendance any more
popular with the villagers, and the Sugao school merely sustained
enrollment at the former level.

In 1923 a comprehensive Primary Education Act was passed.
At this time, the nationalist struggle for independence had increased
social and political awareness and more attention was paid to

An exercise period at school. The village's primary school has been in operation for nearly one hundred years.

The Sugao kindergarten has few toys or books and no drinking water. It is minimally subsidized with village funds.

education. Educating the so-called lower castes was stressed nationally. This is reflected in a school record in Sugao which states that in 1928 free slates, pencils, and books were distributed to lower-caste children. Two Mahar boys had in fact joined the Sugao school as early as 1892, but they and the Mahar students that followed were segregated from the others in the classroom until 1930. This practice of segregating the Mahar students was prevalent in many villages until quite recent times. Although compulsory education was introduced in the city of Satara in 1921, it was not made compulsory in the rural areas of Satara District until 1946.

By 1930 the Sugao school had an enrollment of some ninety students, and the villagers volunteered to construct a new school. It is significant that, although village people do not easily cooperate in a group endeavor, they organized a collective effort, volunteering their labor to build a structure to house the school. It was located adjacent to the Bhairava temple, perhaps in the hope of eliciting the god's cooperation in the education of the young. This structure consisted of about sixteen hundred square feet of enclosed space, divided into five classrooms, and about one thousand square feet of covered veranda. It was occupied in 1931. It also serves today as a common gathering place for the villagers on special occasions, such as the night I projected slides I had taken of Sugao.

In 1943 there were four teachers—a Brahmin, a Maratha, a Muslim, and a Christian—all of whom commuted from nearby villages. A high school was established in 1963, which caused an appreciable increase in the level of education for the entire village. By 1977, 42 percent of migrants from Sugao were educated beyond the eighth grade (see table 4A), as were 14 percent of those remaining in Sugao (see table 4B). In 1977 Sugao's literacy rate was 62 percent, well above the rate for Maharashtra State (47 percent in 1981). The ongoing contact with Bombay may be partly credited for this, as the Sugao migrants to Bombay have generally supported the concept of the school in Sugao.

The content of the syllabi in rural areas differs very little from that of urban schools. Classes are generally directed toward the

Despite its limitations, education is the main avenue to better jobs, usually in the city.

Although primary education is available to all, prospects are still brighter for the children of the well-to-do.

teaching of basic reading, writing, and arithmetic skills, as well as
the traditional social sciences. The natural sciences are taught by
the book; experiments and demonstrations are limited by the lack of
facilities. The learning, as is true of education in general in India,
is by rote rather than by experimentation or critical inquiry. It is
an education well suited to the preparation of individuals to fill
bureaucratic, white-collar, urban jobs and not designed to instill a
spirit of inquiry and innovation. Scant attention is given to
designing appropriate applications of knowledge to rural needs, such
as management of farm accounts, estimation of yields, land records
and legislation, legal writing and its comprehension, and new
techniques in agriculture and animal husbandry. The fact that
teaching is often routinized and pedantic does not, however, negate
the fact that it provides an avenue to city jobs and is perhaps the
only route to advancement available to the depressed castes, for
whom a quota of government jobs are reserved.

With the increased demand for education in Sugao, school
facilities generally have become cramped. Currently the English
High School is housed in a building enterprisingly constructed for
this purpose by a Brahmin family in the village. They now enjoy a
comfortable rent from this property, a reward for their foresight.
The primary and secondary schools are housed in various temples.
These quarters are much too small and lack recreation areas and
facilities such as drinking water and toilets.

Periodically village leaders and migrants working in Bombay
voice their concerns over this situation and discuss ways to create
new facilities. Money raised in 1974 by the Bombay migrants
expressly for the purpose of building a new high school languishes
in a Bombay bank because of a power struggle between village
leaders and the Bombay group. The migrants wished to have their
funds managed by the trust that currently runs the school.
Previous experience with funds given to village leaders for
educational scholarships had not been reassuring, as the funds were
siphoned off for other uses. The stipulation that the new funds for
building and scholarships should be in outside, "neutral" hands was
not well received by the power elite, who construed it as a challenge
to their control of the school system and refused to cooperate. The

money remains untouched, losing its value daily with inflation. It is a tangible manifestation of the rift that develops between men who live and work in Bombay, and who thereby disenfranchise themselves from power within the village, and the elite that remains behind and controls matters of importance to rural life. To some extent the Bombay migrants are seen as "troublemakers," and they are given little opportunity to make changes in Sugao.

Village Teachers

The founding of the high school in 1963 created a few high-status jobs for teachers in Sugao. The high-school teachers are better educated than their primary-school counterparts. Some of the younger ones have college degrees and are generally more urban in lifestyle than the village people they live with. Since the village has acquired such amenities as electricity for domestic use and a piped water system, more Sugao teachers live in the village itself rather than commuting from nearby towns. Because most teachers are newcomers in Sugao they feel alienated and uprooted in their new location. Initially they lack detailed knowledge of the village power structure, but as most of them are from rural areas and are sensitive to political realities there, they know they must be very careful in their treatment of various students and families.

A teacher's position in the village can be difficult. If he or she is too dedicated and earns the trust of the poor, the teacher is seen as a threat to the village power structure. The story of Patil and his wife Kamla, both teachers in Sugao, is illustrative. Patil taught in the Sugao high school and Kamla in the primary school. By 1977 he had been teaching for thirty years and she for twenty-six; during the last six years both had taught in Sugao. When I met Patil he was no longer teaching in the Sugao school, having been transferred to another village about five months earlier at the instigation, he claimed, of village leaders who were uneasy about his popularity with poor families and students.

Kamla had been trained as a teacher in an era when women's education was not common because her father, also a teacher, believed in the education of females. Life was difficult for her because, in addition to her job at the school, she had to do all the household chores. Domestic work outside one's own home is considered low-status labor in the village, and it is never easy to hire someone. Of course she had to be appropriately hospitable, and offer tea and refreshments when visitors called, as they did in some numbers since the Patils were popular teachers. Being "too busy" to be hospitable is not an acceptable excuse. Furthermore, Kamla was pregnant when I met her. In the teaching profession women are allowed three months for maternity leave. After this period was over, the Patils planned to find someone to care for their child until it was a year old, at which time it would be taken to school with the parents just as their five older boys and one girl had been. Professionalism does not stand in the way of procreation in Sugao! They hoped to obtain teaching positions in the same village, and were unhappy about Patil's transfer because, they claimed, their troubles were the fruit of doing their jobs too well for the comfort of vested interests in the village.

Another husband-and-wife team of teachers in Sugao is a young Muslim couple, Yusef and Habiba Khan, who are better educated than the Patils. Both have college degrees and teach in the high school. Educated Muslim women are so rare that it was especially surprising to find Habiba in Sugao, but, again, she had a father who supported her education.

The Khans are relatively modern in outlook, and husband and wife relate to each other in ways that are at odds with the normal pattern of interaction between the sexes in the village. Yusef can be seen at times helping with household chores or chatting with Habiba in the evening as if she were his friend. They told me that they are careful not to flaunt their relationship in the village. When Yusef is helping to clean the house or doing other "women's work," they close the shutters and lock the door. In the eight years I have known them they have moved their household to three or four different locations in the village. They do not own a house in the village and their landlords always worry that they may acquire tenants' rights. After a few years they are always asked to move. The Khans acutely feel the lack of other couples with whom they have enough in common to become friends. Their sense of alienation is easy to understand, but difficult to remedy.

Teachers from outside the village can hardly be blamed if they keep a low profile most of the time. They are not well paid, they live in whatever housing is available, and they lack the support of extended family that is the mainstay of village society. They are watched closely by the village elite. For single women who are posted to such villages the situation is even more difficult and complex, particularly in the matter of finding appropriate housing. Even educated young girls in Sugao are critical of women teachers who become active in larger village matters. I remember being surprised when my housemate Suma commented in passing that Habiba was "too forward," poking her nose into village matters that were not her concern.

Instead of becoming role models and people to whom villagers might turn for advice, teachers in many instances are isolated from village concerns. Most simply endure their two- or three-year posting in the village and try to obtain a transfer to a place closer to home. Teachers from the village itself usually fare better. The two in Sugao at present come from well-to-do families. Since they have an intimate knowledge of Sugao politics, they have a better sense of when to take a stand on an issue and when to keep a low profile. Unfortunately, since they are also landowners, they seldom oppose the village elite.

Male Versus Female Education

Despite its shortcomings, a high school or college education has become essential for men seeking employment or advancement in the city. A high school diploma has become necessary to obtain work even in the textile mills, for which the requisite qualifications were traditionally low. Advanced training in an Industrial Training Institute (ITI), one of which is located in nearby Satara City, usually leads to a relatively good job in private industry. White-collar jobs such as teaching and supervisory positions naturally go to those with the qualifications to fill them. Educated urban youth are often the first to get such jobs.

Cash cropping has increased in the village, and it has become important for farmers involved in it to be able to read and write, in order to assess the pros and cons of new government schemes, and to keep informed about such matters as market prices, new seed varieties, inputs, and methods. Although education in its present form is not oriented toward the needs of the farmer, it increases his ability to cope with changing situations.

In addition, since the introduction of the British method of recording land rights in the 1860s and 1870s, the legal system has increasingly controlled property relationships in the village. Arbitration of disputes by the village *panchayat* has disappeared, and recourse to litigation through the formal courts to settle land disputes and other issues is increasing. A farmer must therefore be literate in order to keep abreast of laws that govern property or affect his life in other ways.

As elsewhere, persons well versed in legal matters and able to afford the cost of litigation, both in time and in money, are those who tend to benefit most from it. In Sugao such well-informed individuals tend to be the better-educated, wealthier farmers. Some individuals of the poorer castes have obtained desirable jobs in the city because they were educated and qualified. These persons have been able to improve their housing and standard of living in Sugao. Slowly this is making a cumulative impression on the villagers.

Women too have benefited from the high school in Sugao. In 1958 only two women in the village had more than a seventh-grade education, as families were reluctant to send their daughters to the high school in Sirur. When the Sugao high school opened, a few women teachers were assigned to it. For both these reasons, female enrollment rose dramatically. By 1977, 6 percent of the female population of the village had a high school education and illiteracy had declined significantly. In 1942, 96 percent of the females over seven years of age were illiterate; by 1977, this figure had dropped to 51 percent. In 1977 women comprised 42 percent of students completing primary education, but only 11 percent of secondary-school graduates. Higher education for women was still extremely rare. Despite the fact that during my tenure in Sugao more girls attended primary school, 15 percent of village girls between ten and sixteen years of age were working on farms. Young girls are discriminated against in their access to education even at the primary-school level. This is a national characteristic borne out by the fact that in 1981 girls constituted 39 percent of all students enrolled in primary schools (Ministry of Information and Broadcasting 1983, 51).

Increases in literacy have not benefited women to the extent that social reformers and development planners once hoped it would. Fundamental changes in women's values, orientations, and aspirations have not occurred and the basic family unit in the village functions more or less as it always has. Social roles have hardly changed and few job opportunities for women have materialized. Only in teaching have women found salaried jobs in Sugao, and these positions are few and hard to get. Rural women, even if allowed to seek jobs by their family, find it difficult to compete with their city-trained counterparts.

The two female primary-school teachers and the one high school teacher in Sugao are outsiders. For a time an educated Sugao woman, Ratna, ran a kindergarten that the village subsidized minimally, but the funds were discontinued and the nursery closed. Although Ratna tried to reestablish the nursery on a private basis it was a difficult task. She had no toys, play facilities, books, or even a source of drinking water for her three- and four-year-old charges. I observed her trying to teach them the alphabet in the heat of a summer afternoon as they clustered together in a small temple in the village. It was tiring just to watch the proceedings, and I feared that the village leaders would never encourage Ratna's initiative. Upon my return in 1982, much to my surprise I found the kindergarten once more in operation. It had lapsed when Ratna married and left Sugao, but village funds had been allocated to pay another teacher. A young, educated, Neo-Buddhist woman who had married into the community now had the job.

Although many more girls now attend high school, the education of women appears to be a response to an increased demand for educated brides. A Secondary School Certificate (SSC) is considered valuable in arranged-marriage negotiations with educated grooms. A college education, on the other hand, appears to be a disqualification, since it is difficult to find a sufficiently educated mate in the rural network. Educated males also tend to demand more in the way of marriage gifts, if not an outright dowry.

The landowning Maratha families attach social stigma to women who have jobs and earn money. That is considered "men's work." The girls themselves do not view education as a route to financial and personal independence. They are more concerned with "widening one's horizons" and "increasing one's social worth," ideas imbedded in the liberal arts tradition of the West. Marriages are arranged by matching the relative social and economic status of two families, and the girls tacitly accept these prevailing norms. In poorer families, girls receive little education; they work from childhood, with their parents, as agricultural laborers.

Education also has limited significance in the daily routine of a married woman. Women do not use their learning to help their children with their studies, to read for pleasure, or to keep in touch with outside events; a woman reading a book is a rare sight in Sugao. The prevailing sentiment is that there should be something more productive for her to do. Younger, educated women are discouraged in subtle and not-so-subtle ways—often by older, illiterate women in their joint families—from making use of their education.

Few women are members of the village library, and despite the rise in female literacy I never saw a woman enter the *panchayat* office to read the daily newspapers. This is due largely to the social stigma that would be attached to any woman who mixed so freely with men in the office. But, even if separate newspapers were obtained for women, it is unlikely that many would avail themselves of them, for social attitudes encourage educated women to hide their learning. Daughters-in-law, in particular, are forbidden to read books and newspapers, join the village library, or speak out on any issue publicly. On one or two occasions, as I wandered around the village in the middle of the day, a time when young daughters-in-law are sometimes at home alone, I came across a woman reading. Thus caught, she invariably hid the book or magazine and displayed some embarassment at having been discovered.

At times the influence of education has actually been detrimental, leaving women less suited for village life. Formal education often downplays the significance of manual skills and the importance of agricultural work; it is geared toward the attainment of white-collar jobs and based on middle-class values. After years in school, women find it difficult to adjust to the backbreaking work in the fields. On the other hand, school does not provide such agricultural, business-related skills as keeping accounts, helping in farm management, or looking after technical matters. An educated village woman, therefore, often can no longer do agricultural labor, is not trained to be productive in farm management, and is unable to secure white-collar work.

A small number of educated Sugao women have found jobs in Bombay, but all their gains have been made in the city. Within the confines of traditional village society, education has not made any appreciable change in the roles defined for women. No doubt they have benefited from such less tangible effects of education as wider horizons and a tolerance for differences. But these changed perceptions, if they are to be internalized, must be reinforced by confirmation from society at large; this has not occurred in any obvious way.

Education for men has meant increased opportunities to migrate to the city for white-collar jobs. Better-educated male migrants from Sugao have been able to move from manual work in the textile mills to supervisory and civil service positions. On the other hand, almost no single females have migrated for work. Of the Sugao women living in Bombay in 1977, most were married and only eleven were working, just four more than in 1942. Of these eleven, five were cooking meals for village men, basically an extension of their traditional tasks in the village. Often they were in this business out of economic necessity, having been widowed or abandoned; most have acquired a male patron to support and protect them in this activity in the city (see H. Dandekar 1983B).

Only two Sugao women have escaped the traditional female role. One is a policewoman; the other, Vidya, is a practicing *ayurvedic* (indigenous system of medicine) doctor. The critical ingredients in their escape were strong initiative on their part, backed by an intellectual capacity to acquire the needed skills and the moral support of a senior, male, family member. Vidya was supported by her father partly because he had six daughters but no sons.

Although the success of these two women is grudgingly recognized in Sugao, they are not generally regarded as positive role models for others. Upper-caste men feel that, if a woman is working, it is because her men have been unable to support her. Educated independent women are viewed with suspicion. The women teachers in the village, for example, are carefully scrutinized; if single, they are subjected to a great deal of unwanted attention from various men estimating the extent to which the woman is "loose" and available.

The picture painted by Vidya of her daily life in Bombay indicated that she had restricted her vision to a narrow professional goal and denied herself a personal life to attain it. When I asked her if she would ever return to Sugao to practice, she shuddered and said, "They would eat me alive back there. If I set up a practice, I would be giving out services and medicine on credit that would never be paid and I would be personally harrassed by men. I don't have a brother or a husband to protect me from the attentions of even the most illiterate, who will regard it as their right to bother me, and my father will eventually get old."

That Vidya has accumulated enough savings to buy a one-room house in Sugao has not escaped the attention of the villagers. One man reluctantly commented to me that higher education like hers is a useful thing. However, he could not help adding that Vidya was in her thirties and still unmarried—a very undesirable situation. In general the cultural ambiance of the village is not supportive of women's aspirations, and those striving for a professional existence have to sacrifice their personal lives. A cultural ethos of independent working women is not on the horizon in Sugao, and better education has not been instrumental in promoting it. Looking at Sugao from this vantage point, it appears that until social, cultural, and economic changes occur in the village, more educated, "outside" professionals will not fit easily into rural life. The local elite with its vested interests will continue to be the dominant force in decision making, and an educated counter group will be lacking.

Notes

1. This is reflected in the title of Stephen Heyneman's paper, "Investment in Indian Education: Uneconomic?" (Heyneman 1979). This work includes a long bibliography of publications on this topic.

2. Maharashtra was a major focus of reform movements in general and the education of women in particular. Karves's school for destitute girls at Hingne and the SNDT college in Bombay are examples of institutions developed during this period.

3. This history of schools in Sugao is based on Kamat (1968).

CHAPTER 5

WOMEN'S WORLD

The Sugao world is a man's world. Women's voices are conspicuously missing in the body of literature on rural Maharashtra. There is a reason why even in perceptive books like Dandekar and Jagtap's *Gaon Rahati* the central figures are male, often upper-caste landowners. Women have roles in the stories that thread through the novel; they are victims or wantons, temptresses or tragic, sacrificing martyrs. But, the conditions underlying their behavior are not easily comprehended, the sketches having been drawn from the vantage point of upper-class men. This is true in much of the literature on rural Maharashtra. Most researchers are men; they write about the man's world they observe and are a part of in the village.

I had been in Sugao for some time before I began to hear the woman's perspective on various matters from the women themselves. In my initial household interviews it was usually the men who answered my questionnaire. Since I asked about assets and income, women often seemed reluctant to take the responsibility of responding, and, if the man of the house was away, she would ask me to come back when some responsible male was around. In time I realized that the woman's retiring stance reflects the role that Sugao society desires her to play. I was told by Priya and Suma, my house sisters, that they felt constrained by societal pressures to refrain from activities I considered routine: riding a bicycle, talking at length with women friends, reading newspapers, and going to town to shop or see a movie. I tried to develop a receptive ear for the things women began to tell me, and in time, as friendships developed, I began to probe for their reactions to different issues. Gradually I realized that, in the face of impetus for change, village society has successfully maintained the traditional roles and positions of both men and women.

Generally it appears that control over economic resources, access to lucrative or less arduous jobs, and societal recognition of an individual's decision-making and action spheres in village India are stringently delineated by the institutions of caste and family. My observations indicated that in the village these institutions are as much economic as societal. Furthermore, although they control both men and women in rural society, they appear to have fettered women much more, decreasing their chances of benefiting from change by narrowly circumscribing their interests and interactions. Caste and family strictures have been much more instrumental in controlling women's time and labor and in maintaining their traditional roles. This has been important for the continuing viability of subsistence farming, which requires ready and inexpensive labor, most of which is provided by women and children in the farm family.

The Significance of Family and Marriage

Most marriages in India, and nearly all marriages in rural areas, are arranged by the family. Marriage is as much an economic arrangement as a personal one. Great consideration is given to the process of finding suitable mates by matching individuals to their exact caste and subcaste. The marriage system operates to find a match between a man and woman of similar economic backgrounds and education whose families have, as far as possible, equal status within their communities. Within this range of possible partners, the marriage arrangement is influenced by an individual's attributes. For example, the eldest son of a wealthy family possessing much land will have more women to choose from than one who is the youngest son of a land-poor family. Eldest sons have more power than younger ones in management of the joint family, and families with a good deal of land are more desirable than those with less. Similarly, if a woman is educated and beautiful, she is more likely to be accepted by an affluent family or a better-educated man than if she is neither.

However, such personal attributes in a woman affect the choice of a husband only at the margins of a selected and well-screened range of possible individuals. Before marriage, a woman's position is completely defined by the social status and caste of her father and her family. After marriage, it is determined by the status of her husband's rank in his joint family. Thus marriage is not an easy means to a dramatic, upward shift in a woman's status since the choice of a partner depends largely on her family's caste and its political-economic status in the community. A woman thus has little ability to change her personal status in society. At birth she inherits the position that accrues to women of her family, and the status of the family she marries into is also largely determined by this position.[1] Although it can be argued that this is equally true for men, finding a suitable husband for a woman is generally considered a major hurdle for a woman's family, but not so for a man's. The institution of arranged marriage makes a woman a burden to her family, but not a man to his.

There are no legal intercaste marriages in Sugao, although long-term liaisons between individuals from different castes have always existed. Social tradition prevents the formalization of these relationships. Because the Yadav and Jadhav families of Sugao, who constitute 55 percent of the village population, consider themselves of the same *devak* (subcaste) group, they do not intermarry. The other castes in Sugao are numerically much smaller. In 1977, 70 percent of Sugao's population of 2,583 were Marathas (upper-caste Kshatria), 6 percent were Neo-Buddhists (former untouchables), 7 percent were Dhangars (blanket weavers and sheep herders), 11 percent were various castes of traditional artisans, 3 percent were Muslims, and 3 percent were Kaikadi (basket weavers), Wadar (masons), and other depressed castes also considered untouchable (see table 1). Most of the families within these castes are blood related and do not intermarry.[2]

Since intercaste marriage is not practiced, almost all Sugao residents marry partners of the same caste from other villages. The young bride who comes to Sugao enters a village where she has no friends or blood relatives to support her emotionally. Through marriage she becomes a member of an alien family in whose midst she must create a niche for herself by leading an exemplary life. The stress is on conformance to the dictates of the village's social order and any signs of rebelliousness or initiative on her part are looked upon with disfavor by the family and village elders.

A woman is responsible for maintaining the family honor. Any suspicion of infidelity on her part is severely condemned. There is tremendous pressure, especially on higher-caste women, to be uncritically loyal to the family and dedicated to its "honor." Any deviation from the socially accepted norms for female behavior, any suspicion of sexual or emotional infidelity, can bring ruin upon her and her paternal family. I once observed a woman, who was managing her family farm alone, being questioned by her loafing teenage son about her whereabouts and activities that day and the reason for her trips to Wai. The family honor was felt to be at stake and the young son, who was doing nothing productive for the family, felt free to question his mother, the breadwinner.

Although society does not allow upper-caste widows to remarry and forbids intercaste marriages, it is very sanctimonious in condemning liaisons, intercaste or otherwise, between men and women who by custom are not allowed to formalize their relationship. Women are especially critical of other women who have strayed from the narrow path, even though they recognize that rural women often have no other means of survival. In 1977, I knew of at least three intercaste liaisons, all of which were de facto marriages. The fact that a legal marriage is not performed often proves detrimental to the woman's long-term interests.

There is great pressure on higher-caste women to make their marriages work because in these castes remarriage of widows is not sanctioned or practiced. A woman cannot remarry, even if she is widowed in childhood before the marriage is consummated. All men, on the other hand, are allowed to remarry. Consequently, there were 176 widows and only 28 widowers in Sugao in 1977, while at least 22 men had two wives. Although lower-caste women are allowed to remarry, second and third marriages are given lower status than first ones. Women married more than once cannot participate in certain rituals. Lower-caste men can freely remarry and any number of sequential marriages is equally sanctified.

In response to new laws raising the legal age of marriage, or for other reasons, age at marriage has in fact increased for both males and females in Sugao, and there are now far fewer child marriages. Child marriage was prevalent in the recent past. In 1942 almost 30 percent of the seven- to sixteen-year-old girls in the village were married, and often very young girls were married to men who were thirty or forty years older than they. Sometimes these girls were widowed in their youth and not allowed to remarry. In 1977 only 2 percent of the seven- to sixteen-year-old girls were married, an appreciable drop. However, this still leaves women many years of fertility in marriage and numbers of children per woman have not decreased. In 1977, women over age thirty-seven had an average of four living children, and those aged twenty-seven to thirty-six, still of childbearing age, had an average of three living children. Despite education and increasing age at marriage, women remain tied to childbearing, child rearing, and family tasks in their young adulthood and are hardly exposed to the larger world outside. Traditional work patterns and joint family relationships continue unchanged, providing few opportunities for women to develop an independent role.

As noted above, the security of a woman's position in her marital home depends on her loyalty to the family. In this the bearing of a son to perpetuate the family is critical. If she does not bear a son, her husband may remarry with the full force of societal sanction behind him. In this case, the first wife becomes almost an outcast and sometimes is forced to return to her father's house. Table 5 gives some indication of the numbers of women who leave Sugao for this reason. Most permanent outmigration of women from Sugao results from abandonment or some other circumstance that forces a woman to return to her former home. Usually she does not own productive assets such as land, has little education and few skills with which to obtain a job, and if she is of high caste remarriage is not permitted. Returning to her parents' home is an uneasy compromise. Even there she remains outside the mainstream of family life and its related functions and ceremonies, which are the major social activities of the village. For a man, maintaining a marriage is not as important and the consequences of failure are not as dire.

Social and Work Spheres

The confinement of a woman's sphere to the home is physically reflected in the lack of space in the village where women can socialize and the restricted radius of their travel for daily work. Although men congregate in the evenings at various places to gossip and smoke a *bidi* (an indigenous cigarette), women do not. I was often asked by younger women to linger a while longer in the area where women relieve themselves. Knowing that there were few other places where they could freely talk to me, I would try to comply until my legs rebelled at squatting or the smell and the flies became intolerable. In the house, under a mother-in-law's eyes, these same women were mute. Restricting women's interactions to members of the joint family facilitates efficient functioning of the family farm. The joint family is an organization well suited to subsistence farming as practiced in Sugao because the mix of women's and children's labor required at different times in the agricultural cycle is provided in-house.

In the joint family the male and female hierarchies are very rigid, with the women's hierarchy secondary to that of the men. In the women's hierarchy, the mother-in-law is dominant and the newly married wife is at the bottom. In higher-class families, the women's world consists exclusively of cooking and cleaning, with some of the older women going to the fields to supervise the labor. Higher-class families take pride in the fact that their women do not work in the fields. In the middle-income, smaller, farm families, women do the domestic work and toil in their own fields. In land poor or landless families, they do the domestic work and in addition toil as agricultural laborers on other farmers' lands.

Women prepare meals in dark, smoky kitchens that have hardly changed in hundreds of years.

The stove, all the essentials for cooking, and a basket for the baby.

The daily chores of drawing and storing water, cleaning the house, cooking, cleaning utensils, and washing clothes have changed very little in the years since development efforts were initiated. There is no tapped running water in any of the houses in the village, no bottled gas for cooking, and kerosene is in short supply for stoves. The daily meals, their method of preparation, and the utensils used have changed little. Cooking is still done over smoky, wood-burning, dung-plastered *chulas* (stoves) that leave utensils sooty and hard to clean. Cheap aluminum utensils are beginning to replace the traditional brass ones, and they are even more difficult to clean as the metal is softer and is easily pitted and scoured. The well-to-do buy stainless steel. This, apart from being more functional, has become a new indicator of social status. *Bhakari*, a thick unleavened bread made from *jowar* or *bajra* (varieties of millet) is still the staple food, although wheat is now more readily available from the ration shops and people eat *chappatis* (a thinner unleavened bread) made from it. There is no bakery in the village, but six home-based grocery stores in Sugao stock a few biscuits and loaves of bread obtained from the market town. This leavened, Western-style bread is relished by the Sugao residents.

Modern conveniences such as *gobar*-gas would provide clean cooking fuel and ease women's chores, and they are within the reach of the more affluent farmers of Sugao. Technology that improves working conditions for women is not valued highly by their men, however, and few families have a kerosene stove or even a smokeless *chula*. Meals are cooked in dark, smoke-filled kitchens, an environment that has a detrimental effect on the eyesight of the women. In the poorer families cow dung, small sticks, and twigs used for fuel have to be scavenged, usually by the women. In addition, women from poorer families must work as laborers and face the chastisement of the landowners if their domestic tasks cause them to be late. Despite all of this, they get barely enough to eat. If there is a shortage of food, priority is always given to the men in the family; the women have to be satisfied with whatever is left. Women are brought up to neglect minor ailments and do not attend to their own health problems until they become serious. The changes that have most eased women's daily chores are the piped water system and the two flour mills.

In the daily routine of household and farm work, women are closely watched by the family. The daughters-in-law, when new to the village, are dominated by their mothers-in-law. They are discouraged from forming friendships with other women in the neighborhood. New friendships are made surreptitiously at the water taps or in the fields where women relieve themselves. They have very little independence or cash on hand to initiate any action on their own, and innovation or independent actions are criticized as being too "forward." If a woman desires a few trinkets, or even a few more cups of tea, she obtains them only at the discretion of her mother-in-law. Young brides, and sometimes older women who have failed to acquire much status, will steal and sell a bit of grain for money to spend on a bangle for themselves or a hair ribbon for their daughters. Apart from a few pennies earned by raising chickens and goats, most women have no control over money or use of other assets.

Lack of decision-making power is pervasive. As mentioned above, although 25 percent of Sugao's farms are cultivated by women, there has been little change in their roles and responsibilities. All management decisions are a male prerogative, and women do only the most routine agricultural tasks. In some of the large landowning families, the senior women will oversee farm laborers. When wages are paid at the end of the day, however, whether in cash or a share of the crop, in most cases a male will come to the fields to oversee the payments.

Landownership

Although women have legal rights of inheritance, in practice most land is inherited by males. In Sugao, the prevailing sentiment is that village land should stay in village hands. Wives of Sugao men are considered outsiders because, for reasons mentioned above, they generally come from families outside the village. If a woman is widowed and has no heirs, Sugao men fear that the land will be inherited by outsiders. Daughters, since they are destined to be married to outsiders, are not even considered as claimants in land inheritance, whereas every son automatically acquires a share.

Thus, all Sugao women—sisters, mothers, or wives—are outsiders in terms of the land inheritance system.

Land is practically the only means of earning a living in the village. Its control and ownership is therefore central in determining economic status and power. In 1977 there were 399 landowners, of which only 30 were women. Barring three cases, all these women owned less than two acres each. Less than 3 percent of Sugao land is owned by women, mostly widows with no sons. Even then, the land owned by women is usually managed by men. Women who try to till their own land are often insecure and find it a precarious task, not only because they lack management skills but because they are cut off from the male grapevine through which farm practices and problems are discussed.

When a woman acquires a title to some land, many male farmers watch for an opportunity to acquire it on legal or technical grounds. A newly widowed woman who gains legal title to land often lacks experience in farm management. If she is from a well-to-do family, she may in fact have spent the bulk of her time in the house. Even if she has worked in the fields, she generally has not been included in management decisions and planning. Women, especially the older ones, are largely illiterate and traditionally have been discouraged from assuming responsibility. They therefore find it difficult to suddenly assume the responsibilities of a farm. During the early, critical period when she is finding her feet, a woman who acquires land may be duped and robbed of her acreage.

My hostess, Bharatibai, was the only woman in Sugao who owned as much as 7 acres of land. She was left a widow with no offspring some nine years ago. Since then she has had a hard time establishing a legal right to her land and stopping various relatives from taking it away from her. Her brother and, more importantly, an old friend of her husband from the city helped her in this. Subsequently she was able to establish her right to 5.5 acres of nonirrigated and 2 acres of irrigated land. She has had legal possession for four years, during which time she has had some unsavory experiences. The first year she leased the land on a share-cropping basis under which half the produce was to have been

With so many men residing in Bombay, women are responsible for
all but the heaviest farm labor.

paid to her as rent. She had little to do that year but take her
water buffalo to graze and see that she was not cheated. She *was*
cheated, however, the tiller spiriting away a *quintal* of this or that
before the division was made. If one loses as much as a sack of
peanuts the loss is considerable in the village economy.

The next year she tried to farm herself, calling upon her
brother to help with the sowing and an old servant to help at
harvest. During this time many well-to-do farmers tried to
persuade her to sell her land or give it to them for tilling. The most
insistent among them was a first cousin of her husband, a man
known as Mukadam (meaning "chief" or "captain") among the
Jadhavs. Now, in 1985, she has decided that she cannot cultivate
the land effectively herself and will give it to a new family each
year on a share-of-the crop basis. Still, this is at best a tenuous
arrangement. At any moment she could be taken advantage of
financially by someone more knowledgeable. She can barely read or
write and has great difficulty comprehending legal documents.
Without her husband's friend, who is versed in legal matters, she
would be lost. Mukadam is anxious to acquire her land. Since
Bharatibai is an outsider and has no offspring who can claim Sugao
blood, he feels she has a moral claim only to the product of the land;
its ownership should not be allowed to pass to an outsider such as
her brother.

Agricultural Labor

Women constitute 75 percent of the agricultural labor force in
the village. Until recently they were paid two-thirds the wages of
men. Since 1982, with the scarcity of male labor in Sugao, wages
have risen for men but not for women: now women earn only a
third of what men do for a day's work in the fields. Women
laborers do not operate more independently and in a wider social
realm because of their lack of capacity to earn income. They
usually come from the poorer families and their income is generally
consumed immediately. The day's earnings are taken to the store
in the evening and spent on the commodities required to make the
evening meal. There is usually little food stored in the house, and if

a woman does not find work one day the family does not eat that night. Therefore the female agricultural laborer never acquires the surplus funds that might allow her to make decisions regarding investments. On the other hand, an agricultural laborer enjoys greater social interaction and is psychologically better able to function in the larger world than her sheltered, higher-caste contemporary.

By the nature of their tasks and of their social ambit, rural women remain isolated. Even the agricultural laborers do not view themselves as a group with shared interests. Their poverty renders them particularly vulnerable to pressures so that, even when they work as a group, they cannot help each other to any large extent. A sick member of a *toli* (work group) may be helped with her line of weeding or allowed to rest while the others finish her task. However, if the owner is dissatisfied with any woman's work the team leader will usually drop her since the other women cannot afford to lose their employment. Some landowners also exert other controls over select members in the group; for example, one woman's son may be employed by the owner as a yearly servant or she may have received credit in the form of grain. Such personal obligations inhibit the emergence among agricultural laborers of a sense of solidarity. Their condition of marginal poverty leaves them with few options for mobilization.

Choices for Men and Women

The fact that 50 percent of Sugao men work in Bombay, leaving their wives behind to look after their children and attend to the land, does not have a significant impact on the work or spheres of interaction for most of these women, especially if they remain in the joint family system. Joint families continue to exist in Sugao. In 1977, almost 53 percent of all the families were still joint (see table 2). If a husband remits money to Sugao, it is sent either to the male acting head of the joint family (a brother or father) or to the responsible female head, usually the mother-in-law, who looks after day-to-day affairs.

If the joint family happens to be land poor, however, the economic imperative for remaining joint is not so strong and the family may begin to split into nuclear units. Some cases of this may be seen in Sugao, especially among the artisan and Neo-Buddhist families. When this occurs a woman may have some cash on hand with which she buys the daily necessities for herself and her children. However, a woman generally does not feel secure living separately this way. She often lives in a room that is part of the old joint-family house, in which case her actions are monitored with even greater vigilance to ensure that normal conventions of proper behavior are not transgressed. Infringements are noted and will eventually reach the husband's ears.

On examining men's and women's worlds in the village it is clear that, although men are governed by many of the same social constraints that limit women, they generally have a wider range of activities in their daily routine and a more active social involvement outside the immediate family and the village. They deal with management, marketing, and disposal of farm surplus. Men in Bombay send packages to Sugao containing clothing, tea, sugar, cosmetics, and toys. Thus men control a major portion of any surplus funds. A successful marriage is not essential for a man's survival. He inherits land, the major productive resource in the village; he has access to the village grapevine, better mobility, and more opportunities overall, even if he does not belong to a large landowning family. In general, educating a son is of higher priority than educating a daughter, so that in families where resources are scarce the son will be allowed to attend school while the daughter will not.

If the social atmosphere in the village becomes oppressive, a young man can move to the city. The question of a woman's honor, her chastity, and her credibility to the community at large as a potential marriage partner prevent her from making similar moves. In the past only destitute women moved to the city where they survived by serving meals. Most were forced to establish a liaison with a man. Women who survive in this fashion were and are maligned by villagers who look upon them with critical and

The *Tamasha*, an annual play, is considered lewd and not appropriate for female viewing.

The troupe travels from village to village. Donations from individual households support the yearly performance.

jaundiced eyes. Gossip abounds. Thus, rural society discounts and devalues women who show initiative.

Men have a wider field for social interaction. They are not required to do domestic work. Once a day's agricultural tasks are complete, they are free to gather at the common areas, smoke a *bidi*, or go to the village library to gossip and read the newspapers. They go to Wai on the weekly market day to sell farm products and may have lunch in a hotel, or, if they can afford it, see a movie. It is not customary to take a wife along on these expeditions. Some women go to the market towns, and occasionally see movies, but they do so surreptitiously. If a woman frequents theaters or is seen in Wai too often, people comment upon it, since her trips are seen to have less legitimacy than a man's. In the matter of extramarital relations people tend to wink at a man's philandering, whereas a woman who has an affair is considered spoiled and fallen.

Men's recreation is active. They wrestle at the annual village festival, they do an exercise dance called *legim*, and they are active in the evening religious singing called *bhajans*. If a woman attends the devotional singing too often, however, it is adversely noted by the community. Only men are allowed to watch the annual play that comes to the village, the *"Tamasha,"* which is considered lewd and not appropriate for female viewing. This is particularly grating to some of the better-educated women because the play is supported by donations from each household.

Women's recreation is more passive. During festivals they cook and make ceremonial visits to all the temples. There is little physical activity except during *nag panchmi*, the yearly festival, at which time women practice their singing and dancing for a week or two by moonlight when the domestic chores are done. But even this activity is not really carefree. Their songs are filled with dire warnings, bad omens, and a compendium of a woman's duties to her family. When social rules are broken, the retribution described in these songs is harsh.

Thus, one finds that what rural society asks of women and what it obtains through social, caste, and family pressures is dedication to the perpetuation of the family and the economic and social system of the village. The rural woman's life is brutal. It is confined to childbearing, child rearing, and performing the backbreaking tasks of domestic and agricultural labor. Although life for rural men is arduous too, its rigor is tempered by the fact that in general men have more choices and better control over their destinies. Caste makes a difference in the amount of work that is called for; higher-caste individuals do not have to work as hard to earn their basic subsistence. Men of higher caste have more control over their futures than men from lower castes. But it does appear that in all castes most men have more control over their lives than women do.

Notes

1. This state of affairs has been a constant for Indian women. For a historical analysis of women's position, see Desai (1957).

2. For a historical discussion of marriage rules, dowry practices, and marital relationships in Maharashtra, see Desai (1980, 71–79).

PART II

WORK IN SUGAO

CHAPTER 6

MAN AND LAND

Land is the most prized possession in Sugao. Ability to own land is intrinsically linked with family ancestry and sex. A combination of being male and from the right family—Jadhav or Yadav in Sugao—can make one an "insider" as opposed to a "guest," or worse yet, an "outsider."

Landowners hold onto their land, cherish it, and never give it up easily. To lose land is to have a lifeline severed. To become landless and perhaps forced to leave the ancestral village renders one virtually casteless over time. The village will forget you and your family, and no one will be able to vouch for your pedigree when it comes time to arrange marriages for your children and grandchildren. A stake in the village land system and its society is much more than an economic need; it is a social and cultural necessity not to be lightly abandoned.

Pride of landownership and the sense of representing the village to outsiders is clearly apparent to anyone who walks through the agricultural fields. It was especially so at harvest times when landowners would call out to me from one field or another and invite me onto their land to taste fresh peanuts, green tamarind plucked from the tree, or other delicacies. When the millet was just tender, I would be summoned to snack on the young ears, which the owner would flash roast over a fire of twigs. It was delicious food, eaten with a squeeze of lemon and a sprinkle of salt and powdered red chili. Young corn and wheat, I discovered, are also very good eaten like this, sitting in the dry dirt, the air balmy, the wind in your hair. On such days, when the rains have been timely and the harvest good, life in Sugao seems idyllic.

Land has a reassuring effect on its owner. I noticed particularly that some farmers, who were not informative or interested in answering my questions when I cornered them in the village, were much more cooperative in their fields. In the morning their excuse would be that they were anxious to get to work; in the evening all they wanted to do was smoke a *bidi* and chat with other men. I learned to catch them at noon in their fields, when the sun was high and hot, a much more reasonable time to sit and stretch one's legs in the shade. In the absence of eavesdropping neighbors, I usually got detailed information about their land, crops, animals, yields, and other assets. It obviously was reassuring to be on one's own land, where possession was clear and one could answer the inquisitive stranger's questions with less trepidation about the advisability of doing so.

Landownership in the Deccan has historically been vested in small peasant proprietors, called *ryots*. Unlike the *zamindar* system of Bengal, Maharashtra's *ryotwari* system of individual peasant proprietors is somewhat more egalitarian.[1] The earliest village communities in the Deccan consisted of small bodies of joint proprietors who were called village Thalkaris (*thal* referred to the land attached to a settlement). The Thalkaris were joint proprietors of the village itself and its attached land. This position amounted to absolute sovereignty. Although villagers paid taxes and owed allegiance to the local sovereign, the community itself was autonomous in all its internal affairs.

Joint proprietorship did not mean joint ownership of village land or even joint cultivation. It is doubtful that the land was ever jointly owned or cultivated; if it was, it gradually became subdivided into ever-smaller holdings of subgroups of the original families. In its external dealings with outside forces such as the sovereign, however, the village community of Thalkaris presented itself as a single unit. In Sugao, the Yadavs, Jadhavs, and Dhangars were once joint proprietors, and to some extent they regard themselves as such even today. Moreover, this special status is acknowledged by the other groups in Sugao.

As more powerful and alien kingdoms came to rule the Deccan, the joint proprietor system began to break down. Each landlord came to hold title to his land at the behest of the sovereign and thus became a tenant of the government. However, the special status of the Thalkaris continued to be recognized. They were called Mirasdars, acknowledged as descendants of the old village proprietary body, and their rights to their land were regarded as inalienable. Only unoccupied or deserted land belonged to the government in the sense that it could be disposed of as the rulers wished. The tenants to whom such land was given were known as Upri, and their claim to the land was contingent upon the payment of taxes.

Land tenure of village servants such as the Mahars was akin to that of the Mirasi except that it was based on satisfactory provision of services to the village community. Such land tenure began to be called *inam*, meaning gift, or *watan*, meaning duty or service. *Inam* land was free of revenue assessment. The state, by exempting these lands from revenue payments, contributed in a sense to the provision of essential services to the village community. The village was thus self-sustaining, communal lands having been set aside to pay for communal services. In fact, the state later adopted this system to compensate its village and district officials. The *patil* (village headman) and the *kulkerni* (village accountant) were paid with *inam* land. In Sugao there were always two headmen, one from the Yadavs and the other from the Jadhavs, and two accountants to take care of the two groups. The *deshmukh* (district collector or governor) and the *deshpande* (district accountant) also were allowed to hold tax-exempt private land in various villages in the district. These revenue-free lands, earmarked to pay for essential government functions of the state, also came to be known as *watan* or *inam* lands. Finally, the state made another type of land grant, which took the form of revenue from a particular parcel. Such grants were made by a ruler to maintain a secular or religious office, for past services rendered, or sometimes on whim. Such grants were conferred by every ruler to demonstrate authority and consolidate power.[2]

In 1773 the entire land revenue of Sugao, along with thirty-six other villages that surrounded the nearby fort of Pandavgad, was granted to a warrior named Raste by the prime minister of the Maratha Empire. The revenue was earmarked for the upkeep and maintenance of the fort, of which Raste was the commander. In 1802 the Rastes donated the revenue from Sugao to support a religious festival held in Wai. But neither the original grant of Sugao revenue to the Rastes in 1773 nor its assignment to the Wai festival in 1802 affected the Mirasi tenants in Sugao or the *watan* or *inam* tenures of many village servants, officials, and temples. The grant to the Rastes did not affect the internal organization of the community or its relation to the village lands.

The British Period

At the beginning of the nineteenth century, when the British took over administration of the country, the proprietary land rights of the Yadavs, Jadhavs, Dhangars, and Kochales who were Mirasdars were transferable. The land could be sold or mortgaged. The rights of the Mahars and other village servants to their *inam* land were not transferable but could be mortgaged. This was also true of land reserved for temple and mosque maintenance. As far as possible, British administrators were anxious to avoid any changes in this system of revenue collection. For example, the new British government recognized the Rastes' right to the entire land revenue of Sugao. Occupancy of land was allowed to all tenants as long as they paid the land assessment.

In time the British administration carried out systematic surveys and compiled land records. Sugao was surveyed in 1876, later than most villages in the Satara District, because it was an "alienated" village (one whose land revenue had been allocated to some party other than the state, in Sugao's case to the Rastes). Settled conditions followed the establishment of British rule. Transfer of land was made easier by the land survey and land records, as a result of which a number of plots changed hands in Sugao.

The British land survey made it clear that decisions as to which lands should be revenue paying and which revenue free had to be more systematic. In 1920 the hereditary office of *kulkerni* (accountant) was abolished and replaced by a salaried village accountant called the *talathi*. Revenue collection in Sugao became part of the general revenue administration in the district. By 1931 the government had taken over the entire village administration and the Rastes had ceased to have any connection with it.[3] The rents on *inam* land remained unchanged, but the revenue assessments of other land were increased. Obviously the British were losing a considerable amount of revenue to *inam* tenure, but they wished to avoid radical reform. *Inam* tenures therefore continued until the end of the British administration in 1947.

Post-independence

When the independent Indian government took office it began to abolish *inam* tenure under the new constitution, on the grounds that the services for which revenue-free land tenancy had been granted were no longer being performed. The *inams* of the *kulkerni* and *deshpande* were abolished in 1950, personal *inams* in 1953, and by 1959 all inferior service *inams* had been abolished. Abolition of the inferior service *inams* changed not just the services these families rendered to the government but also those they rendered to the village on the *baluta* system. By 1978 *baluta* payments and service by artisans such as the *ramoshi* (watchman), *mahar* (village servant), and *koli* (water carrier) were discontinued. *Patil* (village headman) *inams* were next to go and *patils* began to receive a salary from the government. In Sugao today, little remains of the old order of lands granted in return for the rendering of services.

A switch to cash or in-kind payments for work performed has permeated the personal arrangements between artisans and cultivating families. More and more farmers prefer to pay cash for a personal service such as a haircut. The cultivators grumble about the payment of *baluta* to religious functionaries such as the *gurav* (priest) and the *kumbhar* (potter), and it seems likely that these arrangements too will soon entirely disappear. Other arrangements that were essentially barter agreements (food in exchange for work) have been gradually replaced by cash payments. Consequently, service artisans in Sugao have lost the assurance of being able to earn a living that they had as *balutedars*.

Thus, since independence the village system has changed from a basically autonomous unit that provided for most of its needs internally to one more tied to the regional administrative system and increasingly subject to outside laws and the influence of the state. The traditional system of land distribution and tenure, structured to support a certain number of artisans, has been undermined by legislation affecting such tenure. Gradually the village has become more monetized and less autonomous.

At independence the new national government was acutely aware of the importance to rural society of control and ownership of land. In 1941 more than 86 percent of the population lived in the countryside, of whom more than 82 percent depended on agricultural cultivation and labor as their primary occupations. In Sugao in 1942, 86 percent of all workers were employed on the land. It was not simply a question of who depended on the land for his or her livelihood, but also of who owned and controlled it. The independent government of India, in an effort to initiate egalitarian development, and under some political pressure to do so, introduced legal measures aimed at increasing access of the rural poor to land. Land-reform legislation of various types was introduced, most of it after 1950. Its goal was to increase both equity in distribution of benefits and efficiency of production in agriculture.

In 1977 I calculated farm size within each community group in Sugao, adjusting for irrigated and nonirrigated land (in these parts irrigated land produces four times what can be grown on equivalent nonirrigated land). In 1977 farms of over twenty acres were owned almost exclusively by Jadhavs, Yadavs, and their "guests." All Mahar farms, on the other hand, were under five acres, and 60 percent were under one acre. Thus most of the

Some of the villagers' most pleasurable meals are taken in the fields.

A Sugao farmer stacks a portion of his harvest.

community is virtually landless and depends on agricultural labor for its livelihood. This is not a new state of affairs. The Mahars have always had very little land and with successive generations the situation worsens. Kaikadis and other depressed groups who recently arrived in Sugao are too poor to acquire any land to cultivate or even to live on, and are allowed to squat on richer farmers' land in return for services. Legislation has been ineffective in breaking the link between low social status and land poverty.

The average size of farms has been decreasing in Sugao. In 1942 only 37 percent of the farms were smaller than five adjusted acres (one irrigated acre equals four nonirrigated acres). This figure increased to 44 percent in 1958 and 53 percent in 1977 (see table 6). There is thus a growing number of smaller farmers in the village. On the other hand, although the number of farmers with twenty or more acres of land has decreased from 12 percent of the village families in 1942 to 10 percent in 1958 and 6 percent in 1977, this 6 percent continues to control 34 percent of the village land. Although the number of larger farmers is decreasing, those that have remained large now have bigger farms.

There was no major shift in the location of land belonging to various groups in Sugao between 1918 and 1977 (see table 7). In this table the increase between 1958 and 1977 of land held by the Yadavs and Jadhavs merely reflects the legal transfer of grazing lands from the Rastes to the two groups that had formerly enjoyed de facto use of them. By and large most communities maintained their old plots of land and acquired very few plots in areas belonging to other communities. The Yadavs were the more aggressive group and to some extent they seemed to be spreading into the Jadhavs' land, but this shift was neither rapid nor dramatic.

The impact of legislation on land distribution in Sugao was minimal for various reasons. The legislation to abolish *zamindari* and the placing of a ceiling on the size of landholdings were attempts to redistribute land from hereditary and absentee landlords to the tillers of the soil. Since Sugao was under the *ryotwari* system, the *zamindari* legislation had little effect on landownership in the village. The impact of land-ceiling legislation, too, was insignificant. Given the historical evolution of small peasant proprietors under *ryotwari*, land was already extensively subdivided and few families had holdings that exceeded the ceilings imposed. Those who did had relatively small holdings and were able to divide them (as did families in other parts of the country) so that land held in common was legally subdivided among family members. However, they continued to cultivate the land jointly, which was technically legal. Some members of these families lived and worked in the city, and their land was cultivated by the joint family in Sugao. They were de facto absentee landlords, which is not legal under tenancy legislation. However, only three or four of the leading families in Sugao have resorted to this, understandably so, and its eradication would hardly have a dramatic effect on the overall landownership and distribution pattern in the village.

Tenancy legislation was another intervention by the new government meant to improve the position of agricultural tenants who were cultivating land under various arrangements. New tenancy laws fixed minimum rents, improved security of tenure, and finally gave tenants the right to purchase the land they tilled.[4] The impact of much of this legislation on practices in Sugao was slight. In 1957, although land records indicated that 20 percent of all the arable land in Sugao was in tenants' hands, much of this was leased to them by families such as the Rastes or by temple *inam*-holders at nominal rents that were actually lower than the maximum regulated rent. In fact, only 5 percent of the total arable land in Sugao was under real tenancy, and less than 1 percent of the tenants were paying regulated rent. The remaining 4 percent paid a half-share of the crop. In Sugao, between 1947 and 1957, after more than ten years of tenancy legislation, the extent and type of tenancy remained unaffected; most tenants continued to pay the customary half-share of the crop. In 1982 this was still the rent charged by Bharatibai for the land she was leasing to tenants.

In 1957 the government radically amended the Bombay Tenancy and Agricultural Lands Act of 1948. This amendment stated that "On the first day of April 1957 (hereinafter referred to as Tiller's Day) every tenant shall be deemed to have purchased from his landlord, free of all encumbrances subsisting thereon on the said day, the land held by him as tenant." In effect, the amendment put the force of law behind the slogan that the soil belonged to the person who tilled it. Accordingly, all tenants subsisting on any land on April 1, 1957, immediately became owners of the acreage they cultivated. Ownership was no longer permitted for any use except personal cultivation or nonagricultural activities. Naturally this shattered the traditional concept of man-land-state relations so deeply embedded in village minds. The Yadavs and Jadhavs' belief that as descendants of the original settlers they had unqualified and inalienable proprietary rights to Sugao land had been respected by all governments prior to the British. Even under the British the Yadavs and Jadhavs clung to the belief that, whatever the government might say or do, their special right to Sugao land allowed them to use it any way they liked, subject only to the payment of their tax assessment.

The new law was a rude shock. To occupy agricultural land a farmer not only had to pay taxes on it, but he had to cultivate it himself. Sugao landowners reluctantly yielded to the dictates of the new order, realizing that if they did not personally cultivate their land they might lose it. The new law provided for this, and the machinery of the government could enforce it. During the hundred years of British administration Sugao landowners had acquired a respect for land records. They treated them as sacrosanct, and believed that if land was not noted in their name in the Record of Rights, they had lost it.

A field check of tenancy in Sugao, undertaken by the Gokhale Institute in 1959–60, revealed forty-two tenancies that were not recorded. The tenant farmers tilling the land were unwilling to admit that they were tenants. Of the twenty-five landlords who were leasing land to them, eighteen did not reside in the village. In some cases not a single member of the owner's family lived in the village; in others, the wife and children or some invalid member were left behind. Most of the landowners who lived in the village were widows or elderly persons. In all cases land was leased under the guise of service contracts. The tenants insisted that they were either working as farm laborers or under contract to do bullock work. In some cases the service contracts were even formally executed. Thus it appeared that tenancy had found a new form in which to survive.[5]

In 1977, twenty years after tenancy legislation was passed, I made a field check of the situation in Sugao. By this time land-to-tiller legislation had been fully implemented and there was no legal form of tenancy. The villagers knew this and had seen some ownership pass from landlords to their tenants. Landlords were therefore extremely reluctant to allow anyone to till their land, and, even if there was a tenant cultivating it on a share-of-the-crop basis, neither the landowner nor the tiller would admit to this arrangement. Other individuals, too, were reluctant to discuss the subject.

Landlords resorted to this share-of-the-crop arrangement with great trepidation. Rent was, as before, a half-share of the crop. The tiller and the owner shared the costs of fertilizer, manure, seeds, water, electricity for powering water pumps, and the cost of threshing and processing. Often such arrangements were made only with close relatives and even then not continued from year to year. New arrangements were negotiated often, the landlord fearing loss of land on some legal technicality if he permitted two or more years of sub rosa tenancy to the same individual.

This state of affairs was particularly problematic for women farming on their own. As a rule, despite legislation giving daughters an equal share in family holdings, land is in practice inherited only by the males. In 1977, a few women had inherited land, one being Bharatibai, my village hostess. She was always anxious about whom to lease her land to from year to year. She had few managerial skills and little of the technical know-how required to cultivate land on her own. After a couple of not too successful years of trying, during which period she claims her efforts were sabotaged by men who wanted to buy her land, she began to lease her acreage on a year-to-year basis for a half-share of the crop. Each year she agonized over the choice of the next tenant, for it had to be someone she could trust not to jeopardize her ownership rights. Even close relatives could not be completely trusted in this matter. But since land is scarce there are always farmers willing to take up tenancy, even under the half-share arrangement, and ready to deny that they are doing so if confronted about it for any legal purpose.

In 1977, 15 percent of Sugao land was informally acknowledged as being cultivated by tenants for a half-share of the crop. Discounting the Rastes' personal lands, which are barren and used only for grazing, this figure was reduced to 3 percent. Sixty-six percent of the remaining landowners in Sugao were cultivating their property on their own and 19 percent were cultivating it with hired labor. My field observations indicated that at least a quarter of the land worked by hired labor probably was concealed tenancies. Thus, sub rosa tenancy in Sugao in 1977 involved from 3 to 22 percent of total land under cultivation. This situation probably persists today.

In addition to the three land-reform measures discussed above—land ceiling, rent control, and land-to-the-tiller legislation— the new Indian government passed the Bombay Prevention of Fragmentation and Consolidation of Holdings Act in 1947. This act had two objectives: to prevent further fragmentation of an individual's holdings and to decrease the existing fragmentation by helping farmers exchange holdings of equal value with adjoining neighbors so that land could be concentrated into fewer but larger plots. The argument was that consolidation would make for larger plots and more efficient production on each holding. Further fragmentation was to be discouraged by not allowing subdivision when a "fragment" would be created.[6]

The economic rationale behind consolidation was that, if the fragments of land a cultivator owned, which were generally scattered throughout the village, could be gathered together in one piece, he could farm more efficiently. Guarding crops at harvest time, irrigating efficiently, and using machines to plough and till might all be possible. On the other hand, consolidation of all the holdings of an individual farmer was seldom feasible because the different plots vary in quality. Owning various types of land allows for cultivation of diverse crops which need different amounts of rainfall. In this way a farmer minimizes his risk of losing all his crops in any one year.

A subsistence farmer grows a little bit of everything he can to provide for his family's needs directly from the land, to reduce his need for cash, and to minimize the risk of losing everything in a bad year. Thus, even if a subsistence farmer's land is consolidated into one or two parcels, he may subdivide these into mini-lots to raise different crops. On these subdivisions rational farming techniques cannot usually be applied. Therefore, even if land were to be optimally consolidated, it is doubtful that a more efficient form of agricultural cultivation would result as long as subsistence farming is the general practice.

Consolidation efforts were not enthusiastically received in Sugao. Such efforts were not implemented in the village until 1971, and as late as 1975 village records went by the old survey numbers. In 1976, for the first time, an individual's holdings were identified by the new consolidated block numbers. A glance at landholding statistics on Sugao illustrates the need for consolidation. A study of Sugao holdings in 1960 showed that the village lands, consisting of over two thousand acres, were divided into 2,544 separate parcels. Taking into account differences in soil quality, it was estimated that 2,369 of these plots, owned by 355 cultivators, could theoretically be consolidated into 881 parcels.[7] Plot statistics for the village in 1977, after consolidation measures had been implemented, showed 1,801 separate plots, 303 under 219 single proprietors and 1,498 owned by 475 joint proprietors. Apparently there are still opportunities for further land consolidation in Sugao.

To understand the complexities of what occurred during the consolidation process in Sugao, I studied the detailed transactions concerning a number of plots of some irrigated land on the right bank of the Chandraganga. This area was irrigated with water channeled from the stream and was mostly owned by Yadavs. It consisted of 177 effective plots, of which 43 had changed ownership under consolidation to form larger, contiguous blocks. Originally plots in this area were tiny, partly because it is irrigated land, which is generally extensively subdivided. The 43 transactions resulted in 30 consolidated blocks, which, even after consolidation, were under "standard size" (defined as one acre) and classified as "fragments." It is apparent that the consolidation exercise did not appreciably increase the size of holdings; 87 percent of the plots remained under standard size and 74 percent were under one-half acre.

Consolidated blocks cannot legally be divided. However, I found at least two cases where plots had been informally subdivided between cousins who cultivated them as two separate parcels. My field survey was made just one year after consolidation of holdings in Sugao. Over time more plots will be similarly subdivided on the basis of verbal agreements, since they cannot be so apportioned legally. Denied a mechanism for documenting these divisions, the strong-arm elements in the village will probably over time appropriate land from the timid and less able.

Such takeovers had already begun in 1979 when I revisited Sugao. A farmer from one of the Dhangar families followed Mr. Jagtap and me around the village and asked us to visit his house to discuss a problem. It turned out that in the consolidation process his small fragment of prime, irrigated land on the right bank of the Chandraganga had been given to his neighbor. In lieu of it, by oversight or collusion, he had received a clearly inferior piece of property. He had made several trips to the *taluka*, district, and regional offices, and had bribed various officials, but he had not been able to have the matter resolved in his favor. Even the man who had received the land admitted that an error had occurred, but land records are land records, and he intended to keep his new holding.

The Dhangar wanted to continue his fight to regain his fragment of land, but not being well-to-do he could hardly afford the expense. Literate but unable to understand the legalities and impeded by unhelpful bureaucrats at every step, he seemed exhausted and helpless. But there was no giving up; if he lost his land, he would lose his family's only means of survival in the village. The Dhangar was also sentimentally attached to that particular plot. His family had owned it for generations. His case is illustrative of the manner in which an impersonal government official can make a mistake, or be bribed to make one. If there is no internal accounting or sense of justice in the village society, then the poor and less powerful suffer. The minimal success of consolidation can be partly explained by this reluctance of villagers to exchange ancestral land.

Thus, one finds that land-reform legislation in Sugao has had little success in changing patterns to benefit smaller farmers and tenant cultivators. In fact, to some extent abolishing tenancy has led to less productive agricultural practices. Given the ideology of increasing equity and distributing resources in rural areas, the rationale for land reform appeared sound. In implementation, however, given the persistence of subsistence farming and landownership patterns that do not easily change, land reform appears to be delivering less than was hoped for.

The tenacity of traditional land-man relationships in village India is a force to contend with in economic development planning. Land is scarce, there is competition for its ownership, prices are rising, and intrigue and rivalry are common when plots come up for sale. Availability is advertised only by word of mouth, and thus ownership usually remains within the same village subgroups. Furthermore, every farmer knows that, given half a chance, a neighbor or other villager will rob him of his land. There are always numerous cases of land litigation. Not surprisingly, any move to change existing landownership patterns is regarded with suspicion and distrust by the villagers. Small farmers are less able to afford litigation and are not as aware or informed of their rights. Given a choice, they would rather maintain the status quo than jeopardize their holdings for some uncertain, dubious benefit.

Consequently, between 1920 and 1977 there was very little change in the proportion of cultivable land in Sugao owned by each community group, with one exception. Under the land ceiling and tenancy acts the Yadavs and Jadhavs obtained land from the Raste family and other absentee Brahmin landowners. Otherwise landholding among the various groups is extremely static. This fact is particularly significant when one considers that land is the most important productive asset in rural areas. Thus it remains true in village India that, despite planning efforts to the contrary, an individual's opportunities for increasing assets and improving material well-being are closely circumscribed by the community and by the stratum of society into which he is born.

To summarize, land reform was introduced by the new Indian government to distribute land more equitably among the rural population and to consolidate parcels so that agricultural production could become more efficient. The major categories of land reform were aimed at eradicating large holdings belonging to landlords; reforming tenancy legislation so as to fix minimum rents, improve security of tenure, and give ownership of land to the tenant; and consolidating fragmented holdings. Conditions in Sugao illustrate that land-reform measures have not appreciably changed ownership patterns. Families such as the Rastes and Deshpandes, who did lose substantial areas, had in fact already relinquished their rights before reforms were introduced. On the other hand, tenancy legislation has not substantially improved the position of former tenants. In fact, it has become more difficult for land poor farmers to obtain parcels. Those who once might have been willing to lease land now choose to cultivate it, albeit not at full capacity.

Consolidation of holdings has been achieved to some extent, but there is room for improvement. Farmers resist consolidation efforts because they are emotionally attached to their ancestral lands, and fear that shifts in ownership may result in loss of good parcels in return for less desirable ones. It also has been argued that consolidation may not necessarily lead to greater efficiency in agriculture. Fragmentation of holdings and cultivation of a multiplicity of crops can be useful in spreading risks. The overall impact of consolidation programs, even those that are effectively implemented, will be marginal as long as subsistence farming remains the norm.

Despite the various attempts at land reform, there has been little change in distribution patterns in Sugao. Poor groups like the Mahars have stayed poor and have acquired no new land. Legislation has basically shifted legal ownership from absentee owners to the Yadavs and Jadhavs. The number of small farms has increased but the larger farmers have obtained a greater percentage of village land. Distribution is skewed, and growing more so, a bleak prospect for the future of the poor in Sugao.

An unforeseen effect of tenancy legislation, one that can be seen in Sugao, is that land once available for rent has been taken out of circulation. Many of those families in which all adult males are working in Bombay (in 1977, 112 of the 399 cultivating families) would formerly have leased their lands to a tenant. These lands are now being cultivated by the women in the family who stay behind in Sugao. In three of these families, in fact, even the women live in Bombay, returning to Sugao just for sowing and harvesting. They harvest whatever crop has managed to grow during the *kharif* (the season following the monsoons). Such haphazard cultivation is not common but exists mainly because the landowner is afraid to lease his land to a tenant, and does not want to sell it, but must work in the city to support his family.

Notes

1. *Zamindars* were revenue collectors for the Moguls who were given outright, by the British administration, the land from which they used to collect taxes. Their holdings therefore were large and often cultivated by serfs or tenant farmers under oppressive conditions.

2. The description of Sugao is drawn from V. M. Dandekar's unpublished notes, Gokhale Institute of Politics and Economics. For a generic description of this system in the Deccan, see Desai (1980, 1–29).

3. It is worth noting that this change in the administration of Sugao was implemented more than a hundred years after the British established it in neighboring villages because Sugao revenue had belonged to the Rastes. The hundred-year delay in introducing the new order in Sugao illustrates the

reluctance with which the British encroached on the existing internal relationships of villages.

4. The Land Revenue Code adopted in 1871 by the British government did nothing to regulate rates at which land was rented. These had been fixed historically by the landlord at any amount and in any form he chose, including the provision of services by the tenant. Since land was scarce, the landlord was dominant and would often levy extra charges on his tenants. The Bombay Tenancy Act of 1939 and an amendment in 1946 abolished such additional levies and established a rent ceiling for the first time. This was set at one-fourth of the crop (or its value) for irrigated land and one-third of the crop (or its value) in other cases.

    Most land leases in Sugao were for a share of the crop. Despite laws to the contrary, the share was uniformly set at half the product of the land, whether irrigated or not, and there were few cash rental agreements. This half-share seems to have been agreed upon uniformly throughout India and is an indication of the high premium on landownership. This is in stark contrast to conditions in the new countries of the Western world where land was much more freely available. In 1952 a notification was issued that fixed the maximum share-rent in Satara District at one-sixth of the crop. This legislation had no impact whatsoever on the share-rent in Sugao. Landlords continued to blithely set it according to custom, at half the crop. In response to this, in 1956 an amendment was passed abolishing all rents in the form of crop share, and at the same time prescribing the maximum and minimum cash rents in terms of multiples of the revenue assessment. The rents for all the lands in the Wai Taluka were set at five times the revenue assessment.

5. This historic analysis draws heavily from unpublished notes, a rough draft manuscript, and data collected by V. M. Dandekar of the Gokhale Institute of Politics and Economics.

6. A "fragment" was defined as any plot smaller than a plot of "standard size," which in Wai Taluka was set at two acres of dry land, one acre of irrigated land, or one-half acre of rice land. Standard-size (one acre) plots were to be created by severely restricting transfer of existing fragments to prevent their perpetuation, and by stipulating that they could only be sold or transferred to contiguous holdings. In addition, consolidation proceedings were to be promoted in the villages to eliminate scattered holdings, and a new system of consolidation block numbers was to replace the old survey numbers.

7. For a detailed case study of the effects of consolidation on Sugao land, see H. Dandekar (1978, 130–36).

CHAPTER 7

MODERNIZATION OF AGRICULTURE, MONETIZATION OF THE ECONOMY

The hustle and bustle of everyday life in Sugao revolves around farming. The agricultural cycle is geared, in the Sugao farmer's mind, to the moon and the astrological sign (of which there are twenty-seven in the Hindu calendar) ascendant at the time. Village activity changes with the agricultural season, the pivot around which village society is organized.

Along with better health care and modern medicine, the development decades have brought high rates of population increase. Despite this, Sugao's resident population increased only from 1,621 in 1942 to 2,583 in 1977 (1.8 percent per year), a much slower growth rate than that of Maharashtra State, where population has grown by more than 2.4 percent per year since 1951. This is mainly due to the migration of Sugao men primarily to Bombay; by 1977 there were almost as many Sugao men earning a living outside as there were in the village itself.

The population increase in Sugao has led to decreasing land-to-person ratios. Whereas in 1942 there were 1.34 acres (.54 hectares) of land (unadjusted for irrigated and nonirrigated) for every person in the village, by 1948 there were 1.06 acres (.43 hectares), and by 1977 this had shrunk to .84 acres (.34 hectares). It is not possible to increase the amount of land available for farming in Sugao because even the most marginal arable land is already under the plough.

143

At the village's present level of development, and despite migration to Bombay, Sugao's farms can no longer fully support its residents. Furthermore, those who stay in the village have little choice about how to support themselves. The rural economy has not diversified greatly, and farming one's own land or working as hired labor are the major occupations in the village. This is made clear in table 8, which gives the main occupations of Sugao workers since 1942. More Sugao workers (90 percent) now depend on agriculture and its related activities than ever before.[1]

The fact is that most Sugao farms are not large or fertile enough to fully support a family. Faced with this reality, Sugao farmers, like those in other villages in Satara District, have two options: remain in the village and augment income from their subsistence farms with locally available work, or migrate. In 1977, almost 50 percent of the village men were living outside Sugao but maintained their families and households in the village. Out of a total of 399 landowning farm families, 75 (19 percent) had no men living in the village and another 22 farms belonged to single or widowed women. Ninety-seven (or 25 percent) of Sugao farms were cultivated primarily by women.

Because of the traditional *ryotwari* system, and the social control exerted over landownership, most villagers working in agriculture are owner-cultivators. Over the years land has been divided and subdivided among family members so that, in 1977, 399 of the 493 Sugao families owned land. Table 6, which gives the size of landholdings, shows that many are miniscule, and the owners virtually landless. However, even those with tiny parcels cultivate them diligently, both because the land is ancestral and sacred, and because it is usually the only asset that will provide them some security in their old age.

Farming in Sugao in 1942

In 1942 most farming in Sugao was for subsistence, that is, cultivation was primarily for family consumption. These farms were operated mainly by family members who provided the bulk of the labor, augmented by reciprocal work-sharing arrangements between landowning families. Thus, to own land in Sugao was to have some assurance of work and a livelihood. A farm-business survey by the Gokhale Institute in 1938 calculated that of the total workdays put into agriculture 65 percent were contributed by the family, 15 percent by mutual exchange between landowning families, and only 20 percent by hired labor employed at peak times on a casual basis.[2]

Agriculture was primarily dependent on rainfall, which in the *mawal* region where Sugao is located is generally sufficient for a good *kharif* crop. (The *kharif* season is the main growing season in winter following the monsoon rains.) Only about 15 percent of the land was irrigated, by small earthen dams built across the stream. The first rains were always anxiously awaited, the monsoon often making the difference between survival and starvation. Soils in Sugao are of three main types: the medium to deep black soil found on river and stream banks, which is rich and suitable for garden crops; *malran* or lighter soil suitable for *bajra* (a variety of millet); and red or laterite soil, best suited for rice or fruit. Soil type and availability of water determine the mix of crops cultivated in the village.

In 1942, *bajra*, interspersed with pulses that mature and are harvested earlier, were the main *kharif* crop of the village (see table 9). Wheat, gram, indigenous *jowar*, and safflower were grown in the *rabi* (spring) season. Cash crops such as sugarcane, chili peppers, fruit, potatoes, and turmeric were cultivated on only 8 percent of the farmed land. Cereals were grown on 77 percent of the land and pulses on 12 percent of it. Thus, food-grain production predominated. Of the gross value of total agricultural produce, 35 percent was sold for cash while 17 percent was used for in-kind payments.[3] The rest, almost half the production, was kept for home consumption or for use as seed.

In 1942, as is indicated in table 2, many farming families were joint or extended families in which a number of brothers and their wives and children would live, cook, and eat under the same roof and cultivate the family lands together. This organization was well suited to subsistence agriculture because it provided, within the family, the needed combination of female, male, and child labor necessary for cultivation of a given set of crops.

Post-independence Changes

Following independence, improving the productivity of agricultural land became a major goal of rural development. The government's efforts were directed toward boosting production through cultivation of more land, enhancing the quality and extent of irrigation, inducing changes in the cropping pattern so that more cash crops were produced, and seeing that high-yield, hybrid seeds were used along with chemical fertilizers and pesticides.

In Sugao there was little additional land that could be brought under cultivation. However, production could be increased by improving irrigation. Reliable year-round irrigation allows the cultivation of several crops a year, of crops that have higher yields, and of crops that sell for higher prices. The total land area of Sugao is 2,691 acres, of which 2,175 are cultivable. Records show that in 1904 about 330 acres, or 15 percent, were classified as irrigated. Most of this resulted from eight earthen dams across the village stream, supplemented by a few wells. The earthen dams were washed away annually during the monsoons and reconstructed communally by the farmers who used them. Sugao farmers have been irrigating their fields since the village was first settled. They have developed a complex water-distribution system by which each plot of irrigated land is allocated a certain percentage of the available water.

Recent public investments have improved the delivery of this water. In 1965 the state government rebuilt, with permanent masonry construction, four of the eight earthen dams. These need little maintenance. In 1977 government officials claimed that thirty-four additional acres were irrigated in Sugao as a result of this construction, but my field observations did not confirm this. Water supplied by the improved dams was more reliable but remained available only to those who previously had a claim on it.

A double bullock team, plowing, and sowing.

Harvesting *jowar*.

The extra water often was wasted because the farmers let it drain onto the road. The farmers were afraid that if they shared with their neighbors in good years, the neighbors might claim a share when times were bad (indeed, some easement laws might allow them to do this). As a result, the improvement of the traditional dam system of irrigation in Sugao has not increased the amount of irrigated land.

Wells are the other form of irrigation in Sugao. Most improvements of existing wells have been made, or new ones have been dug, by individual farmers. Between 1942 and 1977 the number of working wells in Sugao increased from thirty-nine to fifty. In the 1970s the government made low-interest credit available to land poor farmers to enable them to construct irrigation wells for their lands. But the few small farmers in Sugao who availed themselves of such loans found the funds insufficient to allow digging wells deep enough to reach water on their plots. These farmers found themselves in the unenviable position of having used their land as collateral for loans which did not help them increase their income.

Their experience has deterred others and farmers are extremely reluctant to use land as collateral for loans. This has effectively precluded the smaller farmers from taking various loans made available to them under other government schemes. In spite of legislation that makes moneylending at the village level illegal, borrowing at 100 percent per annum from local moneylenders is still the most common way that villagers, especially the poor, obtain cash. Generally this is in the form of small loans used to meet some emergency.

During a major drought in 1972, the government financed construction of percolation tanks in each village. Percolation tanks are shallow reservoirs which help retain monsoon surface waters. The water thus stored percolates slowly into the ground for some four or five months. Thus the water table in surrounding areas is higher for a few more months of the year and the village wells are better replenished, providing enough irrigation water for two crops.

In addition, wet crops such as rice can be grown in the percolation tank itself.

Some wells in Sugao within the range of successfully completed percolation tanks in neighboring Vele and Chandak villages increased their water supply considerably, some owners claiming that they had year-round water, whereas before their wells were dry half the year. One of these farmers was so enthusiastic about this improvement that he insisted I visit his plot to investigate the feasibility of taking some of this additional water, by plastic pipe and gravity feed, to his other plot half a mile away. He is a good example of the way enterprising farmers will rise to the challenge of expanded potential.

The percolation tank built for Sugao was originally not very successful. The earthen embankments gave way during two successive monsoon seasons and were not rebuilt for several years. In 1979, however, and again in 1982, I observed that the embankment had been reconstructed and reinforced in masonry at the critical pressure point. The villagers were pleased with its effect, claiming it had improved the water table of the village wells. Unfortunately, some of the poorer farmers in the community have paid disproportionately for this.[4] In addition, the main benefit of the percolation tank—raising the water table and increasing the available supply of water in wells within its range—has accrued to those who have wells, generally the more affluent. These farmers have used the extra water to make the switch to cash crops such as sugarcane that have higher market value.

As mentioned in chapter 3, the electrical grid was extended to Sugao in 1964. The extension of electricity to villages can be seen as both a political decision, illustrating the independent Indian government's concern for upgrading village life, and as an economic development strategy. While most villagers have not opted, or cannot afford, to employ electricity for domestic use, most farmers with water sources on their land use electricity to run irrigation machinery. Forty-five electric pumpsets have been installed by farmers on their wells. Thus, the state's infrastructure investment in electricity has stimulated private investment in irrigation. The replacement of bullock-driven *mhots* (irrigation devices that lift water using a leather bag) by electric pumpsets is pervasive now in Maharashtra, so much so that it is difficult to dissociate the rhythmic sounds of motors from memories of walks taken in the village fields. Those who own enough irrigated land to afford electric pumpsets are usually able to buy fertilizers as well. These well-to-do farmers now grow high-return cash crops such as sugarcane. Farmers without these resources cannot enter this new arena. At the same time traditional relationships of barter, and in-kind payments for labor, are atrophying. As a result the poor must increasingly look outside the village economy for a means of survival.

Farming in 1977

At first glance, farming practices in Sugao do not appear to have changed much since the 1940s. Traditional tools and equipment, from small scythes and trowels to bullock-powered wooden ploughs, continue to be used. However, agricultural extension programs in the region, facilitated by the partial increase in water availability, have resulted in a shift of cultivation on wet lands to cash crops. Sugarcane, a voracious consumer of water and fertilizer, has, with the establishment of refineries and the assured market they provide, become one of the most profitable crops in the Sugao area. In addition, extension programs have encouraged increased cultivation of such improved crops such as hybrid *jowar* and hybrid peanuts, which give higher yields per acre and have shorter maturation periods.

Aggregate data at the district level indicate that the major crops grown in Satara District are sugarcane (on irrigated land), *jowar* (the staple food in the area), rice, wheat, lentils (the main source of protein in the local diet), fruits, vegetables, peanuts, chili peppers, and cotton. Crops that are produced in surplus and exported from the region are coriander, peanuts, peanut oil, turmeric, chili peppers, onions, and garlic. Imported articles include groceries, wheat, cloth, building materials, and medicine. Wholesale trade is concentrated in a few centers such as Satara, Lonand,

Phaltan, and nearby Wai. The economy of Sugao is typical of the district and reflects the production pattern described above.

Aggregate figures on agricultural production are generally based on village-level statistics. Theoretically, the *talathi* keeps records of crops grown on each separate plot in the village every year. In practice, the *talathi* often compiles these records in the comfort of the village office. The Sugao *talathi*, who disliked village life, fabricated figures at his home in Wai by repeating the information recorded the previous year. Thus, in many cases the official crop record changes very little over the years regardless of what is actually grown.

As a check on this, I did a field survey in 1977 of crops grown on 177 plots of irrigated land and compared it to a field study of the same plots done in 1965. The comparison illustrated the growing monopolization of good agricultural land by sugarcane and the decrease in crops such as turmeric and sweet potatoes. It also revealed an increase in double-cropping as a result of better irrigation.

A comparison of the 1942 and 1977 cropping patterns in Sugao shows the following significant changes in crops: an increase in cash crops such as sugarcane, peanuts, *kharif jowar* (a hybrid variety of *jowar*), *rabi jowar* (the indigenous variety grown on irrigated land), and broad beans (a black bean called *ghevada* in this area); a decline in cultivation of sweet potatoes and turmeric (which were once profitable cash crops but were destroyed in the severe drought of 1971); and a dramatic drop in the cultivation of *bajra* (another kind of millet), once a staple food grain of the village (see table 9).

These shifts have altered the balance of a cultivation cycle that evolved through hundreds of years of small refinements. They have led to a greater dependency on outside inputs such as fertilizer and seeds, have disrupted traditional methods of maintaining the condition of the soil, and have led to a decrease in the variety of foods consumed in the village. A typical peasant meal eaten morning or evening in Sugao now consists of fresh millet bread with some pickle, a vegetable (if any were interspersed among the cash or cereal crops), or a thin *dal* (lentil soup) or *usal* (spiced bean dish). Often poorer families will have only bread for their meal.

By 1977 almost one hundred acres of irrigated land, 4.7 percent of all the agricultural land in Sugao, were planted with sugarcane, up from .7 percent in 1942. Sugarcane needs generous and regular applications of both water and fertilizer, both of which are paid for in cash. Therefore only the richest farmers can afford to take the risk of planting it. It requires more than a year to mature, at which time the return on investment is among the highest for any crop grown in this region. A total of 15 percent of the land was being used to grow cash crops, while 76 percent continued to be devoted to cereals. Of these cereals, *bajra* was being displaced by *ghasar matki* (another type of millet that can grow in less fertile soil), which took up 9.4 percent of the land, and hybrid *jowar* which occupied 8.7 percent of the land (up from 1.5 percent in 1942). This switch in millet type from *bajra* to *ghasar matki* is an indication of deterioration in soil quality since *bajra* is the preferred cereal and farmers will grow it if they can. In addition, as villagers grow more hybrid *jowar*, they claim they have to buy more animal fodder because the stalks of the hybrid are inferior.

Alterations in cropping patterns are resulting in other changes in diet and soil quality in Sugao. For example, the sweet potato is a root vegetable that used to be a staple food during the rainy seasons.[5] Harvesting this crop required deep digging, which insured beneficial turning of the soil. With the decline in its cultivation, the soil is no longer deeply turned, and its quality has deteriorated.

Hybrid *jowar* has a shorter maturation time than the nonhybrid millets it is displacing, so it is not possible to intersperse it with pulses. As a result, cultivation of pulses declined from 12 percent in 1942 to 3 percent in 1977. Also, in contrast to such grains as wheat, rice, and millet, improved strains of lentils are not yet available. Since yields per acre for lentils are low, farmers are switching to other crops. This reduction is unfortunate because lentils are the major source of protein in the village diet. Lentils also help maintain soil quality by fixing nitrogen in the soil. The fact that fewer nitrogen-fixing plants are being grown means that alternative fertilizers must be applied if the soil quality is not to deteriorate further. One such alternative is animal dung. The supply of organic manure in the village has presumably grown with the increase in animal population. In Sugao, unlike other areas of India, this is carefully collected and applied to the land. Night soil is not used as a fertilizer in the area (although some Sugao farmers said they had seen it applied in other villages with fine results and expressed a willingness to consider its use), but people do maintain compost pits in which they put dung and other organic wastes.

The decline in pulse cultivation and increase in fertilizer-dependent cash crops has resulted in several changes. The proportion of cash sales in the gross value of agriculture increased from 35 percent in 1942 to 60 percent in 1977, mainly as a result of the increase in sugarcane production. Hand in hand with this, the cash component of total farm expenditures also increased from 45 percent in 1942 to about 70 percent in 1977, and the way this cash is spent has changed significantly. Property taxes and other government-related expenses now account for only 5 percent of total farm expenditures, down from 18 percent in 1942. A phenomenal increase in the purchase of inorganic, chemical fertilizers now accounts for 25 percent of total farm expenditures with additional outlays for hybrid seeds, potato seeds, pesticides, electricity, and agricultural equipment such as pumpsets.

Although sales of agricultural products and monetized exchanges have increased, the farms are still operated as production-cum-consumption units. Not a single farm specializes in the production of one cash crop. Farmers grow the grains and fodder they need for personal use; then, if there is land to spare, they raise a cash crop. Most farms continue to be worked primarily by the family, although casual labor is hired during peak times, as it was in 1942.

Although I have not made a systematic analysis of the cropping patterns in Sugao since 1977, more casual observations of the village during visits up to 1982 suggested that little had

Cutting sugarcane.

This diesel motor runs a sugarcane crusher.

Farm laborers stoke the fire at the cane crusher.

changed. The impact on farming of the textile industry strike and the subsequent return of some of the adult men from Bombay to work on the land would make an interesting study, one that I have been unable to undertake as yet. Villagers told me in 1985 that the return of the men had resulted in more dynamic farming practices. Some of these farmers have been investing in improved irrigation and are experimenting with new crops. If this is true it suggest that the migration of men to Bombay does in fact have negative consequences for agricultural productivity in the village.

Farm Size and its Effect on Production

The average size of farms has been decreasing in Sugao. In 1942 only 37 percent of the farms were smaller than five adjusted acres (one irrigated acre equaling four nonirrigated acres). This increased to 44 percent in 1958 and 53 percent by 1977 (see table 6). Adjusted acres are useful for comparison purposes and all references to landholding in this chapter will be by adjusted acres unless otherwise specified. Thus, there is a growing number of small farmers in the village. On the other hand, while the number of farmers with twenty acres or more decreased from 12 percent of village families in 1942 to 6 percent in 1977, this group continues to control 34 percent of the village land, only slightly less than the 36 percent it controlled in 1942.[6]

The smaller farmers in Sugao grow mostly cereals, pulses, safflower, or peanuts to be consumed at home. If they own additional land beyond that required for subsistence, they may grow broad beans or hybrid *jowar* for cash sale. Few small farmers, and none of the village Mahars, own bullocks. Most of the bullocks are owned by the larger farmers. These are hired by the smaller farmers for ploughing.

Good crop yields depend on ploughing and tilling the land at critical times. A bullock owner will first work his own farm and then rent his animals to those with whom he has an established labor-sharing arrangement. For example, in many cases three farmers, each with a pair of bullocks, will harness all three teams to a heavy plough and deep-plough each other's holdings. Finally, they will do the work for others. Cash payment for this service is the rule, but cash alone is not sufficient to procure priority service in an economy where reciprocal arrangements are still paramount.

Since Sugao, like most hamlets in this region, is a nuclear village in which houses are closely packed on a central site in the midst of agricultural fields, distances to outlying farms can be three or more miles. The bullock cart is still the major means of transporting goods between the home and the fields. Ownership of a pair of bullocks and a cart confers status, besides facilitating cultivation by transporting seeds, manure, pesticides, and the harvested crops.

Small farmers' access to credit is poor and they are not capable of bearing financial risks, so experimenting with new crops and agricultural practices is difficult for them. For example, it is nearly impossible for a small farmer to take up sugarcane cultivation. Even cultivators with five to ten acres can afford to put only an acre or so into sugarcane, assuming they have access to sufficient water. Often they lack the cash to buy fertilizer. Even if they can manage all this, at harvest the cane must be processed within hours of its cutting to obtain the peak yield. Ownership or availability of a bullock cart or a tractor to transport it immediately to a processing plant is essential.

Thirty farmers in Sugao sold sugarcane to the refinery in 1977, not one of whom owned less than 5 acres of land; in fact, twenty-four of the thirty owned more than 12.5 acres. Sugarcane cultivation is the de facto monopoly of large farmers. The increase in cash income for the village as a whole, mostly the result of increased sugarcane cultivation, thus accrues mainly to those with larger landholdings. In Sugao, few of the large farmers have more than 2 acres of land planted in sugarcane, and only five have as much as 4 or 5 acres. These five have the biggest farms in the village, owning from 15 to 25 acres each, including 5 to 10 acres of irrigated land. They are the power elite in the village. Two of them own *gur*-making units and flour mills, and three own tractors. The chairman of the village *panchayat*, the head of the village cooperative society, and the cooperative's secretary are all from these families; people claim that they use these positions to their extended families' immediate advantage.

Like small landowners, women farmers cultivating land by themselves are relatively disadvantaged, the more so if they own small farms. More and more farmers and agricultural workers in Sugao are women. As table 8 shows, in 1977 women constituted 65 percent of farm workers in Sugao. The fact that 25 percent of the farms are cared for by women and children alone has not made these women more independent in their lifestyles.[7] Generally, they have continued to do the day-to-day work, while a man, either a male relative in Sugao or the owner himself (who returns at critical times) makes all the management decisions.

Villagers of both sexes insist that, when farming is left solely to the women, productivity suffers. Various cultural and social factors prevent women from operating the farm optimally. Traditionally women in Sugao do not work with bullocks; they do not even untie the bullock and take it to graze. When the man is away, the bullocks are stall-fed until he returns. Women are often afraid to guard the crops at night during harvest time or to insure that they get their full share of irrigation water—a chore that often involves sleeping all night beside the canal. Such tasks are essential to protect one's interests, since at present the village farmers act competitively rather than cooperatively. Finally, since men and women do not interact socially in the village, women are cut off from the grapevine, a vital source of farming information. It is difficult to estimate how many of the difficulties confronting women farmers are due to lack of ability or strength, or to an unsafe environment, and how many stem from the traditions and expectations of their society. What is important is that at present the whole village, including the women affected, believe that they cannot do the work alone.

With increased male migration and the illegality of tenancy, more women are farming Sugao land alone, and more of the farm work requiring bullocks is done on hire. This latter trend is also a result of the deterioration of the joint family and the consequent

A farm laborer feeds cane into the crusher.

Gur (processed sugar) cools in bucket-shaped molds.

fragmentation of landholdings, which leaves the new nuclear families with too little land (and other assets such as housing and farm sheds, feed, and cash reserves) to warrant support and maintenance of bullocks. Villagers also claim that tilling is not done properly by hired bullocks, for the laborers who drive them do not care how well or evenly the land is ploughed. If this is true, and field observations seem to confirm it, then more and more of the village lands are being less profitably cultivated. The proportion of families that owned land but possessed no bullocks increased in Sugao from 47 percent in 1942 to 62 percent in 1977.

Farm Labor

As mentioned earlier, most Sugao farmers try to do all the farm tasks with their own family's labor. Hired laborers are usually employed when the workload increases, for example, at times of weeding or harvest. Traditionally, farm tasks have been fairly clearly divided between men and women. Most management decisions are made by men, who also do the heavy work such as ploughing, sowing, and threshing, which requires the help of bullocks. Women perform the day-to-day chores such as weeding, thinning, and harvesting. Although children have always worked on the family farms, the use of child labor has decreased, largely because better access to education is being provided and its importance is coming to be recognized. Whereas 25 percent of seven- to sixteen-year-old children worked in agriculture in 1942, only 10 percent did so in 1977. More boys than girls have been escaping the drudgery of the farm by going to school because villagers think that educating a son is an investment; the daughter, after all, will only marry and live with her husband's family. In 1942 some 60 percent of the children working on farms were girls; in 1977 almost 80 percent were.

With decreasing land-to-person ratios, more people have been working as agricultural laborers as a primary occupation. In 1942 only 9.5 percent of agricultural workers were laborers, but 11.3 percent were in 1958, and 16.6 percent were by 1977. Of these laborers, 72 percent were women in 1977 (see table 8).

Migrant workers outside their makeshift hut. When their work is done, they must leave the village.

A yearly servant from the Dhangar (goat herder) caste.

Agricultural labor as a secondary occupation for a family also increased by 1977.[8]

Agricultural work is highly seasonal. At harvest time and during weeding and hoeing there is a labor shortage, and farmers coerce landless and land poor workers who are beholden to them to work in their fields first. In the interim there is little work and laborers go hungry. Available agricultural work varies from 120 to 150 days per year. Wages are higher for men than for women, and there is work for more days of the year for men. Consequently, women laborers, on the average, earn half of what men do. Up until 1979, women's wages were generally two-thirds of men's wages. This difference in pay has existed since at least 1937, when women were paid 19 *paisa* per day (100 *paisa* equals 1 *rupee*) and men 30 *paisa*. In 1977 women were paid Rs. 2.50 and men Rs. 4.00.

Given that prices rose sixteenfold between 1937 and 1977, there was some decline in the real wages of agricultural workers over the forty-year period. The discrepancy between wages for men and those for women has been increasing, as fewer and fewer men are left in the village who are available for casual day-labor. In 1982, because of this scarcity of male labor at peak-demand periods in the agricultural cycle, men received Rs. 7.00 to Rs. 10.00 per day for farm labor, while women received only Rs. 3.00 for a day's work.

Life as an agricultural laborer in Sugao is at best precarious. In the slack season agricultural laborers often come begging to the doors of the larger farmers asking for odd jobs or advance payments of food. Those farmers who have a stock of grain can make such advances to the laborers they trust, thus they always have enough indebted laborers for hired help in season. A large landholder has many such means of ensuring loyalty from agricultural laborers. He can lend money to a worker at a time of crisis, or he can hire one of the laborer's family members to work in his flour mill, *gur* factory, or other enterprise. He may have a lien on the laborer's land. In some instances he can be a reliable and fair employer whom the laborers like. If he is not, the laborers must still work for him, if only to pay off the debts they have incurred. The small and marginal farmers, on the other hand, have little leverage in recruiting laborers in the peak season and often have difficulties harvesting their crops on time.

Apart from agricultural labor hired on a daily basis, there is a system of bonded or attached labor that exists to varying degrees in different parts of India. An attached laborer contracts himself for a year's work to a family in return for a predetermined annual wage paid in cash or in kind. No limits are set to the number of hours or kinds of work he must perform; consequently this system can become extremely exploitative. There were only a few such attached laborers in Sugao in 1977, but I was able to observe two of them closely. They belonged to poor sheep-herding families from a village east of Sugao in the drought-prone part of the district. They worked for a woman who was a hard taskmaster and noted for her acid tongue. They worked seven days a week, twelve to fourteen hours a day and were often fed leftover food and bread that was specially made for them from inferior grain. In return they received five to ten days of vacation per year, food, clothing (one T-shirt, two shirts, one pair of sandals, and one set of pajamas), and a cash payment of Rs. 500. At prices current in 1977, this amounted to U.S. $161 per year. An attached laborer is in effect a servant; his workload and material conditions depend completely on the inclination of his master. By 1982, there were almost no attached laborers left in Sugao, but the practice is more common in other parts of the state.

Monetization of the Sugao Economy

Of all the farming families in the village in 1977, 31 percent (25 percent of all the families in Sugao) claimed to be self-sufficient, that is, producing all their basic food requirements. Slightly less than half, 47 percent (38 percent of total families), had deficits of one to six months, and 22 percent (18 percent of total families) had even larger deficits of six to twelve months. Most farms larger than 3.5 acres were self-sufficient, and the majority of farms deficient for six to twelve months were smaller than 3.5 acres.

Almost 40 percent of all the families in the village who were buying food in 1977 purchased it at the ration shop. The government's establishment of ration shops in villages has helped some of the poorer families to survive; however, the switch to more cash transactions and to lower production of grain (due to allocation of land for sugarcane cultivation) has forced these families to buy grain in the first place. Most of the customers at the ration shops are small farmers. Formerly, if they worked as agricultural laborers, they were paid in kind, usually in food grains. Nowadays, the large farmer often prefers to pay for farm labor in cash, because he can afford to store the grain and sell when prices are high, thus getting a greater price per unit of grain than he can by using it to pay his laborers. By contrast, until recently, wage payments in cash for men and women remained fairly constant, increasing only slowly and lagging behind market prices so that the larger farmer benefits from paying cash to his workers. Although the pay for male laborers had increased by 1982, the pay for women was still quite low. This is significant given that women constituted 72 percent of those whose primary work is agricultural labor.

Food sold in these shops comes from towns such as Wai, where grain is collected from the surrounding region and distributed to the ration shops. The grain is often of an inferior variety, since it is levied from farmers at a controlled price. Farmers tend to grow hybrid varieties, which give higher yields but are less relished, to meet this quota. The rich farmers usually try to grow enough food grains of the preferred indigenous variety for personal consumption, and the farmers buying from the ration shop are firm in stating that they would rather eat the indigenous varieties as well.

Often the village poor do not have sufficient cash to buy the minimum quantities sold in the ration shop. For them the day's work pays for that night's meal. Ration shops do not sell food on credit. This is a problem on nights when the laborer has found no work and has no money. These families, about 17 percent of the village population, are forced to buy their necessities daily in the private shops in tiny amounts. Even salt, one of the cheapest ingredients, is bought in miniscule quantities. Since the poor must buy at the private stores, paying two to three times the price of food purchased in larger quantities, they pay the highest prices for generally inferior foodstuffs. Another 17 percent of the population are able to buy food in larger quantities (sacks of grain, gallon tins of oil, etc.) either in the village or at Wai, where one gets the best value for one's money. Naturally this is the preferred way of making up food deficits, and families that receive remittances from Bombay are often able to make such purchases.

Of the families that produced surpluses in 1977, those who sold them in Sugao tended to own less land (5 to 12.5 acres) than those who sold them in Wai. The nine families with holdings of 12.5 to 20 acres, a mere 2 percent of all cultivators, sold their produce as far away as Poona or Bombay where the prices were highest. Smaller farmers, with less to sell, cannot afford to travel very far to seek a better price. Thus, in a cash-crop economy where monetary transactions predominate, the subsistence farmer fares badly and is progressively being squeezed out of his occupation as a cultivator.

In 1977 about 75 percent of the total consumer needs in Sugao were met with cash purchases. At least two factors explain this figure. Most families lacked sufficient land or livestock to meet their total requirements for grains, milk, and vegetables. Also, there has been a shift to using city-made or processed products. This has had an adverse impact on the village economy. Cooking oil from outside the village, for example, is cheaper than oil from village-grown seeds, and therefore has supplanted the local product. The price difference stems from the fact that the new hybrid varieties of peanuts now cultivated in the village require higher pressures for oil extraction. The oil press in the city is larger and more efficient. In addition, the hybrid varieties of peanuts have been developed for eating rather than oil production, so villagers have cultivated and sold them for this purpose and bought the more refined cooking oil from the city. The villager is disadvantaged in this transaction because the refined oil is less nutritious than the unrefined local product. In addition, when oil was pressed locally villagers kept the leftover peanut cakes, an extremely nutritious

fodder for their animals. The villager forfeits this by-product when
he buys oil from the shop.

Sugar consumption has undergone a similar change. More
villagers are buying refined sugar produced in large factories in the
towns, which is more expensive and less nutritious than the locally
produced *gur*. Other products from the city have made similar
inroads into the village market. Plastic footware, soap, cosmetics,
medicine, tea (the consumption of which has jumped tremendously
in the last thirty years), metal ware, and tobacco have all
supplanted village products. The value of manufactured goods
purchased by Sugao people almost doubled in real terms between
1942 and 1977.

Cash, then, has become more important. But in agriculture
only the large farmers have been able to enter the cash economy
and profit effectively. The land poor and landless are not so
fortunate. They cannot supplement their income in local
nonagricultural activities because that sector of the rural economy
has traditionally been small, and, as villagers have increasingly
bought city products, village-level production has shrunk even
further. Fewer and fewer opportunities exist to earn a living in
nonagricultural endeavors in the village, while the amount of cash
needed to buy agricultural inputs and consumer goods has continued
to rise.[9]

Increased monetization and the problems it presents to land
poor people in Sugao are disturbing. If the current direction of
development continues, the village will become more and more
dependent on the city. The small subsistence farmer will gradually
be squeezed out of the village and will be forced to look for a niche
in the increasingly restricted urban economy. The brisk rate of
urbanization in India is partly the result of such disenfranchisement
of the rural poor.

Currently Sugao people are eating less protein. They are
reducing the variety of crops they raise for personal consumption in
an effort to maximize production of cash crops, and are paying for
this with monotony in their diet. Obviously the "improvement" of

agriculture in Sugao involves more than an increase in the market value of agricultural products. It is necessary to grow more food grains, not just cash crops, and to provide for their distribution, so that more food is available for the villagers themselves, and so that there is an improvement in the nutritional content and diversity of their diets. The objective should be not the modernization of agriculture for better production of cash crops, but improvement in the quantity, quality, and diversity of the food available for consumption to rural as well as urban people.

The development literature on agricultural transformation is replete with examples of investments made in improved technology and infrastructure that do not deliver anticipated benefits. Sometimes the sociocultural fabric of the rural community and the unwritten rules by which it is sustained are not understood and therefore not accounted for. The programs fail to achieve their explicit objectives. At other times the questions of who will benefit and how the distribution of the benefits will occur are not addressed. Often the poorest are left out. Agricultural labor is largely unorganized and cannot obtain payment for services rendered in keeping with the general rise in prices. Often the agricultural laborer survives only because he can buy food at controlled prices at the ration shop. To be truly termed "development," the agricultural transformation of rural areas must extend beyond the parameters currently established so that local consumption of food for rural people is tangibly improved.

Notes

1. In 1942, 86 percent of all workers were employed in agriculture. By 1977 this figure had grown to 90 percent, an increase not merely in relative importance but in real terms, the numbers of workers rising from 763 to 1,165.

2. Figures extrapolated from Farm Business Surveys by the Gokhale Institute of Politics and Economics, executed in 1938. This information is available in the form of manuscripts and field notes.

3. For a case study that refers to the attrition of in-kind payments in two villages in Maharashtra, one of which is Sugao, see H. Dandekar and Brahme (1979, 122–43).

4. On previous trips to Sugao, I was told by those who had to give up land on the site of the tank that more suitable locations existed but they were owned by farmers who had enough political strength to get the tanks located elsewhere. One finds that often the poorest farmers end up having their lands confiscated for projects like the percolation tank because they are least able to manipulate the political system to their advantage. This seems to be another characteristic of development efforts: often the poorest sacrifice scarce resources such as their land for projects that contribute to their community's well-being.

5. The villagers make some traditional, flavorful dishes from sweet potatoes, for example, *kiise*, shredded sweet potatoes sauteed in spices with ground peanuts, and *kapp*, sweet potato slices in a syrup of *gur* (unrefined brown sugar). With the changes in cropping patterns these dishes are not made as often, and a less diverse diet has resulted. For recipes for these typically Maharashtrian dishes, see my *Beyond Curry: Quick and Easy Indian Cooking, Featuring Cuisine from Maharashtra State* (H. Dandekar 1983A).

6. Thus, although the number of larger farmers is decreasing, those remaining have gotten bigger, and inequality between the rich and the poor has increased. This skewed land distribution among the large and small farmers is illustrated again by the fact that the bottom 40 percent of landowning families control decreasing amounts of village land (10.7 percent in 1942 versus 9.6 percent in 1977); and that 80 percent of the families control less than 50 percent of village land (49.8 percent in 1942, 46.7 percent in 1977).

7. Detailed case studies of women in Sugao, including women farmers, were compiled during my residence in Sugao in 1976–77, 1979, and 1981–82. I am completing a book on the

impact of development on rural women in India. Some aspects of women's roles in Sugao are elaborated in H. Dandekar (1983B).

8. The farm households with a second occupation were 39 percent, 36 percent, and 43 percent of those with farming as a main occupation for 1942, 1958, and 1977, respectively. Of these, persons working as agricultural laborers as a second occupation increased from 40 percent in 1942, to 56 percent in 1958, and 73 percent by 1977.

9. For a comparison of rural industries in one small and one large village in Maharashtra, see H. Dandekar and Brahme (1979). Sugao is the small village in this study.

CHAPTER 8

NEW AND OLD INDUSTRIES

As burgeoning urban populations and the proliferation of squatter settlements overload services in the city, policy makers have been searching for ways to keep people in the countryside. Strategies that have been developed to stem migration include some programs to stimulate decentralized rural industries and others designed to support traditional artisans in their family occupation and help at least to postpone their displacement by modern industry. Such development efforts in India have aimed to diversify the rural economy to create more jobs outside of agriculture, in the belief that increasing and diversifying employment in the countryside, particularly in rural industries that have backward and forward linkages to the local economy, would make the rural economy more viable and self-reliant. This would help to keep people on the land and prevent their migrating to overcrowded metropolitan areas.

Several programs to support and diversify rural industries have been implemented in Maharashtra, and their impact on a typical village in the Deccan can be gauged by looking at the nonagricultural work opportunities in Sugao and the ways in which they have changed. Sugao, quite typically, has never received a concentration of government funds in pilot projects to stimulate nonagricultural employment opportunities. Nonagricultural activity in Sugao has been providing a livelihood for proportionally fewer and fewer workers, declining from 14 percent of village workers in 1942 to only 10 percent in 1977. Despite overall population

171

increases, the actual number of workers occupied outside of agriculture in 1958 and 1977 has remained the same at 130 (see table 8). This is noteworthy, given that numerous schemes to stimulate rural industries were introduced by the government during this time. Nonagricultural work in Sugao since 1942 can be classified into broad categories: traditional artisan services and production, agro-industries, animal husbandry, trade, and finally the more prestigious white-collar and other salaried jobs. The availability of work in the different categories has varied over time, and has differentially affected, in beneficial as well as detrimental ways, the lives of Sugao workers from all income strata.

Traditional Artisan Industry

Traditional artisans in Sugao have either produced certain goods needed by the village community or provided services. The former generally produced goods necessary to agricultural cultivation. This included the making and mending of ploughs, other agricultural equipment, and bullock carts by *sutar* (carpenters); the production of leather *mhots* (buckets used in irrigation) by *chambhar* (cobblers); and the making of reins, whips, and ropes by the *mang* (rope makers). Services were provided by the *navi* (barbers), *parith* (washermen), and *mulani* (butchers), all of whom catered to the personal needs of individuals and families. Others such as the *ramoshi* (night watchmen), *gurav* (priests), or *mahar* (village servants) provided services needed by the village as a whole.

Historically the traditional artisans were an integral part of the village community. They were consciously drawn into the village economy through the reserving of certain village lands (*inam*) to pay for communally needed services, and through the *baluta* system of bartering artisan services for a fixed share of the agricultural product. When *inam* land tenure was abolished under federal land-reform measures, the services rendered by the artisans also stopped and the *baluta* system, which was a personal arrangement between the cultivator and the artisan, atrophied.

In Maharashtra State the *baluta* system is fast disappearing. In Sugao, as late as 1938, about 7 percent of the total cereal production was distributed as *baluta*. By 1959 the *inam* land legislation had been passed and the Mahars, who traditionally acted as village servants, had converted to Buddhism and refused to work as scavengers for the village. They also stopped begging for bread in the village each night, which was part of their traditional ritual. By this time only 3.7 percent of the total cereals produced were given in *baluta*, and by 1966 this figure had dropped to 1.8 percent. By 1982, except for religious functionaries and the carpenter, cobbler, and blacksmith, most artisan services were being rendered on a cash for service basis (H. Dandekar 1978, 188–234).

As the village economy has become more monetized due to the raising of commercial crops, *baluta* services have also declined in importance. Some traditional tasks in agricultural cultivation have been displaced through mechanization. Because the traditional role of the *balutedars* is gradually disappearing, these nonagricultural workers have had to diversify their productive activity, switch to cash payments, or migrate to the city. Between 1942 and 1977, the number of working productive artisans has remained stationary except for the *kaikadi* (basket weavers) and *mang* (rope makers), who have increased and managed to support themselves by expanding their market range. They hawk their products in the surrounding villages or in the local weekly markets. However, they are one of the poorest groups in the village, barely managing to eke out a living. Generally, expanding agricultural production and monetization have not increased opportunities for the traditional artisan. On the contrary, it has undermined the claims he formerly had in the old village order to at least a bare subsistence. Some artisans have been more affected by these changes than others. For some there has been a role to play in the new world; others have not been so fortunate.

Carpenters

Of all the artisans, the carpenter has been least affected by changes in village life. This is due to the fact that, despite the three

tractors and one mechanized thresher in operation in Sugao, the use
persists of wooden ploughs, other wooden implements, and bullock
carts. The carpenters continue to provide maintenance and repair
services, but they are increasingly paid in cash rather than *baluta*.
In Sugao only two carpenters are partly supported with in-kind
baluta payments.

Kisan is a case in point. A carpenter by caste, his family is
one of the original *balutedars* of the village, now split into three
units, headed by three brothers, each having a share of Sugao's
baluta houses. Kisan is a *balutedar* for thirty or forty families. The
rest of his income is derived from contracts to build houses. He
served an apprenticeship with a relative in Satara, so he knows
how to build furniture and houses more like those of the city. He
would like to make and sell furniture, but says there is no demand
for this sort of thing in the village. Most of Sugao's furnishings
were brought from the city by villagers working there. Nor can
Kisan get a loan for this activity from the banks. The Wai
Panchayat Samiti office would loan him money to buy better
equipment for his traditional trade, but no funds are available to
buy wood to start a new business, since the *balutedar* aid scheme is
not allowed to finance such ventures. This is a good example of how
bureaucratic rules, necessary though they may be, serve to stifle
initiative and creativity on the part of the recipients and limit the
effectiveness of a program.

Vilas, my assistant in the field, and his father were also
carpenters by caste. The father did a major portion of the *baluta*
carpentry in the village. Vilas helped with this when he was needed
and also worked half a day as the village postman. He was
constantly trying to augment his income in various ways. He
bought old wooden tea crates in Wai and converted them to
household shelves. He bought thirty-kilo molds of *gur* from a local
producer for Rs. 2 per kilo and retailed it at Rs. 2.25. He wanted to
open a shop to sell kindling wood in the village, but this would have
required a minimum investment of Rs. 1,500, money he did not
have. Also, he was leery of setting up any substantial business in
Sugao (another possibility was a tea stall) because, lower in status
than the landed Yadavs and Jadhavs, he would be forced to grant

In recent years cash payments have been replacing *baluta*. This has forced artisan groups such as the carpenters to diversify.

The Sugao potter's main product is tiny clay pots used in religious ceremonies. There is little potential for expansion.

them credit on purchases. Often such debts are never paid, and in his case they would have driven him out of the trade. Vilas's family had no land. In 1977 he became extremely sick, had to be hospitalized, and was forced to take a loan of over Rs. 800 to meet the medical payments, which has indebted him for many years. This is the fate of most of those who depend on nonagricultural activity in the village. They manage to eke out a living, but unexpected expenses force them into debt.

The four remaining carpenter families in Sugao have either switched to construction work or are paid in cash. One family started building houses in the early forties and invested the profits in land. By 1977 this family had diversified: the father had a cycle rental shop, the son, Shivaji, maintained a dairy business and an electrical repair shop, and the mother and younger brother ran one of the two *paan* shops in the village (*paan* is the digestive snack, of chopped betel nut wrapped in a betel leaf, which is eaten after a meal). The *paan* shop had to be open from 7 A.M. to 10 P.M., and the profit from it was only about Rs. 5 per day. The other *paan* shop in Sugao also carried on an illegal trade in hashish and country liquor, but I was told this family's business was "clean" (and their profits commensurately low).

Shivaji also ran a loudspeaker business, which was particularly brisk in the wedding season. He started with an investment of Rs. 3,000 (U.S. $353), which he used to purchase loudspeakers, *mandaps* (decorative enclosures), record players, and so on, and he had been adding to it. In 1977 he had about Rs. 5,000 worth of equipment which he used in some sixty engagements a year, charging Rs. 75 for a wedding needing a loudspeaker and *mandap*; Rs. 20 for a religious *puja* using only a loudspeaker; and Rs. 10 for a *barsa* (name-giving ceremony for a baby), where only a loudspeaker was provided. He claimed he was making a profit of Rs. 2,500 per year. For jobs outside the village he usually had four trained people on hand, whom he paid Rs. 4 per day. His business ranged as far from the village as Khandala Taluka; he traveled by the State Transport Bus or in a rented bullock cart if he had to take a lot of equipment. As far as I was concerned, the blaring out on celebration days of "film music" on rented sound equipment such as Shivaji's was a new bane on rural living. The villagers, however, appeared to have adopted this custom with delight. At weddings the microphone was often used to give a running commentary that could be heard throughout the village; there was no escape. An account of who had given what to the bridal pair was often included. Shivaji profited from this trend in village celebrations, but his family illustrated with their various enterprises that survival in nonagricultural activities in the countryside calls for both farsightedness and agility.

Rama, another Sugao carpenter by caste, had been blacksmithing for years, since he could not get enough work in the village in his traditional occupation. Actually, he was a jack of all trades, keeping ducks, chickens, and a horse, which he rented for marriage ceremonies. (It is a tradition in some castes that the bridegroom arrive perched, however precariously, on a horse.) Rama was also a stonemason. He had three small children, one son and two daughters, and had had himself sterilized so that there would be no more. He was leery of taking bank credit for any business venture because the experience of others in the village had shown him that he could lose everything if he defaulted. If he had expanded his activity, it would have been in the poultry business, but as it was he had barely enough room to house his family. A poultry farm requires a sizeable investment, especially if it is of the modern type.

Helping people from this landless artisan group enter into nonagricultural business requires far more money than is offered under the current programs. Rama is an intelligent, good-humored man, well aware of the possibilities of diversification and development, but limited by his assets and social status. Even the carpenters of Sugao, one of the few artisan groups that seems to have a viable base in the village, have to struggle and be quite ingenious to make ends meet.

Cobblers

Traditionally the village cobbler maintained and supplied *mhots*, reins, and other leather articles to farmers in return for

baluta payments. During the sixties, with the advent of electrical
pumpsets (there were forty-five in Sugao in 1977), *mhots* went into
disuse and the demand for some of the cobbler's products
disappeared. In 1977 only one cobbler practiced his traditional
occupation in Sugao. Four other men of the cobbler caste had
migrated to Bombay where they worked in the textile mills. One of
them did minor shoe repairs on a sidewalk in Bombay to earn extra
money. He did this, at the same location, for over sixteen years.
From discussions with other researchers in the city, I learned that
this utter lack of upward mobility in informal-sector work in
Bombay is fairly typical. The city allows for survival in these petty
trades but does not present unlimited opportunities for growth.

Plastic footware has become common in Sugao, further eroding
the market for the cobbler's product. Villagers buy plastic
footware, not because they prefer it to leather, but because it is
cheaper. Most villagers are aware that plastic sandals do not last
as long or feel as good as leather ones, although outsiders have
made the condescending judgment that the villagers do not respond
to the aesthetics of leather ware, but ready cash is in short supply
and leather sandals cost four or five times more than plastic ones.

Potters

Traditionally the village potter worked with local clay and
horse dung to make the containers used for storing water and grain,
as well as tiny pots and lamps needed in religious ceremonies. As
cheap aluminum containers from the city have become readily
available, demand for the potter's products has been shrinking.
Potters in some areas of Maharashtra have switched to related
industries such as brick and tile making, which tap larger markets
(H. Dandekar and Brahme 1979, 122–24). But, since Sugao is in a
rocky, hilly area, clay is not available in sufficient quantities, and
this transition was not an option for the village potters. In 1977
only one potter still plied his trade in Sugao, and that rather
minimally. The son who used to help him in this work had
migrated to Bombay to find another occupation. The Sugao potter's
main product is the tiny clay pots that are used in various religious
ceremonies. His pottery is rudimentary, low-fire eathernware with

little potential for exploitation as a handicraft. The potter himself is a downcast man who is barely surviving in Sugao. When his wife died, leaving him with small children, he did not immediately remarry, as is the norm. Bharatibai explained this by saying that no one would give him a woman because he was so poor. She concluded, as if it were a last indignity, that "he has to pat his own *bhakari*." Cooking is woman's work, and a man has sunk low in village eyes when he has to make his own bread.

Traditional artisan activity as a whole is on the wane in Sugao. The government program for *balutedars* extends credit to artisans for the purchase of better tools, equipment, and raw materials. But most Sugao artisans feel that there is no longer a large enough market for their traditional products, and that the government scheme does not provide funds to allow them to start alternative businesses.

Traditional Village Services

Such traditional village artisans as the *navi* (barber), *parith* (washerman), *mulani* (butcher), and *sonar* (goldsmith) once catered to the personal needs of individuals and families. Others such as the *ramoshi* (night watchman), *gurav* (priest), and *mahar* (village servant) served the needs of the village as a whole. Those artisans who rendered service to the village at large were paid through the use of *inam* lands; those who worked for individual families were paid under the *baluta* system. The decline of the *baluta* system has meant that the various artisans either switch to cash payments or try to perform other needed services.

Ramu, the barber, came to Sugao in 1962 to take over the house of his father-in-law. The "house" was just a shed, looking very temporary, made from wattle and with a thatch roof. However, it was equity enough to induce Ramu to make the move. The tools necessary for Ramu's trade are few and simple: an old-fashioned razor, a hair-trimming machine, a comb or two, a nail cutter, a brush, a sharpening stone, some soap, oil, and talcum powder. In 1977, when working for cash, he charged twenty-five *paisa* for a shave and fifty *paisa* for a haircut. If he was working on the *baluta* system, he received ten kilograms of grain for cutting one man's hair and shaving him for a year, and six kilograms of grain for cutting a child's hair. Thirty or so families paid him *baluta*, a sack or two of grain plus a little of the other produce each farmer grew. The rest of his business was for cash.

The Mahar, or Neo-Buddhist, community is another group providing traditional village services that has had to find other means of earning a living. Most do agricultural labor in addition to tilling their own land. Few work in nonagricultural activities. One of the families, however, that of Bhagwan, has been doing masonry work for some years. This family is noteworthy because it has a history of leprosy, although the head of the family now appears to be cured. In spite of this, the family continues to struggle to better its position in the village. Bhagwan has barely one-sixth of an acre of land and owns one water buffalo. He learned the masonry trade from his father and takes contracts for house construction. In the year preceding the 1977 survey he had completed six houses, all in Sugao or surrounding villages.

Bhagwan has one married daughter, whose husband is a textile worker in Bombay. She lives with her husband and spends her time scouring the city's garbage heaps looking for odds and ends she can sell to junk dealers. When Bhagwan told me this in front of his small, sparsely furnished house, he shivered and said, "We don't feel good about it, her sifting through all that filth, one basket to another, to pick out a scrap of a rag here, a piece of plastic there." His oldest son is in Satara City at the Industrial Training Institute, trying to finish a two-year course so he can get a job in a factory. A second son has been apprenticed to a local carpenter. When this son completes his training, Bhagwan's family will be skilled in all aspects of house construction, including wood framing. Currently most of Bhagwan's houses are of mud and stone construction. Masonry work pays about Rs. 10 per day. He pays male workers Rs. 4 and females Rs. 2.5 per day, more if the labor is hard. In recent times brick work has become popular with his clients since it is cheaper. He has had to acquire different skills and equipment to accommodate this trend.

Construction of an eight-*khan* house with an upper story cost Rs. 1,000 in 1977. Bhagwan's profit from such a house was between Rs. 100 and Rs. 200. Bhagwan knows how to estimate and will contract according to brasses of work to be done (Rs. 130 to Rs. 150 per brass of brick work, or Rs. 200 per brass of stone work in 1977), or he will quote a lump sum per *khan* (an Indian unit of measure, being the area between two spanning joists, which is approximately five by ten feet). He buys bricks from a mason in Sirawal, some miles away, who charged Rs. 500 per load in 1977, a truckload consisting of about 2,500 bricks. Stone is quarried locally and may be purchased from the farmer who owns the land from which it comes. Sand is taken from the village stream and the cement comes by bullock cart from Wai. Bhagwan would go into contracting on a larger scale if he had more working capital. Presently he requires an advance from his customers in order to buy the necessary raw materials, which means he cannot mark them up.

The only other person who was employed outside of agriculture in the Neo-Buddhist alley in 1977 was Pralhad, who worked in the village flour mill and carried on a small trade in tobacco. He bought tobacco in Wai and sold it at the weekly markets in Sirur and Kudal, and in small amounts in the village. Most of these Mahars, the former village servants, are forced to eke out their livelihood if they stay in Sugao.

Some *inam* lands, such as those dedicated to the temple and mosque, continue to be kept revenue free for that purpose. *Guravs* (priests), for example, still hold *inam* lands, and manage to scratch out a living from the land and from *baluta* payments for religious services, which have not fallen off as dramatically as those of the other service castes. But I noted among the villagers some discontent about the priests' demand for grain. The end of their *baluta* payments will come in time.

There are two Gurav families currently in Sugao. Between them they share the village's *baluta* payments, one depending upon the Yadav families and the other upon the Jadhavs. Each has half an acre to an acre of *inam* land, and one family has bought irrigated land for itself. In return for the *inam* land, the Guravs maintain the temples of the god Bhairava and his sister Laxmi. They also perform the *puja* (daily services) and preside at various religious functions. They are required to make plates and cups from the leaves of certain trees. These are presented to *baluta*-giving families, and used in serving large numbers of people at feasts and marriages. The Guravs claim that they must wander farther and farther into the hills to find the leaves they need since the forests have become depleted.

The son of one of the Gurav families has been trained as an art teacher and has a job in a high school. He and his high school educated wife are reluctant to commit themselves to carrying on the Gurav function after the parents' death because they find it demeaning to go from door to door asking for grain or offerings. This couple, however, is better equipped to give up the Gurav trade than is the other family.

The butcher, or *mulani*, continues to practice his traditional trade in Sugao. Every Sunday one or another farmer has a goat slaughtered. The meat is sold immediately to the various families who have put in claims for it. The *mulani* charges for the number of animals slaughtered; the fee is paid by the owner. The close social relationships in the village prevent the butcher from starting a meat business of his own. Dagdu, a Muslim, is one of the Sugao *mulanis*. He lives with two of his four wives. Having more than wife is sanctioned by his religion and allowed by the state. One of his daughters from a previous marriage lives with him. Although she is only nine, she is useful. Rather than attending school, she watches the family's animals and takes them out to graze.

Dagdu's is one of three Muslim families (offshoots of an original single family) who have charge of the *inam* lands reserved for the support of the mosque. This land is governed by a trust located in the city of Kolhapur. The trust inspects the mosque every year to assure that it is being appropriately maintained by Dagdu and the other two *inam*-receiving families. Theoretically there is a system of rotation whereby two of the three families hold the land each year, so that each has land for two years and none for a third. In practice, the head of one of these households has become quite successful in the truck trade in Bombay, and, until recently, when he abducted the wife of a Jadhav man from Sugao, he supported his mother and the rest of his family comfortably on these earnings. Now he mistreats them because they complain about his behavior. He has left the *inam* land to the other two families, who are quite poor.

Dagdu gets two *rupees* for butchering one animal; this is comparable to what a female agricultural laborer earns for one day's work in the field. Dagdu claims that the villagers are very particular about the kind of meat they will buy. It must be the meat of a male goat, a she-goat will not do, and they have to see "the whites of its eyes." He therefore does not buy an animal, butcher it, and then sell it so as to get a higher profit for himself. He explains that it is different in the city, where you can buy an old she-goat for Rs. 30 or so (it has about ten kilos of meat), and after butchering sell it for between Rs. 8 and Rs. 10 per kilo, making a tidy profit. Such entrepreneurship is not feasible in the village under present social conditions.

Sugao's *sonar* (goldsmith) was never on the *baluta* system, although in some parts of Maharashtra goldsmiths do function as *balutedars*. He is one artisan who is always busy in the village, and he and his sons and their families live comfortably, if austerely, off the business. They manage so well because they are skillful and have been able to attract clients from many surrounding villages. During the day the goldsmith's house usually hosts a small group of women clients and would-be clients who sit chatting and watching the work underway. This is one of the few places in the village where women from different clans may spend some time together.

Agro-industry

Smaller household industries, such as bullock-powered oil presses and small sugarcane crushers with tiny *gur*-making units, were squeezed out of the village economy by mechanization. There were four large *gur*-making units in Sugao in 1977, all of which had sprung up in response to increases in sugarcane cultivation. In the crushing season, they provide jobs for village laborers and for some migrant workers from drier regions. While some units use oil engines to run the sugarcane crushers and pump the cane juice, and others use electric motors, the basic method of making *gur* is very simple. Over the years the technology has changed very little.

One of the existing *gur*-making units was bought in 1966 at a cost of Rs. 10,000 (U.S. $1,177). The cost of maintaining the machinery is high since the crushers have to be replaced every three or four years. Last time, the owner complained, it cost Rs. 3,000 for new crushers. The cost of running the unit is fairly high; raw materials such as lime, hydrox, and castor oil, for example, cost Rs. 1,356 in 1977 for a four-month season. At that time the cost of electricity for each pail of *gur* was Rs. 4, and labor charges were Rs. 7 per pail when eight people were employed (two to feed fuel, one to test, and five to work the crusher). Sometimes the *gur*-making unit is rented to adjacent villages, at a price of Rs. 22 per pail. A unit makes a profit of about Rs. 4,000 in a season. Profits in the *gur*-making business are good if one has the means to start and maintain it. All the Sugao units are owned by affluent farmers in the village.

During the year I lived there, the *gur* units in Sugao were limited to working at a fraction of their capacity because the government had committed the supply of local sugarcane to the cooperative sugar factory ten miles away. Since sugar factories are technically cooperatives, and because they produce sugar for export, they are a protected industry. As a result, the local, labor-intensive, decentralized *gur* industry, just the sort of economic activity that should be promoted by rural development programs, was under seige. However, on later visits to the village I noticed that the *gur* units were in operation once again, the owners having prevailed in the courts.

The trend is indeed toward the village supplying raw agricultural products like sugarcane and ground nuts to the large manufacturing units and buying back processed goods like sugar and oil. A family that ran a bullock-powered oil press in Sugao in

1942 was displaced when a mechanical oil crusher came to the village. The family was forced to migrate to Bombay. They acquired some capital there, which the eldest son, Vithal, invested in a small grocery store in Sugao from which they are trying to earn a living. Their traditional business was displaced both by a change in technology, which introduced more mechanized equipment, and by stronger marketing links with nearby urban centers.

Although there are a number of small, home-based, grocery stores in Sugao, only three or four of them, including Vithal's, make enough profit to support a whole family. Opening in 1971, and financed by retirement benefits accrued during Vithal's eleven years on the Bombay police force, his shop owes its success to his tenacity and a daily routine of hard work. Vithal's first shop failed because he extended too much credit to his customers. He was able to begin again, however, and this time, having learned the knack of doing business in the village, he was successful. He superstitiously moved this second shop from one end of his two-room ancestral house to the other, so that it is now situated directly over the site of his father's old oil press. He feels that this move has been an auspicious one.

Vithal works alone in the shop, keeping it open from 8 A.M. to noon, and from 3 P.M. to late evening. Every other day he bicycles to Wai, where he buys supplies, packs them onto the back of his bike, and rides home. It is hot and dry at noon, when he makes this trip, except during the monsoons when the road is even worse, and the ten- to twelve-mile uphill ride to Wai is not easy. Once a year he hires a bullock cart and takes it to Wai, which costs Rs. 20 for the round trip. There he buys a cartload of salt for Rs. 100. This he can sell during the year for Rs. 150. Profit margins are small in Sugao and capital may be tied up for long periods of time. Sometimes Vithal bicycles to the towns of Khandala and Sirur for other purchases. He prefers to cycle rather than buy a ride on a truck because, he says, truck drivers know that a trader will be carrying money, and he is afraid of being robbed.

His store is full of every type of provision: spices, treats for children, stationary, utensils, medicine, and so on. One can ask for almost anything, and he will hunt around and eventually find something to meet the need. In setting up the shop Vithal had to invest in many kinds of containers (such as large tins for grain and oil), in weights and measures (Rs. 100), in a license to sell kerosene (Rs. 100), and in a license to sell tobacco (Rs. 20). But the shop's popularity rests mainly on its ample provisions, replenished frequently by Vithal's trips to the city.

A few new pieces of agro-processing equipment such as threshing machines and flour mills, all owned by the Jadhav and Yadav families, do a brisk business, but apart from these no new industry has been established in Sugao to provide agricultural inputs, process agricultural produce, or meet evolving consumer needs.

Consumer Goods

Some traditional industries that thrived in Sugao on the basis of local demand for consumer goods have been eliminated. It is illuminating in this context to examine the fate of Sugao's goat-blanket weaving industry, which dates back to at least 1690. According to records found in the Poona Archives,[1] in that year taxes were collected from forty-three houses in Sugao and from five wool-weaving and six cotton-weaving looms. In 1940 there were fourteen Sugao families involved in weaving blankets, in buying ready-made blankets from other weavers in the region, and in selling them in distant villages along the Konkan coastal strip. Wool was bought at a regional market in the area. Later, when an export market for this wool developed in Bombay, city merchants came to the regional market and bid up the price of wool.

With their limited working capital, Sugao weavers could not buy as much wool at this inflated price. Their annual output of blankets decreased and they failed to make a sufficient profit in the business. The yarn spinners who processed raw wool for these weavers ceased their activity as well, since they could profit more by selling raw wool to the Bombay merchants. As a result of the export market in wool, Sugao's weaving industry was practically defunct by 1980, with only one family fully involved in the business and two others working in it part time. The weavers, with their rural-based profits, simply could not compete with the urban market.

Increasingly, Sugao weaver families are sending their men to textile mills in Bombay where they get jobs operating power looms. They are saddened by this state of affairs. They take pride in their skills and would prefer practicing their traditional craft to sweating out their days in the Bombay mills, but the economic forces are too strong. They once formed a weavers' cooperative to buy raw materials in bulk and sell blankets in larger quantities, but even this did not give them sufficient leverage against the urban demand.

The dilemma of the weaver families in Sugao is illustrated by the case of Ramchandra. His father wove and sold blankets in the traditional manner until 1950, while Ramchandra worked in a textile mill in Bombay for thirty-eight years. His wife and her mother ran a *khanawal*, or meals service, in Bombay. They are now back in Sugao, and Ramchandra has started a small grocery store that never seems to have much business. He recently disowned his oldest son, Vishnu, for living with a woman he met in Bombay; she is of the Koli caste, which Ramchandra considers inferior. Vishnu got in trouble with the law and had to leave Bombay. Now he is living with his mistress in a makeshift hut in the village, trying to earn a living through an illegal trade in liquor. Because he was born and raised in Bombay, he feels unequipped for, and uninterested in, agricultural labor. He is also at odds with the villagers, who do not look with any sympathy on intercaste relationships.

Ramchandra invested Rs. 500 in renovating his home and establishing a shop in it; another Rs. 500 in buying equipment such as scales, weights, and containers; and Rs. 3,000 for the initial stock. Most of this money came from his retirement fund and from the "sale" of the room in Bombay that belonged to his mother-in-law. He sold this room without her knowledge and she still curses

him for it, as it forced her to return to Sugao instead of continuing
her meals business in Bombay.

Ramchandra goes to Khandala or Wai every couple of weeks to
buy supplies. However, business is not good and he will probably
lose his investment. A few more individuals of the Dhangar
community have started similar grocery and provision shops after
retiring from Bombay. There is not much else to invest in if one
has no land and is getting old. People return with their funds and
invest in a small business, hoping to augment their income at least
marginally.

Bali is the head of a Dhangar family still involved in the
blanket-weaving business. His work and sales pattern is still very
traditional.[2] None of his sons will continue in the trade. He has
three sons in Bombay, one in the textile mill, another in the police
service, and one who works as a clerk in the dockyard. They share
a room in a tenement in the heart of the mill area where several
other Sugao families reside.

Bali has not expanded his trade very much during his thirty-
five years in the business. While he could invest more capital, wool
prices have been rising, and he has too little to make an appreciable
difference to his trade. When questioned about how he might
diversify, he replied that he could sell ready-made articles such as
banyons (T-shirts) and other clothing in the interior villages of the
Konkan, where he travels in the course of his blanket trade.
Although he and his wife obviously enjoy their traditional work, he
sees little future in the business for his sons. Their salaried jobs in
Bombay are more reliable sources of income.

The case of blanket weavers in Sugao illustrates the
multiplicity of problems that traditional artisans and craftsmen face
with the encroachment of urban industrial goods. With the advent
of the more finished, and often cheaper, factory products, the
traditional craftsmen are losing not only the urban market but the
local rural market as well. Rural craftsmen have difficulty
producing goods at prices competitive with the factories. First, they
have problems procuring the necessary raw materials, even if

Like most village artisans, the goldsmiths' workplace is in their home.

Traditional weavers must now compete with producers of cheap, factory-made goods.

produced locally, in the face of competition from large-scale urban merchants who buy in larger quantities and are able to pay more. Second, the craftsman also labors under certain technical inefficiencies, which often results in waste of raw materials. Third, it is more difficult for him to buy raw materials with cash. Transactions at the village level are often on credit, which further depletes his working capital. This poor asset position makes it impossible for him to keep an inventory; thus he is driven to distress sales, which may result in losses. Under these circumstances it is not surprising that household industry is being uprooted in spite of the numerous aid programs offered by government agencies.

One finds similar flows of money from the village to the city in such activities as building construction. Although the housing industry has the potential of being rural based through improvements in local building materials, one finds that the prevalent trend in Sugao is to import materials such as cement, bricks, magalore tiles, and galvanized iron sheets for roofs. Local carpenters, masons, and manual laborers are employed, but no materials are manufactured locally.

Trading

Service trades such as bangle selling, tailoring, and grocery vending have existed in Sugao since 1942. Numerous people in the village own sewing machines, and, although many have at times tried to make a small living by sewing, only three or four individuals are usually successful. Success is largely the result of good interpersonal skills, which allow the tailor to keep the customer happy even if the work does not get done on time, and expertise at tailoring. My friend Rani has run a thriving sewing business from her one-room house since 1975. She averages a profit of Rs. 2 per day. She is busiest around the time of Diwali (the festival of lights and the Hindu New Year) and Yatra (the annual village festival). In these seasons she averages an extra profit of Rs. 60 or more.[3]

Rani with her chili-grinding machine.

Bhikku (far right) and his team in the *mandap* and loudspeaker business.

Rani thinks that she could run another business such as a small shop selling stationary or ready-made clothes. However, she is reluctant to tie up her capital in these goods for a long time. She did expand into chili grinding in 1978, and by 1982 it was a lucrative but arduous business. Her one-room house is dominated by the grinding and sewing machines, the pungent smell of chili powder always tickling one's nose.

Some new businesses (cycle rentals, decorative lighting and music services, radio repair shops, and flour mills) have been established recently. At the time of the 1977 survey there were three cycle rental and repair shops in the village. All the owners complained that there was only enough business in the village to support one cycle shop. Each of the shops had four to six bicycles. Two of the owners conducted business in their houses, while the third rented a room, for Rs. 10 a month, facing one of the main village squares. Rental rates at this third shop were Rs. 3 a day or 40 *paisa* an hour. This shopkeeper said he earns between Rs. 150 and Rs. 225 a month. With all the competition, profits are low. He would like to combine his shop with some other endeavor.[4] One of the other cycle shops has a small grocery store attached.

One person who has been adept at starting various small businesses in Sugao is Bhikku, a man who was largely raised in Bombay. In 1958 his father and mother, both from Sugao, were living in the Kermani Building in Bombay, where his father worked in the textile mill and his mother ran a meals service. Bhikku left school in the seventh grade and learned electronics and electrical repair in Bombay. He claims that he made a lot of money smuggling gold and running hashish and opium from Delhi. He was caught, jailed, and, on his release, banned from returning to Bombay.

He therefore began a radio repair and *mandap* (ceremonial awnings and tents) shop in Sugao. He uses the electronics knowledge he picked up in Bombay, and designs and constructs the ornamental arches and backdrops himself. His *mandaps* are in much demand in the area, especially in the town of Wai, where, as he puts it, "they appreciate the sophistication" of his work. He always wins a prize for his display at the Ganesh festival in Wai. He charges a minimum of Rs. 300 for wedding decorations if he is to provide the entrance canopy, lights, loudspeaker, and music. He has acquired a large selection of attractive *mandaps* and other decorative pieces. Recently he rented a room opposite his present "studio," and opened a small bar which sells local bottled wines and alcohol by the glass. Of the three or four establishments selling liquor in the village, only Bhikku's is licensed. The other operations are sub rosa, one of them in fact serving the product of a home-made still in the fields.

Bhikku is also taking on some light contracting work. He recently rewired the lights of a restaurant in Vele and has bid for the repair and refurbishing of the interior of a small school building in Khandala. He is one of the most aggressive of the new people who have started small businesses in Sugao. His Bombay upbringing may have something to do with his initiative. Most investors in the village unimaginatively engage in some service activity already well provided for. Bhikku always seems one jump ahead.

Most traders felt that, when an opportunity for opening a business manifested itself, far too many people opened establishments to meet the need, with the result that all made meager profits on their investments. No single trader was able to live comfortably off a new opportunity, and all of them had to invest vast amounts of time in order to make just a few transactions. Most of the tailors, grocers, bangle sellers, and so on, practice their trades as a sideline or subsidiary business. There are only three full-time grocers in the village and one tailor. Apparently this is all the village economy can support.

One of the problems of doing business in a closed village society is that inevitably a trader must extend credit to families to whom he is beholden. Often his debtors never pay, and ultimately his capital is depleted, forcing him to close his business. Lower-status castes are especially susceptible to this since they are often dependent on higher-caste, affluent farmers and cannot refuse a request for credit from one of them. As a result, many are loathe to open any retail establishment. Villagers prefer to do business in Wai precisely because it can be done more impersonally, among people with whom one does not have past years of association or future years of expected contact.

Besides the year-round trades, there are some informal, seasonal, and social activities that result in the production of goods needed by the family. In the hot season following the harvest, women gather in groups of four or five to make quilts. Formerly this was done as a mutual exchange of work, each woman getting her quilt made with the help of the group. Nowadays it is more common to hear of a woman being paid for her day's work on a quilt. Women make noodles and other savory snacks cooperatively in the hot seasons and store them for use during the year. This activity is still based on friendship and reciprocity. Other individuals play musical instruments at weddings or other religious ceremonies. Payment for these and other minor activities is fairly small, however, and the volume is insignificant.

The few salaried jobs in the village, apart from those of schoolteachers, are village-level worker (*gram sevak*), postman, electrical line repairman, and a couple of jobs in the two flour mills. Salaried jobs are valued highly by the villagers, as they provide a steady and regular income unaffected by the vagaries of the climate or the moods of the village.

When potentially valuable resources exist or opportunities for trade and entrepreneurship arise, it appears that some villagers, often too many, will endeavor to exploit them. If some demand is not being met, it is probably due to some real constraint on its profitability, and not because no one has recognized the potential. In the most isolated hamlet I have heard residents expound on how they could stimulate tourism in their area if only the government would build a road or provide transport service. The problem is not lack of knowledge or entrepreneurship, but a very small and insecure asset base.

At present, opportunities for expanding the nonagricultural sector in Sugao are extremely limited. With the shift from

A basket weaver and his daughter in their yard.

The cigarette shop on the main axis lane.

subsistence farming to cash crops, a villager sells his product to the
city and buys his goods and services from it. In the process he
becomes more closely linked to the urban complex, and rural
demand is increasingly being satisfied by factory products. With
improved bus and truck service, villagers have better access to the
city and are accustomed to getting goods and services there. This is
so even for the poorest villagers. Their most common purchases—
matches, sugar, tea, cloth, a few utensils, and perhaps a cup and
saucer—are mostly products of the factory and not of the local,
traditional agro-industry. Remittances to the villages come not only
in the form of money but as necessary and luxury goods. Soap,
cosmetics, cloth, kitchen utensils, and even tea and biscuits are sent
from Bombay to Sugao, further depressing the local potential for
trade. Just as the urbanite's preferences lead him to buy imported
goods whenever possible, so also the villager's preferences lead him
to buy city products when he can. The villager who has no
commercial cash crops is left stranded. He needs things from the
city, but has no way of earning the necessary cash.

With the growing integration of the rural and urban
economies, traditional industries are on the decline and few new
industries have appeared. It is apparent that the local market for
services in Sugao has not been expanding rapidly either. In fact,
the only increase in nonagricultural service jobs has been some new
teaching positions at the village school. To succeed, rural industry
must link itself to the urban economy and make a profit from urban
money. Currently there is not enough surplus money in the village
to allow industry to thrive on local demand alone; besides what
surplus does exist is already flowing largely into the city. Contrary
to the popularly held beliefs, a successful rural industry does not
necessarily develop many forward or backward linkages to the
villages around it, since it is generally tied to the urban economy.
Thus, as things stand today, Sugao's destiny is irrevocably tied to
that of Bombay and other cities.

Notes

1. Poona Archives, Innam Daftar, Satara District, section 44, rumals 1625 to 1628.

2. A history of the blanket weavers of Sugao and a description of their trade and its decline is given in Jagtap (1975).

3. Rani's investments in 1977 consisted of purchases of a Merrit treadle machine at Rs. 410 (U.S. $48); scissors, bobbins, needles, etc., at Rs. 50; and buttons, thread, and accessories at Rs. 100; for a total of Rs. 560. Because she conducts her business in her home, separate costs for rent and electricity are not incurred. She charges Rs. 1.5 for blouses, Rs. .75 for petticoats, Rs. 1.5 for shirts and pajamas, and Rs. .75 for underwear.

4. Investment in one of the cycle shops was about Rs. 2,200 (U.S. $259), consisting of five bicycles, four new and one old, at Rs. 1,500; tools valued at Rs. 100; and spare parts costing approximately Rs. 400. This shop was owned by a "guest" of the village who came to Sugao to look after his wife's land. He borrowed the investment money from his former employer, who owned a cycle shop in Satara. He paid 8 percent monthly interest on this loan. He also bought spare parts from this Satara dealer.

CHAPTER 9

ANIMALS AND ANIMAL HUSBANDRY

The animal and human populations of Sugao either share their living space or occupy juxtaposed and proximate quarters. Most families in Sugao own a few animals, one or two goats or maybe a *mahes* (female water buffalo), which provide most of the milk consumed in the area. Separate sheds to house these animals are rare. At night the goats bed down in one corner of the often one-room house, along with a couple of chickens, a cat or a dog, and the human inhabitants themselves.

Kamli (meaning little lotus) was a two thousand pound water buffalo who was Bharatibai's exclusive charge. She occupied the animal shed off the back courtyard of our house, which was relatively large and had such refinements as a separate kitchen and storage areas, and an enclosed courtyard and bathing room (see figure 6). In the mornings when Bharatibai took her out to graze, Kamli would march through the entry room of the house with great aplomb, scattering the people who might be chatting there, and step majestically down the main entrance steps as though they had been constructed solely for her convenience.

Water buffalo need to be cooled down daily with a bath and so are taken out to wade in the stream. They are temperamental creatures, not much more domesticated than their wild cousins who roam the surrounding hilltops and mountains and who are known to procreate with them at times. They have to be approached with caution and respect. Nobody but Bharatibai could easily approach

Kamli to milk her or take her out to graze. With Bharatibai she was a lamb, meekly following her down the village lane on the way to the fields. However, on one occasion when Bharatibai was ill and a man was hired to take her to graze, I saw Kamli, eyes red, lower her head and charge towards the poor man, who clambered to the top of a nearby fodder stack to get away. You had to be nimble-footed to hop out of the way of water buffalo approaching you along the village lanes. Particular animals were notorious for their bad tempers. When I was still a stranger (and had not yet begun to distinguish the human population one from another, let alone the village *mahes*), I once asked a woman, whose *mahes* was rapidly advancing towards me, whether it would charge. "No, no," was the reply, followed by a shrug, "but after all a *mahes* is a *mahes*." There are no guarantees with water buffalo.

Few of us could get near enough to Kamli to milk her, especially after she had had a calf. Then only Bharatibai could approach her for several weeks. The first few days after a calf is born, the milk is thick and resinous tasting. Mixed with normal milk and sugar, and steamed, it makes one of the most delicious desserts I have ever tasted. Milk animals in a household, whether goat, cow, or buffalo, improve the household diet significantly. Milk is added to tea, turned into yogurt, eaten with rice at meals, and given to small children. But if there is no milk animal in the household, most families, even the relatively well-to-do, buy only a miniscule amount of milk to lighten their tea.

The calf was a delightful addition to our household. I spent several hours watching him in the animal shed, learning to use his unstable legs, being fussed over by Kamli, or sitting watching the world with very large, black, blinking eyes. Priya was amused to find me talking to him one evening, and after that, at the end of a long day of interviewing, the girls would ask me if I wasn't going to catch up on my interview with our calf.

An easy familiarity is established between animals and people in Sugao which is markedly absent in most households in the city. Few urban families have pets, but in the village the goats, water buffalo, and other animals are not only regarded as productive

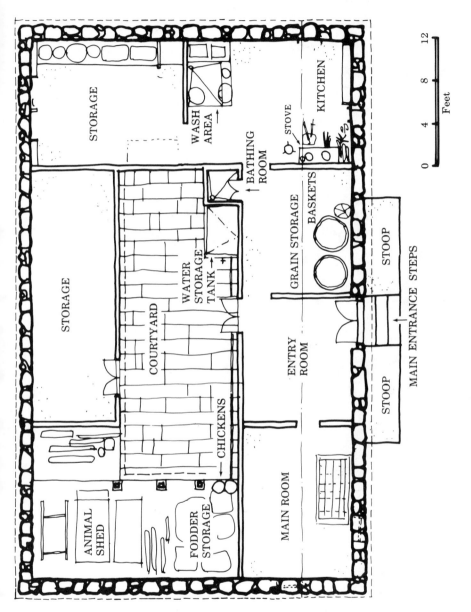

Figure 6: Bharatibai's House

Bharatibai taking Kamli out to graze.

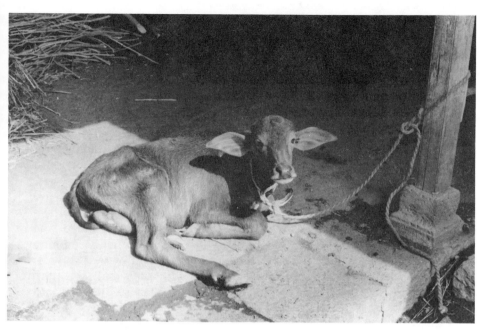
Kamli's calf was a delightful addition to our household.

A farmer and his bullock team.

assets but are treated with amusement and affection. When I showed the villagers slides I had taken in Sugao during my stay (some one thousand people gathered at Bhairava temple on a few hours notice to see "the cinema"), the bullocks and other animals in the background of the pictures were identified by exclamations of "There is so and so's bull, or dog, or water buffalo!"

Bullocks are in fact very important, not only because they are central to effective agricultural cultivation, but because they are a source of prestige for their owners. Men compare and judge who has the best teams of bullocks in the village, and, although no man ever requested that I take a photograph of him with his wife, several men wanted to be photographed with their bullock team. Bharatibai told me that her late husband had been so attached to a particular team of white bullocks that when they died, instead of disposing of their carcasses by selling them, he had had them buried on his land.

The increase in the animal population of the village (from 520 to 712 bulls, cows, and water buffalo, and from 272 to 354 goats between 1942 and 1977) has created great competition for the available fodder. Tremendous quarrels erupt over whose animal grazes on the grass that grows on the bunds separating parcels of land. One animal exempt from this restriction of grazing privileges is the *gaon rehada* (the village male water buffalo). Most male buffalo born in this part of the Deccan are castrated and sold as yoke animals in the coastal plain of the Konkan. The male water buffalo, with his larger, cloven foot, is a more effective yoke animal in the wetter climate and muddier, clay soil of the Konkan. The *gaon rehada*, usually donated by a well-to-do farmer to the village temple, is one of the few uncastrated buffalo in the village. He is allowed to wander, graze, and cohabit freely, in return for which he provides an extremely useful and necessary service to the *mahes* that are kept for their milk. The Sugao *rehada* was sleek and fat and lord of the village, and this was reflected in his assured and proprietary gait through the village lanes and fields.

For the village woman, one of the fringe benefits of working as a farm laborer is that she can take her goat with her to work in the

Dogs, cats, the goat, baby, and the rest of the family share this hut.

Goats are muzzled to prevent them from randomly grazing.

landowner's field, tie it to the embankment, and allow it to graze there. Most of the poorer, female agricultural workers in the village do in fact own a goat or two. The money that women earn from raising a few chickens and selling their eggs, or from selling the goat's milk, has traditionally been considered women's money. This is generally the only money most women in Sugao control. Although money from chickens and goats has traditionally been considered women's money, when a goat is sold for slaughter the money earned is more substantial and men sometimes lay claim to it.

The women and their goats spend a good part of the day together. In the morning and evening you can see the goat following along behind its owner, its mouth muzzled with a string harness devised to prevent it from randomly eating from the fields and hedges it passes and incurring the wrath of the landowner. The goats and kids generally sleep in the house at night. The kids are very playful and entertaining, running up to you, butting you, and nibbling on your fingers and toes. The traditional method to keep them in check and get them out of the way is to catch them and put them under an overturned basket. Then they poke their heads through the holes in the basket, bleat, and stare at you with accusing, pitiful eyes.

While surveying each household, I visited every family in their homes to get a sense of their living space. Many times kids would disrupt the proceedings. On one occasion, the man whom I was interviewing picked up a particularly rambunctious set of kids and shut them up in a cupboard. My questions were accompanied by a plaintive crescendo of bleatings emanating from the depths of the cupboard, a situation too humorous to allow for a serious discussion of the issues I was trying to address. I retreated, catching the man another time outside his home to complete the work.

This sharing of living space by animals and humans is not very healthy for the humans involved. One family I knew consisted of six grown daughters and their mother (the father and oldest sister lived in Bombay) who shared their one-room home with two large goats. There were always goat droppings and an odor in the shared quarters, where meals were cooked and human bodies were washed. I was taken aback at how the goat droppings contaminated the whole living space. Despite the idyllic first impression of life in the rural areas, living conditions for many people are not much better than those endured by people in the city; often they are worse.

Like goats, chickens were allowed to roam casually throughout the house, including the cooking areas. Most households own at least a couple of *gaonthi* (village or indigenous breed) chickens, which are flung a handful of grain at the start of the day and then allowed to scavenge in the streets and alleys. They are a hardy breed, avoiding predators such as dogs and cats with quick flight accompanied by loud squawks and a great flapping of wings. Requiring little care, they are brought in the house at night and bedded down under an overturned basket where they cluck away quarrelsomely for some time before subsiding into silence. You have to watch them closely if you want to find their eggs; they are secretive about where they lay them. Our chicken once surprised us with a brood of chicks which strutted around in our courtyard and went for swims in the drainage channel. Despite our watch over them, only two of the chicks survived the raids of the stray pregnant cat that had taken up residence in our attic.

The village cats are generally wild, aggressive beasts. They steal milk and food in the kitchen and are tolerated largely because they kill rats and other rodents around the grain-storage areas in the house. Cats are not pampered. If they are lucky, they are thrown a crust of millet bread once in a while. But they are adept at fending for themselves. The cat in our attic managed to purloin a neighbor's chicken, which it proceeded to dismember and consume for a few days in the attic over our heads. I remember awakening with a few feathers in my hair and on my face that had floated down during the animal's nocturnal feasts. When the neighbors asked us whether we had seen their chicken, we professed ignorance, not wishing to incur the owner's anger. After the kittens were born and grew to become agile and hungry, the daily battles between them and us escalated. I spent a good deal of time with a stick of sugarcane at hand with which I would charge into the kitchen to drive the kittens away from the food or the milk as it was cooking or cooling on the stove. Tired of their raids, we finally had them rounded up by a well-armed laborer who took them to the mountains and let them go.

Another member of my household was a large, intelligent, country dog named Gullya. He was a noble and loyal animal who attached himself to me and insisted on following as I went about my work in the village. Even when we ventured into the surrounding countryside there was no dissuading him from following along. Two miles out of the village, too late to return him home, we would find him trotting happily beside us, tail held high. His demeanor did not change until we reached the outskirts of other villages, which had resident dogs whose territory he was invading. Then he was between our legs, tail down, leaving us to deal with the unfriendly circle of growling native canines. No leashes or polite owners restraining their pets here. You had to pick up a large stone, make as few threatening gestures as possible, and hope for the best as you skirted the village and went along your way. Once out of range, Gullya would be his sprightly self, tail high, enjoying the country air.

Other animals you had to be careful of in Sugao were the large and unpleasant looking pigs that scavenged around the village. Their main food appeared to be human excrement and they were always found in the areas where people relieved themselves. So eager were they for human offal that they came sniffing when people were still relieving themselves. At night women carried not just the tin of water used to cleanse themselves but large stones to fling at any overly aggressive pig. It was a revolting situation that was simultaneously amusing, if you could distance yourself from this distasteful aspect of village living.

I found that the Kaikadis, the most depressed of the untouchable castes in Sugao, owned these pigs and would slaughter them for a feast once in a while. I blundered in on one such meal, intending to interview one of the Kaikadi families, and noticed them eating meat that looked very bloody and undercooked. Fuel is expensive and the poor family could not afford to cook the meat thoroughly. Even if they knew of it, fear of trichonosis, or any other disease that might be carried by animals fed largely on offal, could not be this poverty-stricken family's concern.

Another, somewhat less depressed group of lower-caste families in Sugao are the Wadars (masons), who are either *dagadi* (stoneworkers) or *mati* (earth movers). They own teams of donkeys which they use in their trade. Once in a while these donkeys would escape and gallop around the village *en masse*, braying at the top of their lungs, their owners in hot pursuit, a hilarious sight if you were not standing in their path.

Into the midst of this small-scale raising of cattle, goats, poultry, and pigs, typical for rural areas of this region, the independent Indian government introduced various programs to stimulate animal husbandry. This was part of the government's strategy of trying to diversify the income-earning opportunities of rural people, particularly of those who were land poor or landless. The Small Farmer Development Agency, under one of its programs, distributed milk animals such as water buffalo and cows, which had been bred for higher yields, to small farmers and landless laborers in villages. The rationale was that these poorer villagers would thus be provided with an additional source of income. Similar schemes were designed to provide such people with improved breeds of chickens, either by distributing such birds or by handing out better-quality fertilized eggs that would be hatched by native chickens. Other programs involved distributing half a dozen female and one male goat to poor families so that they could start a goat-rearing business.

Although these programs appear, at first glance, to be good ways to distribute productive animal assets to poorer families, there are several operational constraints that limit their success. First and foremost, common lands in the villages and the forest preserves around them are denuded and provide meager forage. In Sugao, for instance, it is questionable whether any sizeable additions to the existing cattle or goat population could be maintained on the village grazing land. Before the British rule, there was a greater sense of village unity, and the use of pasture resources was regulated by custom, as the village as a whole felt some responsibility in conserving these natural resources. Today, with the decline of this sense of a community with a shared future, there is little concern for the manner in which these communal lands are being exploited. The hills surrounding Sugao are bare and overgrazed. The forests have been cut for fuel and timber, and the remaining trees have been stripped for fodder. This destruction has accentuated the problem of soil erosion; though individual farmers utilize soil conservation measures on their own lands, communal lands continue to deteriorate. Although the animal population in Sugao has grown, there has been no aggregate increase in agricultural land earmarked for fodder, which indicates that the increased animal population in Sugao is being kept alive at the cost of the existing forest and grazing lands. Despite this, most animals in Sugao appear to be rather underfed. If the animal population is to be appreciably increased in Sugao, the owners must possess some land on which to grow the needed fodder. Most of the small landowners must use all their land for raising food for subsistence. Those without any land are of course precluded from participating in the various schemes.

Second, in a village like Sugao, animal husbandry quickly becomes labor intensive. One individual has to spend almost all of his or her time following the one or two animals provided to the family to ensure that they get enough to eat but do not stray into the standing crops. Fixed stall feeding could be introduced to get around this need and make a viable subsidiary occupation, but this requires investments in stalls and shed space to store fodder, and cash with which to buy the fodder in season. In addition, the recipient must own some land on which to build these structures. These investments would have to be subsidized if poor farmers are to participate in these projects, and this would entail much higher outlays within each program than are currently budgeted.

The same social and economic constraints that prevent cattle rearing from succeeding as a joint subsidiary occupation operate against successful commercial pig rearing. Presently the pigs that roam around Sugao are owned by the Kaikadis and survive by foraging freely in the village. If a scheme for raising pigs

Due to limited acreage and lack of cooperation, communal pastures are bleak and overgrazed.

Poultry raising, the "modern" way. Introduction of new methods and breeds has not always been successful.

commercially in fixed pen environments were promoted, the Kaikadis could not participate since they do not own land to live on themselves, let alone to rear pigs on, nor do they have the assets to construct pigpens. Thus the scheme would be helpful only to the well-to-do and would possibly displace the Kaikadi's current pig-rearing activities.

Similar problems arise in the plans that promote poultry raising in Sugao. The few country fowl that families typically own need minimal care and feeding. If an investment is made in a dozen improved chicks, then suddenly it is necessary to find someone to guard them from predators (both animal and human), and the endeavor becomes too time consuming to be a subsidiary occupation. If one person is not to be tied up all day, a protective coop has to be built and increased outlays must be made to buy feed since the birds will no longer scavenge in the street. This entails an even larger investment. In addition, better breeds of chicks seem to be more susceptible to diseases and die off sooner than the native ones. Some farmers in Sugao had, in fact, invested in fertilized eggs of better breeds only to discover that the chicks were more delicate than the country breeds and succumbed quickly to various illnesses. Furthermore, in the village itself the larger eggs of the improved but more expensive breeds do not fetch a better price than those of the native fowl. For the local market, small-scale raising of better breeds is not cost effective.

Two commercially viable poultry operations (of three hundred chicks each) have been established in Sugao. One of these was financed by capital accumulated in a Bombay job, the other through surplus generated from above-average landholdings in Sugao. These poultry farms are completely locked into the urban markets both for their supplies and services (feed, new chicks, medicines, and equipment) and for their products (eggs and birds), which are sold mainly to a dealer who comes once a week from Bombay. He packs the eggs in cardboard cartons and ships them to large cities such as Poona and Bombay. A government veterinarian comes from Satara to give shots and cut beaks, a free service provided by the state. Spillovers into the village economy are negligible; this scale of successful activity develops very few linkages forward or backward to the village economy.

One new industry in Sugao has been the establishment of milk collecting and sales establishments, which allow the small-scale milk producer to sell his product in the urban market. There are three such dairies in Sugao, one of which is organized to deliver twenty liters of milk daily to the tea shop at Vele. Another, owned by Shivaji, delivers thirty liters to the shop at Vele, and five liters to a cooperative collection truck that picks up the milk at Vele every morning and takes it to Poona.

Shivaji started his dairy in 1974. In 1977 he was paying his suppliers at the rate of Rs. 1.80 a liter in the winter, Rs. 2.10 a liter in the summer, and Rs. 1.70 a liter in the rainy season when the milk usually gets watery. This gives him a profit of 10 *paisa* a liter in the rainy and winter seasons and 20 *paisa* in the summer. To run the dairy Shivaji's day starts at 6:30 A.M., when he has to wash his milk-carrying utensils thoroughly with hot water. Villagers start bringing milk, which he tests, measures, and records in his ledger. This goes on until 8:00 A.M. He transports the milk to Vele by 8:30 in large containers slung onto his bicycle. Sometimes he has to wait until 10:00 for the collecting truck to arrive, which is a nuisance, but he continues to supply the cooperative dairy because it provides him with equipment to run his own operation, such as testing machines that measure fat content and books and ledgers for accounts. The villagers feel that one of the problems with the cooperative dairy is that it pays only once every two weeks; people in the village do not like to wait for payments. Shivaji works hard every day at keeping this business going. On the way back from Vele he cleans out his milk utensils at the stream. Sometimes he pays a man from the village Rs. 4 to make the trip to Vele for him. He is thinking of getting two jersey cows under the Bhumi Vikas Scheme, a rural development program that would give him a loan for his purchase. This would boost the milk production of his dairy considerably.

The success of the dairies in Sugao has resulted chiefly from the evolution of a transport, information, and distribution system that facilitates the collection of milk from the villages and its delivery to various urban centers for distribution and sale. There is little local demand for the milk because the villagers have little cash on hand for such luxuries. Money that could buy milk will also purchase a quantity of grain that is much more filling. The same goes for money earned from selling milk. Formerly, when there were no arrangements for collection, milk could not be sold in any large quantity since the local demand was low; it was therefore usually consumed by the family. Now, since a market exists, it is sold for the ready cash it generates. The result is a poorer diet for the villagers. The same logic of obtaining ready cash operates when the few chickens a family keeps begin to lay eggs. The poorer family chooses to sell the eggs if a buyer is found, rather than consume them. The encroachment of the cash economy into village transactions has thus had some adverse effects on the diet of small producers.

The government-sponsored schemes to stimulate animal husbandry have had some shortcomings when viewed from the perspective of poor people in a village such as Sugao. The schemes generally do not provide a market link to the city or ensure supplies of raw materials such as fodder for cattle raising or feed for poultry. They do not always take into account the capacity of available land resources to bear the additional animal load, nor do they consider the extra manpower required to protect these animals. A more comprehensive and sympathetic understanding of the constraints that operate in villages is necessary before successful schemes to promote small-scale animal husbandry can be successfully implemented.

At present, a minimum amount of land and various other assets are necessary to properly implement many of these programs at the village level. These schemes may generate additional income for villagers who already have some assets, but not for the most needy, the landless and the land poor, for whose benefit such plans are ostensibly designed. The poor are already intensively exploiting whatever resources they can to augment their meager incomes. If their participation in these various schemes is to be increased, it will to be necessary to make these programs more comprehensive, so that they can provide a more complete package of services and subsidies, resulting in changes in the village as a whole. Until then, the people and animals of Sugao will continue to coexist in their ad hoc way, a situation that may be colorful and amusing, but which also needs to be changed.

PART III

LIFE IN BOMBAY

CHAPTER 10

MIGRATION

There is a good deal of coming and going associated with the movement of migrants from Sugao. Of the over 650 Sugao people who were living outside the village in 1977, almost all came home to visit at least once or twice during the year. One of the questions I asked in my Bombay interviews of migrants was how many visits they made to the village every year. One of the textile workers, elbowing his companion in the ribs, answered, "This one goes home all the time. Every flimsy excuse he has, he's off to Bombay Central to catch a bus for Sugao. That's how it is with newlyweds, they want to sit holding the *sari padar* [the loose end of the *sari*, the Maharashtrian equivalent of apron strings] day in and day out! He'll learn. Pretty soon he's going to start complaining about the demands of those back home. They think money and goods grow on trees here. I go home as often and for as long as I can," he continued, "but it's expensive."

Remembering some of the theories in the planning literature about the bright lights of the city attracting the migrant, I asked him if he didn't prefer to live in Bombay. Wouldn't he miss the excitement if he went back to live in Sugao, I wondered. "What kind of question is that?" he said. "There is no question about it. Of course I would live at home if I could make enough money there." Waving his arm to encompass the dirty pavement and the roaring pedestrian and vehicular traffic outside the door of the Sugao *talim* (exercise place) where we were sitting, he said, "There's no excitement here, the air smells of the mills, the food is bad, and there is nowhere to go for a walk that isn't as crowded as this." He was right. It did smell of the mills. We were in the heart of the textile area of the city, and the nearest beaches, which are literally the lungs for congested Bombay, would be packed with the city's population strolling shoulder to shoulder. "In Sugao," he continued, "at least the fields are open and the breeze from the hills is fresh, the *bhakari* made in one's own home tastes so much sweeter than what the *khanawal bai* [the woman who prepares meals for pay] throws on your plate here." Bombay, the queen of India's cities, with its thriving commerce, cosmopolitan and heterogeneous population, more open society, and huge entertainment industry, has little to offer one in his economic class. Working long days in the textile mill, he earns barely enough to maintain himself in the city and his family in the village in a very modest lifestyle. He has little surplus income with which to splurge on the city's luxuries and allurements.

Migration of men from Sugao to Bombay for work is not a new phenomenon. This pattern of migration has existed in Satara District for many years. According to the first Satara District *Gazetteer*, even in 1885, 10 to 15 percent of the men in the district migrated to Bombay (Government Central Press 1963). At that time, however, the migration pattern was seasonal. Jobs in Bombay were relatively easy to obtain, and workers migrated to the city for those six months of the year that followed the *kharif*-crop season, when agricultural tasks were few. Sugao men found jobs as porters in the railways, as coolies on the docks, and, when textile factories were established by Indian entrepreneurs, in the mills of Bombay. By 1942 such temporary or annual-cycle jobs had become much more difficult to obtain. To keep their city positions Sugao men began to remain on the job in Bombay for the whole year. As a result, the migration pattern that has now emerged encompasses the entire life-cycle of a man. An adult male moves out of the village at age eighteen or twenty, usually to Bombay, spends all his working life there, and returns to Sugao upon retirement, bringing his savings to invest in the village.

Such migration out of Sugao has been increasing. In 1942, 17 percent of the resident population had migrated; by 1958 this was up to 24 percent, and by 1977, 29 percent of Sugao people lived outside the village (see table 10). The primary movement of Sugao men continues to be to Bombay. By 1977, however, an increasing number of men had found jobs in the armed forces, mainly the army, and were posted to various regions in India. By 1977 there were almost as many adult men earning a living outside the village as there were men living in the village.

Usually, when the man works in Bombay, his wife and children look after the family lands in Sugao. Before he retires he finds his son a Bombay job, either in his old workplace or in one with better pay or working conditions. A textile worker can usually find such a job in the mill, where his son works for relatives. When possible, he tries to get his son a white-collar job such as a clerk or a supervisor. Once a son is established in a Bombay job, the father can retire, drawing on his pension and other benefits in the village. Remittances from Bombay continue, now sent by the son. In this fashion, having one or more wage earners working in Bombay has become an almost hereditary practice in some families.

One of Priya and Suma's uncles, the man addressed by the Jadhavs as Mukadam (chief or captain of the caste group), was one of the first of the Jadhavs to become established in Bombay. In the 1930s he went to Bombay, working first on the city docks and later in the textile mills. He used his savings to do some moneylending in the village, a tremendously profitable business since monthly interest rates of 10 to 12 percent can normally be charged if one has the spare cash as well as the strong arm required to collect. In addition to making good personally, he found jobs for a number of other Jadhav males from various families, thereby accumulating a good deal of gratitude and power. During his thirty or so years in Bombay he even kept a mistress, on whom he is reputed to have spent a fair amount of money.[1] By the time I got to know Mukadam, he had retired to Sugao, had apparently discontinued his relationship with his city mistress, and seemed content carefully tending the family farm. His son is now working in a textile mill in the city. Mukadam has built a larger house for himself in Sugao, and his financial position is secure. However, because he spent much of his adult life away from Sugao, he is outside the group that makes decisions for the village as a whole, and is marginal even to the group that makes them for the Jadhavs. He would like to get control of Bharatibai's land—her husband was, after all, *his* cousin and therefore the land is his family's land. So far he has not prevailed by either chicanery or persuasion. Despite such problems, the pattern of spending one's productive years in the city and one's retirement in Sugao is common.

Circular Migration

The circular nature of migration from Sugao is graphically illustrated in figure 7, which shows the distribution of resident and migrant population for Sugao grouped by age and sex. In the seventeen-and-older age group there are more women than men in the village. This is the age at which men begin to migrate. The population returns to a more normal male/female distribution in the fifty-seven-and-older age group, by which time most migrants have retired and returned to the village. If the migrant figures are added to the Sugao population, the male/female distribution becomes closer to that of the district and confirms that most migrants from Sugao have been accounted for in the surveys. The figures on those who returned to Sugao from outside jobs between 1942 and 1958 and from 1958 to 1977 (see table 5) indicate that a large proportion of Sugao males who migrate for work do in fact return to the village when they retire.

Very few individuals leave Sugao permanently. The men who left permanently between 1942 and 1958 constituted 1.2 percent of the 1942 population, and the men who left between 1958 and 1977 constituted 4.6 percent of the 1958 population (see table 5). Individuals who left Sugao, having sold their house and land, and whom village residents reported as having settled elsewhere, were counted as permanent outmigrants. The village population was thus quite stable. This fact is important, for it highlights the continuity of village relationships and connections despite what appears at first glance to be a tremendous outflow and turnover in the community as a result of migration to the city.

RESIDENT POPULATION WITH MIGRANT   MIGRANT POPULATION

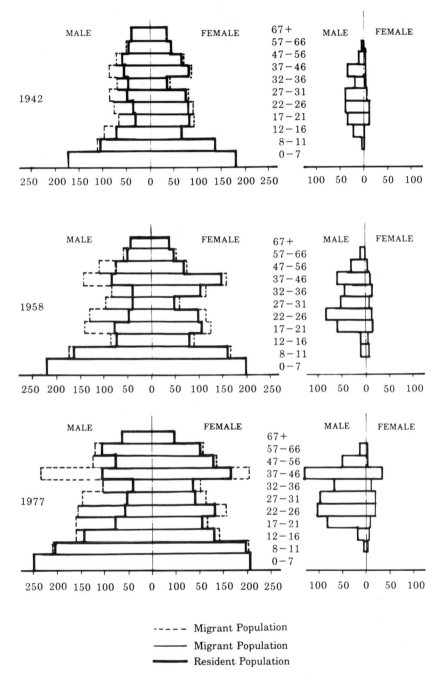

Figure 7: Sugao Population, Resident and Migrant, by Age and Sex

One apparently unusual aspect of permanent outmigration was that a relatively large number of women left the village. Between 1942 and 1958, 1.7 percent of the total 1942 female population migrated; between 1958 and 1977 this figure rose to 5.5 percent. Field investigations revealed that many of these women had married Sugao men and moved to the village, but for one reason or another—often for not bearing a son—had been abandoned. These women left Sugao, most often returning to their parents' or a brother's home.

By comparing the number of females per 1,000 males in rural areas, the extent of male outmigration from a village can be compared with that of a region: the greater the migration out of the area, the more females there are per each male in the countryside. Such an analysis showed that in 1971 rural areas in Wai Taluka (1,129 females per 1,000 males) were sending out more males than was average for rural areas of Satara District (1,062 females per 1,000 males). Sugao had 1,226 females per 1,000 males in 1977, which was above the average for rural areas of Wai Taluka in 1971. The village was thus sending more migrants to Bombay than its neighbors in the *taluka*, probably because of its long-established network of contacts with the city. However, in the same vicinity I visited hamlets and smaller villages with less fertile land, villages that had sent practically all their men to the city. Sugao is thus representative of what can be expected to eventually happen to most villages in Satara District if the job opportunities in Bombay continue to expand. On the other hand, if current trends in the textile industry are any indication, migration will actually level off or even drop as automation is introduced to maintain the competitive edge in the race to export manufactured goods.

Historically, single women have not moved to the city from Sugao to find jobs. The women who do migrate are almost exclusively wives accompanying their husbands to the city. For men the migration is substantially different and predominantly for work. Over two-thirds of the migrant men are married, although the proportion of unmarried males is increasingly slightly. In 1942 and 1958, 29 percent of the migrant males were unmarried; by 1977, 31 percent were unmarried, probably due to the rising age of marriage for Sugao as a whole. Very few of these migrants can afford to take their wives with them to Bombay.

The reason families are left behind in the village is largely economic. Housing in the city is scarce and rents are high. Day-to-day necessities cost more, and the men in the lower-wage jobs cannot support their wives in the city. Some of those with greater incomes felt that they could not continue to help support their extended families if they brought their wives and children to the city. Thus, personal happiness was sacrificed for the good of the larger joint family.

Having "one foot in the city and one in the village" is a necessity for many Sugao families that do not have enough assets to survive solely in one or the other place. The resulting prolonged separations cause emotional stress and hardship in the personal lives of individuals, particularly in the relationship between husband and wife. When a young wife is left in the village with a joint family that does not have much land, cultivation of which requires all the family hands, the joint family tends to split into nuclear families. This is happening in the land-poor Dhangar community. The Dhangars are sending more and more members to work in Bombay, as their village-based weaving industry declines. Joint families are disbanding in the land-poor Mahar community as well.

Often when a joint family is cultivating land in Sugao and has two or three men in Bombay, one of the men's wives will be sent to the city to cook and keep house for the men. Wives of brothers in Bombay sometimes rotate trips to the city so that each brother's wife lives with him for some part of the year. In one or two of these families, the women have started a *khanawal* business in which they cook meals in return for cash payments from a number of village men living alone in Bombay.

Even if there are no sons to take over the city job and not much land to return to in Sugao, most migrants find that once their jobs in Bombay end they have no means with which to go one living there. Few migrants are able to own their living accommodations in Bombay. Even if all they have in Sugao is an acre of indifferent land and a tiny dilapidated house, they can invest their savings in home improvements, in acquiring one or two milk animals, and in better cultivation of their land. The village offers a healthier environment, better food, and a more congenial social life. The climate is good and the lack of such amenities as piped water and sanitary facilities, which so discomfort the city dweller, is not a problem for the returnee since he was reared in those conditions.

There is a theory of stepwise migration that states that the migrant from a village usually moves to the nearest town, and then to the next larger town, as he acquires confidence and an ability to deal with the urban environment. Those who espouse the creation of a hierarchy of urban places to allow for diffusion of development base their arguments on this theory. But it is quite clear from the movements of Sugao's residents that migration to the nearest large town, Wai, with a population of over twenty thousand, is not attractive or popular. There are few opportunities for work in Wai or in other such towns in the area. Poona, the nearest metropolis, which grew tremendously in industrial activity during the 1958–77 period, and which is closer to Sugao than Bombay, has attracted only 2 to 4 percent of Sugao's migrant population. The greater geographical distance between the village and Bombay, where the major migration flows have occurred, has not diverted the flow to closer cities.

The cause of this single leap, as opposed to stepwise migration, is quite clear from the interviews with Bombay migrants. The new migrant obtains work through the contact network of village relatives and friends already in the city, not by venturing out on his own to look for a job in nearby towns. Since Sugao has had contacts with Bombay since the turn of the century, the networks exist for locating jobs for newcomers and places are available where new migrants can live while they seek something better. Sugao has therefore been able to place more men in Bombay than its neighbors, and the contact network in the city remains the dominant factor in the decision to migrate.

Economic Impact of Migration on Sugao

Migration has left few families untouched in Sugao. Even as early as 1942 almost half (48 percent) of Sugao families had at least one person who migrated for work, and 14 percent had two or more people located outside. By 1977 more than half (57 percent) of the families had at least one migrant, and 27 percent had two or more.

By and large, migrants are the better educated, more aspiring, and most adventurous of the village males. A definite selection process comes into play when a family chooses one of its members to go to the city. I was introduced to school-age children and told that this child "is going to Bombay because he has the temperament" to succeed there. Discussions about which of the children should be sent to the city often start early; at times my attention would be called to some infant wriggling in his parent's arms, who, I was told, was talkative or aggressive and should do well in the city. Bombay industries use the services of these aspiring villagers at the most productive times of their lives, often paying them less than the minimum wages needed to maintain a home and family in the city. The migrant manages on these wages by maintaining his household in the village, which is cheaper and more secure, paying instead the psychological cost of separation.

Although the number of families with migrants has increased, the proportion that send remittances home has declined. In 1942, 85 percent of the migrants sent money home; in 1958, it was 81 percent; and in 1977, only 74 percent. This decrease may be linked to the decline in the earnings of migrants working in Bombay: a reduction of 18 percent in real terms between 1942 and 1977 (Brahme 1977). Usually, the individual who leaves the village manages to support himself in the city even if he cannot send money home. So, in effect, migration for some families simply takes a person off the land, leaving one less mouth to feed on village assets but also one less producer. The average remittance to Sugao per year for the 209 families that did receive money from outside the village was Rs. 1,088 per family in 1977. This accounted for 25 percent of the total income for the village for the year, a sizeable contribution to the village economy. Some of the families receiving remittances, particularly those in the land-poor Dhangar and Mahar communities were completely dependent on monthly money orders from outside for buying what they need for daily consumption, over and above what they produce for themselves.

In-kind remittances were also sent to the village. The magnitude of this flow of goods is reflected in the fact that 20 percent of the families in Sugao said that over 50 percent of their need for consumer goods was satisfied by outside shipments. Most of these families were Maratha, either Yadav, Jadhav, Kochale, or guests. The other communities did not appear to send as much home in kind. Such mundane purchases as soap, matches, sugar, and tea, as well as more elaborate items such as clothing, cosmetics, and ceramics, were sent from Bombay. In this way the tastes and preferences of the city are transmitted directly to the villages, and the market for locally produced goods gradually erodes in favor of the city product.

The more affluent families who have members working in the city do not generally need monthly remittances to meet their daily consumption needs. Migrant remittances and savings enable these families to make lump sum investments in major purchases—land, agricultural equipment, and housing—thereby enabling them to increase their asset base and consolidate their dominant position in the village. A major share of money presently spent in Sugao on building new or upgrading existing housing, on acquiring fixed assets, as well as on new industry, comes from the accumulated savings, gratuity, and pension payments of migrants from well-to-do families. Partly as a result of such money flows back to Sugao, and partly because of land scarcity and general inflation, land prices are extremely high. Not only the price of agricultural land but those of house sites and existing dwellings have escalated tremendously.

It is a seller's market in land. Information about possible land sales is transmitted by word of mouth in Sugao, and a buyer must have cash on hand to be able to act quickly. The migrant, residing outside the village, is not a part of the village grapevine that would

Some of the more affluent families use remittance money to build
new homes.

Mahars do the same on a more modest scale, using "sweat equity."

inform him of impending sales; the women in the family, although they live in Sugao, are not included in this male network. Thus the migrant usually misses rumors and is unable to cultivate the seller or bid for the land. In the village milieu, where interpersonal relationships are critical, he is at a decided disadvantage when something as important as a land transaction is contemplated.

As a result of differences in the type of migration for persons from poor and rich families—the latter migrating more out of choice and striving for better returns, the former leaving because of a lack of alternatives—there are differences in the way migrants have adjusted to the city. Most are locked in a circular migration pattern, returning to the village after retirement. A few, the better educated, often coming from more affluent families, are able to obtain a foothold in the city and can begin to consider making it their permanent home, even though most are loathe to give up the connection to the village which validates their caste and status claims.

The migrants from Sugao make substantial contibutions to the basic economic survival of a number of families in the village. Remittances supplement earnings eked out of meager landholdings. They also improve the asset base of some families by allowing lump sum investments in agricultural machinery, livestock, agricultural inputs, and housing. Whether for survival or "development," the migrants and their families pay the price—thirty years or more of separation during the most productive years of a man's life. During this period the village loses its best-educated, most able men to the city.[2]

Over the years the migrant's lot in the city has become more and more difficult. Increased congestion, a deteriorating environment, tighter job markets, and an income that decreased by 18 percent in real terms between 1942 and 1977 are the realities of city life today. This decline is reflected in the fact that remittances per migrant have been falling in real terms, although they still provide a large share of the total village income. The city continues to absorb the surplus manpower resulting from rural population increases. However, this is at an increasing cost—physical, psychological, and economical—to the migrant and his family as well as to the village.

Notes

1. A Bombay mistress is not financially or socially affordable for most of Sugao's migrants; wages are low, the cost of living is high, and peer pressure, even in Bombay, is strong. Consequently, Mukadam's relationship with his mistress was well known to Sugao people, even to young schoolboys. Little remains private in the hothouse of village gossip.

2. The conditions under which Sugao men migrate confirm some of the premises about migration in developing countries and the impact of this on the village community they leave behind. For a wider analysis of village conditions, see Connell et al. (1976).

CHAPTER 11

BOMBAY JOBS AND BOMBAY LIFE

If I had not had a place to start, it would have been a truly formidable task to find Sugao people in Bombay, even for a Bombay native like me. I had been told by Bombay-based villagers that one place to contact Sugao migrants in Bombay was the *talim* (wrestling and exercise place) in the Kermani Building on Arthur Road in the industrial zone. On my first visit I went there. The *talim* is no longer used as an exercise place, although it had been acquired for this purpose long ago by some of the more far-sighted migrants from the village. When I asked why no one used it for exercise anymore, I was told, "People don't eat well enough in the city these days to expend energy on body building." The *talim* now functions as a dormitory for new and not-so-new migrants from Sugao.

In a space about fourteen by twenty feet, a good two-thirds of it covered by four feet or so of red soil, the traditional floor for wrestling, about twenty Sugao people live. Despite this congestion, the space that overlooks the road is rented to a tailor. He conducts his business there, paying, in 1977, Rs. 50 per month to the trust that controls the *talim*. The rent includes electricity, which, he complained, was switched off at 10 P.M. so that the other occupants could sleep. Housing is so scarce that such makeshift arrangements combining business and residential space are constantly made.

Located in the heart of the textile area of Bombay, most of the *talim* residents work in shifts, mainly in the mills; usually residents may be found sleeping there at all hours of the day or night. They

233

bathe under a common cold-water tap, which they share with four or five other such rooms, and water is available only from 5 to 7 A.M. Each person's belongings are locked in a steel trunk; clothes have to be washed in the early morning at the time of bathing. To economize, some workers use the soap and water provided for hand washing at their place of work to wash their clothes at the end of the day. This sort of side benefit is taken into account when a decision to leave one job and take another is made.

The younger, more recent migrants I interviewed at the *talim* in 1977 earned at most Rs. 200 to Rs. 250 (U.S. $24 to $29) per month. With this income they paid for their meals, between Rs. 80 to Rs. 90 per month for two meals a day, the price depending on whether the person got mutton on Sunday and whether he owned a ration card. Tea and snacks cost another Rs. 45 to Rs. 60 per month. What with incidental expenses and trips to the village to take presents of clothing and food, the recent migrant had no surplus money to send home every month. His migration from the village merely lessened the burden on the family land by one person. Some of the better-educated recent migrants had begun to find jobs through the employment exchange and thus were getting into more diverse occupations, although the main method of finding work continued to be through personal networks.

The type of jobs that Sugao men obtained outside the village was gradually changing. In 1942 the bulk of the migrants worked in the textile mills (67 percent) and other factories (4 percent). Such jobs were manual-labor positions with little status and relatively low pay. By 1958, fewer men (58 percent) were in the textile mills, and by 1977 only 41 percent were, although by this time another 10 percent were in other manufacturing industries (see table 3). Thus there was an appreciable drop in the number of Sugao workers employed in textile mills and other factories from 70 percent in 1942 to only 51 percent in 1977. This decline was partly due to the fact that by 1977 almost 11 percent of the migrants were able to find employment in such government services as the military and the police, which had employed negligible numbers in 1942. Because the government, in the interest of equity, had instituted quotas for government jobs for those from depressed and backward castes, a number of educated men from such lower castes as the Mahars, cobblers, and carpenters had obtained such jobs. In 1977 another 12 percent were in white-collar and teaching positions, although almost none had held white-collar jobs in 1942. These positions were more prestigious and paid better than most of the mill jobs held by Sugao men. Thus the male migrants from the village have enjoyed a fair degree of upward job mobility in the last three decades, although the strike in the textile industry in 1982 and its effect on other industries in Bombay may change this picture radically in the years to come.

Much of the upward mobility may be attributed generally to better training and education. In 1977, 10 percent of migrant males had been educated beyond high school, either with some technical training (4 percent) or some college education (3 percent), and some holding degrees (3 percent). Only 8 percent were illiterate (see table 4A). This is a significant upward shift in education levels considering that, in 1942, 52 percent of the migrants were illiterate and none had gone beyond the seventh grade.

Categorizing the educated men of Sugao by community groups, a few of the better-educated individuals from the more affluent Jadhav and Yadav families do remain in the village, where they can be profitably occupied in managing the large family farms. Among the poorer groups such as the Mahars and Dhangars, almost all the educated men leave the village. Despite their training, there is absolutely no opportunity in the countryside for them to get better jobs, increase their incomes, or improve their standard of living. The poorest groups such as the Kaikadis and Wadars are unable to educate their children. Although the school itself is free, the minimal cost of books, stationery, and a set of clean clothes is too much for these families. So the children stay at home and help with the work—basket weaving, herding cattle, guarding crops—and have no option but to resign themselves to their poverty.

The Sugao male who migrates is thus generally more educated than his counterpart who stays behind. He leaves for the city during the most productive stage of his life, returning only upon retirement when his capacity for work is greatly reduced. As a result, urban industries are able to use the best of the rural workforce without having to directly subsidize their training or pay them a sufficient wage to support a family in the city. The migrant and his family, in turn, are just able to survive and maintain their place in Sugao.

Despite the changing occupational structure for migrants, the major source of work for Sugao men prior to 1982 continued to be the textile mills of Bombay. In 1942, a Sugao man could easily find a job operating a loom in a textile mill because the poor working conditions made it an undesirable occupation. Even now, with a much tighter job market, with some string pulling a Sugao man can get a job in a mill. But such jobs are harder to obtain than previously, even though they are generally recognized to be physically arduous and damaging to one's health.

During my stay in Bombay in 1977, I interviewed mill workers from Sugao in all job classifications, ranging from the lowest-paid member of the weaving section (who managed one loom and earned Rs. 350 per month) to the jobber who supervised sixteen automatic looms and earned the most (Rs. 750 per month). Working conditions are generally unpleasant in the mills because the interior has to be kept steamy to prevent the cotton thread from snapping. This, combined with congested housing and hotel food, leads to ill health. I interviewed three men in Sugao who had contracted tuberculosis while working in the weaving section of a mill.

Mill workers are unionized and active members tend to advance more rapidly than those who merely "tear the slip" (pay the dues) each month. The union helps a worker get reinstated if he overstays a leave in the village (a common and recurring situation) and backs him in various negotiations with management. Work is divided into three eight-hour shifts—morning, afternoon, and night—and even the senior workers rotate on them, one month on each shift. No doubt the strike has been instrumental in politicizing the Sugao workforce. Over the years I have observed a greater willingness on the part of the Sugao migrants to talk about working conditions and union matters. In 1977 most of the migrants interviewed in Bombay preferred to talk about Sugao. Such isolation is well nigh impossible to maintain today.

Housing has become increasingly congested in the mill areas. Ten of the individuals I interviewed were either themselves interviewed by Mr. Jagtap in 1958 or had relatives then in Bombay who had been interviewed by him. From these early descriptions it would appear that even in 1958 the housing situation was not particularly good. At that time a room was occupied by six to eight people; the same room housed eight to ten people in 1977. Most of the mill workers live within a few minutes walk of their jobs in the industrial areas of Chinchipokli and Lal Baug, in rooms rented by Sugao people at the turn of the century. Housing in the mill area, although not dilapidated enough to be in danger of collapse, is noisy, congested, and dirty. Although the rooms themselves are kept very clean, the public areas and sanitary blocks are filthy.

The accommodations shared in the *talim* are not much more congested than the quarters of Sugao workers who live in the upper rooms of the same building. The upper story consists of two small ten by ten foot rooms approached by corridors in the front and back of the building, each with a small washing area. Each of these rooms houses ten to twelve people. Some shelflike lofts increase the floor area and allow people to sleep during the day. Although the shift system at the mill relieved the congestion to some extent, my architect's sense told me that spaces claimed as "home" by so many could not possibly accommodate them all. When questioned about this, one of them shrugged and said, "Look, it's embarrassing to tell you since you know us and you know our families and homes in Sugao, but the truth is that on many nights some of us have to sleep on the pavement below. Why hide it, that's the way it is."

Rent varies from Rs. 2 to Rs. 5 per month, depending on the room and the length of tenure of the occupant. Occupancy of these rooms has been in the hands of Sugao people for thirty or forty years. At that time rooms in Bombay were relatively easy to rent, and the first generation of mill hands was able to find accommodations close to their place of work. Today such rooms are impossible to obtain in Bombay; rent control has kept the rent at prewar levels, and transfer of occupancy rights alone (not ownership) cost Rs. 11,000 ($1,294) in 1977. As is usual in such controlled situations, the owner does not maintain the building since he makes no profit from it. So the tenants must make whatever improvements and repairs they need. In the *talim* the rent is turned over to the *talim* trust, which pays the electric bill and other expenses, makes necessary repairs, and keeps the balance to invest in Sugao.

I visited three or four other tenements that also house clusters of single Sugao workers. Barring slight variations in room size and density, conditions were similar to those already described. I talked to migrants who had rooms in the Teli *chawl* (tenement) across the street from the Kermani Building. The municipality has notified them that they must vacate the building. They describe the situation this way:

> The municipality is going to demolish two or three tenements. Anyone who has a room in his name will get a room in the new *chawls* the government will build here. But if you live here as a boarder, you won't get a place of your own. The rents will go up, maybe to 75 or even 125 *rupees* a month. We'll have to live elsewhere until the new buildings are finished. There won't be any "key money" involved. Each tenant will get one double-sized room, 15 by 15 foot—larger than our present 10 by 10. No, we haven't seen any drawings yet, so we don't know what the layout will be like. We'll have to live elsewhere meanwhile. We just don't know how long it will take to rebuild—five years, four years, or two. They will give us space outside the city in Bandra, Ghatkopar, and Andheri [areas from which middle-class people routinely commute are considered "outside" places]. We will have to pay to travel back and forth to work. It's a nuisance to come and go on the railways. Take lunch, for instance. Today the man who delivers lunch boxes fetches the fresh food from here and delivers it to the mill. On the outside

we'll have to make do with less fresh food [with no refrigeration, one must consider where one eats and what].

This building will probably be torn down when the school term is over in June or July. Then the families can move. You know the *chawl* that used to be in front there? [It is now an open space where children play and men congregate to gossip.] That one was torn down almost seven years ago! We have no idea when we'll be able to come back. The people who lived there are now outside the city. The officials say the site is too small for a new building. The government has the cement—that's not the problem. They need the space our building occupies too—then they can build a good *chawl*. When the new *chawl* is finished we will all come back. All of us. It's just a question of which floor we will live on. You'll have to search us out! The new buildings may have five or ten floors.

Obviously the coming eviction will disrupt the lives of many Sugao migrants. For the most part, however, the transplanted villagers think of their Bombay rooms as nothing more than places to stay while they earn their livings. Home is still in Sugao. When a wife accompanies her husband, however, and they have a whole room to themselves, there appears to be a greater tendency to think of their quarters as home. One person who seemed more committed to Bombay, and owned the rights to a room, had this to say:

We've repaired and refurbished the *chawl* now. Mended the balconies, added new beams and columns—the whole structure has been strengthened. Now the work has stopped because of a cement shortage. We have a private contractor. Each room's principal occupant pays 1,100 *rupees*. The owner won't do anything. See the *chawl* that the municipality tore down! It's been five or seven years, and they haven't rebuilt it yet. The poor

tenants are scrounging. The government is in no
hurry to rebuild. We decided we should refurbish
this place ourselves. Five years spent wandering
here and there, and then the rent will go up on
them.

When I asked him what would happen if the mill workers went
on strike,[1] he said, "People like us, from the Deccan—we can go
home, live off the land. Konkan people have no land, so what can
they do? [Land-to-person ratios in the Konkan are even worse than
they are in the Deccan.] In Bombay they have to pay one hundred
rupees to the *khanawal* just to survive. They have a real problem.
It will be difficult for the people of the Deccan, but they will go
home. The land will support them."[2]

Land is in fact the last reliable sanctuary in the eyes of village
people. The major asset the textile worker takes back to Sugao is
his provident fund (a lump-sum payment made at retirement) and
whatever he gets in the form of service or gratuity. Most mill
workers never earn enough to buy more privacy for themselves or
accumulate enough savings and retirement benefits to enable them
to live in the city when they leave their jobs. They generally said
that they would return to Sugao when they retire, and most of them
felt that if they could earn equivalent money in the village they
would prefer to live and work there.

Contract *hamali* (coolie) work is one Bombay occupation that
has employed 5 to 6 percent of the Sugao migrants since 1942.
Most Sugao *hamals* work in the wholesale cloth market, where they
are usually attached to one *seth* (merchant). They move large
bundles of mill cloth on low wooden handcarts, transporting the
bulky, square containers between the mill, the merchant's
warehouse, and the railway, or between one mill and another. I
was told that if he is bright, it takes a man a minimum of six
months to learn how to use his weight to control the heavy handcart
and move it through the astounding congestion of the cloth market
area of Bombay.

A *hamal* maneuvers his cart through the congested Bombay cloth market.

Contract *hamali* work is hard but lucrative. Most individuals take home at least Rs. 700 per month, and in season the earnings are much higher. The working conditions, payments, and job security have improved greatly since the *hamals* unionized in the 1970s. *Hamals* work closely in small gangs, or *tolis*, often on a contract basis, building group solidarity and comaraderie. Schedules are adjusted so that each member can make frequent trips home if he wants.

Most of the *hamals* live in the warehouses of the merchant for whom they work; in being allowed to do this they are entrusted with the care of thousands of dollars worth of merchandise stored there. They do not bring their families to Bombay. When I asked one group why not, since they seem able to afford to do so, one of them said with a grin, "We don't want to spoil our women. Bombay life makes them soft. There is tap water in the room, electricity to be switched on and off at whim, and all a woman has to do is cook for her man and the children. She goes to the cinema and sees the pretty *saris* of the women who live here, and she wants them. We could never get our women to go back to farming and looking after the older people in the extended family!"

Vasant, my assistant in Bombay, was a young man from one of the richest families in the village. He was unemployed, waiting fairly contentedly for the "right job." No sweating in the textile mills for him. His uncle, whom I had met previously in the village, was the leader of the Sugao migrant community in Bombay. He had helped me find Vilas, my Sugao assistant, and now he suggested that it might be mutually beneficial for his nephew and me to work together on my research. Perhaps Vasant would realize that he must work hard if he was to be successful and that opportunities would not come knocking on his door.

To be fair to Vasant, his situation was representative of a certain class of migrants I observed in Bombay, men whose families were well-to-do and educated. They waited and looked for technical or professional jobs, the kind that offer possibilities for advancement. Their relatives in Bombay often supported them for six or more months while they looked. The one college graduate in my Bombay survey, who held a B.Com. degree, spent four years as a shop assistant in the cloth market, earning only Rs. 175 per month, before he was able to get a more suitable job as a senior clerk in a cloth mill, with a salary of Rs. 574 per month. Most of the men who have been in Bombay for twenty or thirty years have managed to find stable jobs and have stayed in them for fifteen years or more. Once a man gets a relatively good job, he tends not to leave the position for prospects elsewhere.

When migrants from the more affluent strata of Sugao society choose to leave the village, they have the economic backing, education, and influential network of relatives and family friends they need in order to bide their time and obtain better paying, less arduous jobs in the city. Those from the lower strata, for example, migrants from the Mahar and Dhangar communities, are forced to leave the village in order to survive. These persons must accept whatever work they can find. If they are fortunate, they end up with jobs in the mills, or, in the case of castes designated as backward such as the Mahars, in positions as sweepers and clerks in government offices, jobs specially reserved for them. If they are not so fortunate they have to make do with whatever odd jobs they can find while they look for better work.

Increasingly, the better-educated migrants from Sugao have obtained jobs in the civil service and in white-collar positions. In Bombay I interviewed fresh recruits in the police service and even one old-timer who had joined when the British were still in India. I also interviewed migrants who had found jobs in the Bombay State Transport bus service (BEST). Although the wage scales are relatively low in these government jobs, there come with seniority such highly valued benefits as allotments of comfortable housing, a provident fund, service payments, health care, and job security. I interviewed one man of the *mang* (rope maker) caste, formerly an untouchable, who has managed to improve his position by educating himself and getting a job in BEST. He had kept his family in the city and educated his daughters, but on retiring he must go back to Sugao, since he has not accumulated the assets, such as a room or a business, that would allow him to continue living in Bombay.

The staff housing provided to civil servants and transport workers with seniority is good. It usually consists of a bedroom, a living room, and a kitchen with a bath and separate water closet. Most people who manage to get such quarters bring their families to Bombay and say they are satisfied with city life. Some men in this group said they would consider severing ties with the village, but most cannot afford to do so.

Since most migrants cannot save enough to buy an apartment or live in the city after retirement, they must retire to Sugao. The educated middle class, however, does manage to gain a foothold in Bombay, and one finds a few second-generation migrants with city educations and white-collar jobs doing precisely that. They have bought rooms in the city and relinquished their rights to land and house in the village, so that a brother or other relative in Sugao may be left with a viable farm. They plan to remain in Bombay after retirement. At this time, however, such cases are exceptions rather than the rule.

When I visited Bombay in 1982, I made it a point to look up Nanu, who had lived in the house two doors from mine in Sugao in 1977. He now had one of the most desirable jobs in the city, that of a policeman. When I asked him how he liked city life he responded with a long emotional speech that seemed to capture the flavor of Bombay life for a young migrant.

> In Bombay, if you do not earn, you have no value. Money is what counts—it's equated with honor. I don't like the rush, the hustle. I feel like a machine. In Sugao sometimes I could stay in bed, take my own time in the fields. Here there is the constant pressure of people. I read the paper in the morning, go for a walk, and eat at noon. I have to help fetch water in the morning at the common tap. In Sugao you can at least get water when you want it, morning or evening, as long as you walk down to the well. Here there is no such choice. You *have* to get it from the tap in the morning.

A *mang* family from Sugao at their BEST housing.

There's no recreation in Bombay. Take the swimming pools, for instance. It's difficult to get into one. People like us can't afford it. I go once in a while but I have to pay 2 or 3 *rupees* to be admitted. In the village I could swim in the stream for free whenever I wanted to. When I have to pay, I try and get my money's worth and I stay there for two or three hours. I take a bath there. It's good.

What do I do for recreation? It's very simple. On holidays I go to the *talim* and chat with Sugao people. On some days I walk the streets for two hours to exercise or go to the Pathar Gym. I don't smoke cigarettes. I exercise where and when I can, and meet with men friends. I feel claustrophobic in the house and spend much of my free time on the street chatting. Once in a while, we plan a trip to Borivli National Park [on the outskirts of Bombay]. I eat at a restaurant once every two weeks or so, no more. I can't afford it.

I earn 550 *rupees* a month. It used to seem like a lot, but the money falls short in every way. I give 200 *rupees* to my sister for food [Nanu lives with his sister and her husband, who are also in the Bombay police]. Even though there is no *khanawal* here, I pay. Tea, coffee, clothing, soap, all add up. If you're late when you're on duty you have to eat outside. You need 2 or 3 *rupees* for "pocket money" every day. I always keep 25 *rupees* with me for emergencies. Everything gets more and more expensive. Now everything is at a "fixed price" in Bombay—5 *rupees* for a kilo of cauliflower—and no bargaining allowed. They want to rob us. They set the price among themselves. Very few people from Sugao develop a *charas* [hashish] or alcohol addition—where is the money for that?

It's a strange life here in Bombay. If you are waiting in line for a bus and someone next to you gets a stomach ache, no one looks at the person. They jump on the bus when it comes—won't take him to the hospital, won't show any pity. One's own life and one's own work—stick to that. I liked the movie *Chakra* by Dalvi.[3] He really captured what it's like in the squatter huts. In the police service we have to go tear down the huts that are built without a license. The people throw stones at us, use foul language, squat everywhere. A shed can appear in a spot almost instantaneously. First there is a curtain, then they throw up tin walls, and before you know it there's a roof! We need to build more *chawls* for the people. The housing enclaves on the periphery of Bombay are good for the big shots—one person or family occupying a whole floor. We need more *chawls* for people like us.

Despite the stories told to the folks back home in Sugao, the daily life of the migrant is far from glamorous. If a man is alone, he shares a room with other men and has no cooking facilities. He arranges to eat two meals a day at a *khanawal* nearby, and buys tea and snacks at the tea shops. In interviews and informal conversations the men complained most frequently of the monotonous, inferior quality of the food.

Running a *khanawal* is one of the few occupations open to women migrants in Bombay. Usually the women who venture into this business are widowed and destitute. They bring their children with them to the city. Through sheer hard work many have built solid businesses, often earning the initial capital by working as domestic servants. In 1977, five women from Sugao were operating *khanawals*. One of them, Chandrabai, has been remitting more than Rs. 100 per month to her son in the village since her husband died some twelve years ago and left her with a ten-year-old child. She was able to maintain control over her land with the help of her brother-in-law, who lives in Sugao. Her son has now inherited the land and is cultivating it while she continues to work in Bombay.

While her meals business is successful, she has not accomplished this entirely on her own. She has a friend (whose mistress she is reputed to be), a Sugao man residing with his wife in Bombay. He enjoys a respected position in Sugao and is considered Chandrabai's protector.

Tanubai, a woman from neighboring Kenjal village, has been in the *khanawal* business in Bombay for thirty-five years. She is in her sixties now and at present serves sixteen people a day, besides her immediate family. Tanubai was married at the age of six to a man who was then twenty years old. She recalls that he used to carry her around on his hip! He died when she was in her early thirties, and, left with young children to raise, she decided to come to Bombay. At first she lived with her husband's brother and his family in a room in the building where she currently resides. She survived by washing dishes and doing other types of domestic work.

After six years of this she was able to get a room of her own and, by borrowing money, invest in the necessary utensils to start a *khanawal*. At first she had only two or three sets of brass dishes (people eat in shifts since no more than four can sit and eat in the room at one time), but now she has enough to serve sixteen or more people. Tanubai rises early. Food bought on ration cards must be purchased at least once a week, and every other day she must go very early in the morning, at 3 A.M. or so, to buy vegetables at the wholesale produce market. On other days she gets up at 5 A.M. and bathes. From then on she is busy, storing water for the day, cutting and preparing vegetables, and making the dough for *chappatis*, a flat bread made from whole wheat flour. Although the villagers prefer a thick bread called *bhakari*, made from *jowar*, it is more expensive, and *jowar* is not always available on ration cards. Therefore the *khanawal* owner compromises by serving *chappatis* for one meal and *bhakari* for another. She makes about five *chappatis* per person, or about one hundred in the morning and the same in the evening, a backbreaking task indeed. The morning meal must be ready by eight o'clock, when the *dubba-walla* (lunchbox delivery man) comes to pick up the meals for those on the day shift in the mills. By eleven everyone has eaten.

After eating, Tanubai takes a short nap and then is off to the flour mill at least every third day to grind grain for the next days' meals. By 3 P.M. she is busy preparing the evening meals, which must be ready by five for the evening-shift *dubbas*. By eight most people have eaten, and she can rest. It is indeed a long and busy day. She pays a person Rs. 8 per month, plus meals and afternoon and morning tea, to wash the dishes every day. She charges Rs. 80 to Rs. 90 per month for two meals a day. The rates differ according to whether a man has a ration card and whether he wants to eat mutton on Sundays. On this income she was making a profit in 1977 of about Rs. 30 to Rs. 35 per person per month. Over the years she has acquired some assets such as her utensils, some jewelry, and her room.

The *khanawal* business appears to be one of the few jobs that village women who are left to fend for themselves can do to survive. In the village a woman would have to find some man, either the brother of her deceased husband, her father, or some other man whose mistress she would become, to protect and support her. It is extremely difficult for a young widow with few or no land assets to survive in the village by herself. In Sugao there was a woman, widowed in youth, who was the mistress of three or four village leaders at one time or another; ultimately, having been cheated out of her assets by one of them, she left for Bombay. She was able to raise her two sons in the city by operating a *khanawal*. Her sons have now returned to Sugao, where one is a teacher and the other runs a bicycle repair shop.

Most of the men who eat at a *khanawal* complain of the monotony and tastelessness of the food. Even if it is "all you can eat," one cannot eat too much, they say, since it all tastes pretty bad. They dare not complain too much, though, since finding a *khawanal* is getting to be very difficult; few women will undertake the hard work involved in running one. Usually a migrant is introduced to a *khanawal* by a fellow villager. Besides their *khanawal* meals, even the lowest-paid individual spends a minimum of Rs. 1.50 every day on snacks and tea. Few people have facilities for making tea or anything else in the communal rooms. Even storage for drinking water is lacking in the *talim*, and residents have to go to a hotel to get a drink of water. If the *khanawals* did not exist and workers had to eat in hotels, all their money would be spent on meals. The *khanawal* is thus a very important institution, one that allows the migrant to survive on his wages and send remittances home.

Only two women from Sugao have managed to obtain white-collar jobs in the city. One woman has a job in the police service, and another, Vidya, is an *ayurvedic* doctor. Vidya is really a product of the city. Her father was in the police service, and, having no sons, emphasized to his five daughters the value of education. Vidya, however, is the only daughter who completed a professional education in the city. Her sisters lacked either the intellectual capacity or the dedication to gain the education necessary for escaping the traditional role of village women. Now they live in Sugao, trying to scratch a living from the land.

Vidya has paid a price for her success. She is prepared to remain single and to pursue her career for the rest of her life; she will not allow a dowry to paid for her marriage and insists on supporting her parents on her income—conditions that prospective husbands are not likely to accept. She has little time to attend movies and plays, or to enjoy the pleasures of reading outside her specialized field. She leads a spartan and narrow life, limited to her profession.

The road to success in the city lies not just through a salaried job. Some entrepreneurs have made good in business enterprises in Bombay. A Sugao migrant named Dharmusheth, for instance, invested his savings from contract *hamali* in a trucking business. Profits were good and now he owns a couple of vehicles. A Muslim man from Sugao has also profited from trucking, and both these individuals hire some Sugao men to work for them. The road to greater profits lies in establishing a business in Bombay, and some Sugao men have mastered the knack.

While conducting my interviews I noticed a young barber shaving people around the *talim*. Later I realized that he was the son of a barber I had interviewed in Sugao. I remembered the

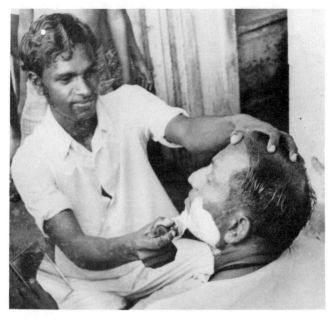

The Sugao barber's son plies his trade at the Bombay *talim*.

Essential, but portable, tools of the barber's trade.

A Sugao cobbler, a mill worker, plies his trade in his spare time at a busy Bombay intersection.

This Mahar (Neo-Buddhist) from Sugao is a security guard at a textile mill.

father mentioning his Bombay son, but I was surprised to find that most of the young man's clients were Sugao migrants. In this case a village relationship was transferred in an only slightly altered form to the city. In Bombay, shaves and haircuts were paid for in cash, and as far as I could judge the urban service was as lacking in sophistication as it was in the village.

I visited the room of one family of five Mahar brothers. They have a house in Sugao directly opposite my village home, and I had often watched their mother, a sweet-faced old lady, always with a friendly smile and wave of her hand for me, scrupulously working to keep her house clean. She usually had two or three daughters-in-law to help, but I rarely saw her sons. This was, I discovered, because they were all in Bombay working at a variety of jobs, one as a peon in the bureaucracy, another selling odd lots of vegetables in the local market. One of their wives always lived in Bombay while the rest stayed at home looking after the mother and working their tiny plot of land. I was struck by the close, continuous contact between Sugao and Bombay epitomized by this family. During my visit they even offered me snacks that had been prepared in the village.

Everywhere I went I was greeted with great hospitality. It was impossible to refuse glasses of tea, lemon soda, sugarcane juice, or coffee. But I noticed that my assistant, Vasant, even when hard pressed, refused to drink or share food with lower-caste people from Sugao. When I asked him about this, he said, "It's all very well for you. I don't really care, but when these people return to Sugao, they will make a point of telling my older brother, quite casually, that I ate with them. My family would lose face. I have a good friend who is a Mahar here in Bombay, but things are more complex in Sugao." He was right. Intercaste relationships are more complex in the village. In the city friendships and alliances are established that could never flower in the jealous village. If caste and class relationships are to be jolted in the countryside, the impetus will probably have to come from the city.

Recreation for the typical Sugao migrant is fairly restricted by economic constraints and social pressure. Free time is usually spent in resting or gossiping with other villagers, mostly about village matters. Only one migrant I met in Bombay was a member of a library; one or two subscribed to a newspaper. Few respondents said that they attended movies regularly. One or two admitted that they drank "a little" on Sunday.[4] Through discreet inquiries I learned that some Sugao men gambled a little and that a couple of them had mistresses in Bombay. However, the life of most migrants is rather tame. Since the men live in such close proximity, little immoral behavior (by village standards) goes unnoticed or uncensured, and this acts as a deterrent to many. Peer and societal pressures in the city seem almost as strong as in the village.

One of the most striking findings that emerged from the survey responses was the tenacious hold of village life upon these migrant workers. Not only does the migrant retire to the village after his time in Bombay, but while he is in the city he remains psychologically and socially very much a part of village society. His recreation time is spent with fellow villagers, and he spends all his vacations in Sugao. If he is one of several brothers working in the city, even the protective structure of the joint family is replicated. He hands over his paycheck to the oldest brother, who gives some of it back for spending money. The elder brother decides how much of the rest to send home to the village and how it should be invested.

There are a few differences between the behavior of men in Sugao and of Sugao migrants in Bombay. The migrants are more cohesive, helping each other to survive in the city. There is an *esprit de corps*, even among those from different castes. They are more inclined to talk freely about personal problems and about the larger political and social world of the village and the city. They are relatively better informed than the village men, though not in any active, participatory way.[5] They are willing to work to improve village life, but are prevented by the resident elites from introducing changes that would in any way disrupt the present power structure in Sugao. Some of the older, more thoughtful men I talked to in Bombay had opinions about the kind of social changes needed in the village, but they felt that Bombay returnees were unable to bring them about. They could not manipulate the rules or mobilize village support as handily as local leaders with years of experience. The wise returnee, therefore, did not try to change the village system in any way.

During his years in Bombay the migrant is unintegrated, subsisting on the edge of city life. Moreover, not only does he play a limited social role in the city, but as the years go by he increasingly becomes an outsider to the village. Economic realities compel him to retire to the village, but upon his return his leadership role in Sugao is severely limited. Although his city experience may have led him to question or even reject the rigid values and social structure of the village, he does not have the necessary moral authority to effect change. His best strategy for survival is to keep a low profile in the village political arena. Migration allows economic survival in Sugao, but the personal costs are high.

Notes

1. The strike did in fact start shortly after this conversation took place in January 1982. Since then the *Economic and Political Weekly of India* has published several articles on the strike, labor unions in the textile mills, emerging trends in the industry, and the industrialists' position. Little has been written about the impact of the strike on the families of the workers and on the home villages.

2. For a comparison of conditions for people from the Konkan and the Deccan, see Patel (1963).

3. *Chakra*, a novel by the well-known Marathi writer Jayant Dalvi, vividly depicts the lives of people in a squatter colony in Bombay. The book was adapted for a movie of the same name.

4. Once I was invited to a Sunday mutton meal, the meat prepared by the men in their room, their *khanawal* lady providing the bread and the necessary ground spices. Two of

the hosts had obviously had a glass of liquor before the meal, which enabled them to relax enough to carry out their duties as hosts. It is difficult to function as a female investigator in this male world, but it is probably equally hard on the male respondents since they are not used to interacting with women and are ignorant of the proper social behavior called for in various situations. Indeed, one of my problems as a woman was deciding how to occupy myself in the afternoon when everyone else was asleep. No one wanted to talk and there was no place for a female to sleep in one of the rooms. Nor would it have been thought appropriate.

5. Until recently, participation in labor unions was perfunctory, limited to the paying of dues.

CHAPTER 12

TODAY AND TOMORROW

The changes that have occurred in Sugao over the last forty years offer a glimpse into the ways in which development has affected the Indian countryside and the microcosm of its villages. The case of Sugao permits some insight into what can be expected to happen in the countryside, to village life, if the present pattern of change continues. This study of Sugao reveals an economy increasingly linked with the larger region around it, with a particularly strong connection to the metropolitan city of Bombay. The village provides not only cheap labor to the city's industries but also an expanding market for the city's exports, receiving in return remittances of cash and kind that allow the village population, which has outgrown the bearing capacity of its land, to survive. This comes at considerable personal cost, however. Whether this relationship with Bombay will persist despite changes in the city's industrial sector remains to be seen. The changes in Sugao have been initiated largely by forces external to the village, but their impact has been affected, at times quite dramatically, by relationships embedded within the village's socioeconomic structure, itself rooted in a long tradition.

The existing connections of Sugao to the region, and particularly to Bombay, are depicted in figure 8. The major flows out of the village have been of adult working men and agricultural products; the major flows back to the village have been those of remittances in cash and kind. An additional, less easily quantifiable, but nevertheless important flow has been that of values and ideas, transmitted from city to village by means of radio, films, and newspapers; through the content of education, government-sponsored extension work, and the philosophy embodied in the various government programs; and by the returning migrants from the city. The village response to new ideas and values from the city has been to try to retain the old ways and traditional relationships for as long as possible. Observations of life in Sugao and interviews with Sugao people in the village and in Bombay suggest that the counterflow of ideas from the village to the city has been rather negligible. New ideas, values, and philosophies have not sprung up in the soil of the countryside to change the ways and affect the thinking of those in the city.

So ingrained is the dominance of the urban, core culture that even the Panchayat Raj, an institution created specifically to facilitate the filtering of local priorities and decisions up the government hierarchy, functions largely in only one direction, in the flow of decisions down through the various levels of government to the village. Acceptance of hierarchy is part of the Indian ethos, most directly manifested in the continuing acceptance of caste and of such hierarchical structures as the government, and in the acceptance of the dominance of urban culture over rural.

Improved amenities such as clean drinking water, better transport and communication, and the availability (albeit with some difficulty) of modern medicines have contributed to an acceleration of population growth. Despite considerable migration to the city, land-to-person ratios have declined in the countryside. In addition, despite land ceiling and land-to-the-tiller legislation, land distribution is increasingly inequitable. In Sugao in 1977, more than one-third of village land was in the hands of 6 percent of the farmers, while more than half of the small (less than five acres) landowners in Sugao together controlled only 16 percent of the village land. This has resulted in two major categories of migration out of Sugao: the well-to-do, who move by choice for better prospects in the city; and the poor, who move by necessity, no longer able to survive on the soil. The savings of the former, accumulated in the cities, have allowed them and their families to consolidate their positions and perpetuate their dominance in the

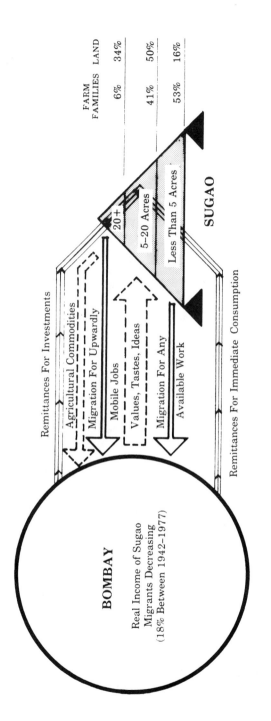

Figure 8: Connections Between Sugao and Bombay

village. The earnings of the latter have been used for consumption and survival, by both the earner in the city and his family in the countryside.

Real income of the Bombay migrants from Sugao decreased by 18 percent between 1942 and 1977 (Brahme 1977). During this time city life grew more difficult, and city jobs became more scarce and therefore more difficult to obtain. Population increases and migration to the city outstripped industrial expansion and the labor absorption capacity of the city-based factories. If this continues, and every indication is that it will (the outcome of the months-long textile strike has illustrated that the industrialists, not the workers, are in control), the potential migrant will be caught in a vise: there will be little increase in opportunity for him in the village economy, and city jobs will be more difficult to obtain and less and less profitable. Eventually, more of those who presently migrate will choose to stay in Sugao and share the poverty there. Bombay will be unable to provide a safety valve for population pressures in the village. Although migration will continue, village production must change so that it can support more of its own people.

How is this to be achieved? There is very little even marginally productive land that has not been brought under the plough. The strategy of increasing land productivity through irrigation is limited by the available water supply, which depends on the monsoons. And, even if the water supply is increased, the benefits, which now pass to the few who already have some water rights, will have to be systematically extended to those who do not. Given the zeal with which such rights are guarded, this will be difficult in Sugao.

Historically, the village has consisted of individual peasant proprietors who tilled their lands independently, with little concern for the common good of the village. Democratic traditions and citizen involvement in civic affairs are not part of the history of Indian village society. The traditional distribution of land between dominant and subordinate groups, and the *inam* system of assuring community services by offering revenue-free land to artisans, maintained a stable system in which village assets were unequally enjoyed. The system was eminently successful in maintaining social inequality while sustaining the community in a dynamic equilibrium. In the old order, every villager had a place where, barring famine or other natural disasters, he and his family could claim at least a bare subsistence.

The British administration did not try to change this set of relationships. And, although the new independent Indian government did, it had very limited success. What was needed was something stronger than the Western social welfare and reform philosophy accepted by the liberal Indian leadership. The demographic balance was quickly changing, a result of the rapid population increases that began in the 1940s. The old order of land distribution became more and more pressured as land became scarce. One not unexpected result of the government's efforts at intervention was that competition and distrust between farmers, and between farmers and tenants, grew. This fragmented the village, further destroying the fragile sense of unity that had existed previously.

Civil courts and a judiciary system patterned after the British one displaced the *panchayat* of village elders, the traditional arbiter of village feuds. The old village *panchayats* were at times repressive, and usually consisted and were biased in favor of the village elites, but they had to temper their considerations with a recognition that the village was one interdependent community and that its individual residents and families had a shared future. The new, more formal, legal system lacks this historical understanding of the reality of social relations in village life. It places even more power in the hands of the elites, who are best able to bear the financial burden involved in using the court system.

Even the minimal collective responsibility which the traditional village system assumed for preserving and maintaining the communally owned village grazing lands and forests has now been shifted to the government. These public lands are badly abused; they are no-man's-land and therefore exploited without concern for the future. The government departments responsible for their conservation find it logistically impossible to protect them from indiscriminate use. The only pressure that can succeed in protecting and revitalizing them will have to come from a local, grassroots recognition of the importance of these lands for the collective good of the village. Only this understanding can create the moral pressure, constant commitment, and surveillance necessary for their preservation.

Lacking this, the pasture lands around Sugao are overgrazed and the hills around the village are completely denuded. The forests have been cut for fuel and timber, and the remaining trees are being stripped for animal fodder. All this has worsened soil erosion. Though individual farmers sometimes invest in soil bunding and conservation on their own land, this does not compensate for the continuing deterioration of communal lands. Subdivision of village lands and the resulting fragmentation of holdings further work against the rational use of the land and the introduction of soil conservation measures.

Despite the attempts at land consolidation, nearly 40 percent of the plots in the village are less than half an acre in size. Unless the land and water resources of the village can somehow be considered as a whole, and unless scientific measures for bunding, leveling, draining, and renewing the forests are designed and implemented, it will be difficult to maintain, let alone improve, the physical resource base of the village. The lack of impact of land-reform legislation on village holdings has shown that it is not a solution to the problem of distribution and rational utilization of village resources.

The problem lies not just in the way natural resources are distributed in Sugao, but in the attitudes of their owners toward each other. In a fiercely competitive environment, one of confrontation and suspicion, each farmer assumes a defensive stance vis-à-vis the rest of the village, spending his energy defending his land and optimizing his return from it. The survival of his family depends on this. At harvest time crops have to be guarded day and night; when fields are being irrigated, the farmer has to guard the sluice round the clock to assure that no one steals from his water allocation. The overall ecology of the village is not

A poor Dhangar must graze his flock on marginal land.

and cannot be a consideration. There is no new social structure to allow for it, nor any remaining tradition that fosters the necessary sense of community.

Farmers with adjoining parcels of land do collaborate during the sowing season, negotiating a planting pattern of complementary crops. There are tangible mutual benefits in doing this. They share the water and energy costs from common wells, trade labor, and arrange to sell cash crops like potatoes and onions in the big cities of Poona and Bombay, where higher prices can be obtained by renting a truck together and sending one or two members of the group to negotiate the sale.

But these farmers know each other and the attitudes of the village people as a whole. No one bothers to plant on the little patches of land surrounding the communally owned wells in the fields, or on the bunds between parcels of land, or in the lanes, streets, and meeting squares of the village. They justifiably fear that they will not be able to keep even a fraction of what they plant in these common lands. The produce probably would be taken by the casual passer-by, the neighbors, or some landless laborer. A greater sense of a collective society, in which everyone can be sufficiently fed, would mitigate against some of this. But the sense of the village as a unit with a collective interest is very slight. As a result, the resources of the village, meager as they are, are suboptimally exploited in an atmosphere of conflict and suspicion. Mutually profitable efforts are not attempted because trust is lacking, a feeling summed up in the Marathi saying about someone who "will cut off his nose to spite his neighbor."

Indian society has been stratified for thousands of years, a hierarchy that has been ritualized and sanctioned by the full force of the Hindu religion. For these thousands of years social status and economic power have gone hand in hand. There has been no equally strong historical precedent legitimizing a more equitable structure. The introduction of a legal system allowed the Indian government to force some changes, in matters of landownership, for instance, but even here the village order has proven to be highly resistant, and the skewed distribution has been perpetuated. As tenacious as the land rights, if not more so, are the bonds that preserve caste loyalties and perpetuate the economic hierarchy that results from them. Presently, there is little to encourage an affluent farmer to share the benefits of development with any but his closest relatives.

Not surprisingly, government programs to promote equity have had little success. Village elites have continued to gain; many of the poor are not better off today than they were forty years ago, and some are poorer. This is true not just in relative terms (such as income distribution becoming more skewed), but also in absolute terms, as in-kind payments of grain and other produce are replaced by wages paid in cash. Rural wages lag behind the increase in market prices, unlike grain and in-kind payments, which are set at a given volume and increase in value as their price increases in the market. Monetization and cash wages represent impoverishment to the village artisan and agricultural laborer.

The flow of agricultural commodities out of the village today includes cash crops, cultivation of which has been encouraged by the agricultural development policy of the government. The more affluent farmers have adjusted best to this economy since they can devote sufficient land beyond that needed to grow subsistence crops and can afford the necessary inputs for cash cropping. Small landowning farmers, unable to take the risks involved, are left stranded. Government programs have tried to help them to take risks—by making credit available for seeds, fertilizer, and well construction, for instance—but these have done little to help the land-poor villagers for several reasons. In some cases the credit offered by the government was acquired by farmers who were actually large landowners, and who changed legal ownership so as to qualify technically for small-farm loans. In other cases, in which the credit recipient was a bona fide small farmer, insufficient credit was extended to buy, for example, all the inputs necessary to increase yields dramatically, or to dig a well deep enough to assure a steady supply of water.

Alternative strategies to help small farmers become more self-sufficient by increasing their ability to provide for their subsistence

needs before helping them to grow cash crops have not been
promoted. The emphasis in agricultural extension has been on
increasing cash-crop yields. The shift to newer crops such as the
quicker-maturing hybrid *jowar* has been detrimental to the diet of
poor villagers since it precluded simultaneous cultivation of the
pulses and vegetables on which the family traditionally subsisted.
The absence of such crops has resulted in an impoverishment of the
family diet. Similarly, the success of so-called cooperatives to
collect milk and eggs from the villages for sale in the city has
resulted in decreased consumption of these foods by rural people.
With the gradual shift toward the consumption of products from the
city, purchased with cash, land-poor farmers have become more
strapped for cash and have been selling whatever they can to the
detriment of their own diets and well-being.

Formerly, the caste structure achieved a stable, if inequitable,
socioeconomic order. Social status and occupation went together
and little occupational mobility was possible, but the village
economy provided for those who were part of that order. The
increased connection of the village to the city and the region and the
monetization of the rural economy have undermined this stability
and the assurance of a legitimate, supported place in the village
order. Caste relationships are gradually being overlaid by class
awareness, and a new economic balance is evolving. The sense of
security traditional village society imparted to all its members,
providing each person with a defined role and an assurance of a
livelihood, has been replaced by general distrust and competition.
In the new order the rich farmers prosper while the poor grow
poorer and increasingly insecure. Unfortunately, this situation is
the foundation on which the desired relationships of tomorrow must
be based.

Although it can be argued that full-scale redistribution of
assets and cooperative effort is the most desirable and efficient long-
run solution to Sugao's poverty, this is unattainable in the present
Indian context. The traditional orientation toward making
individual and family gains, even at the expense of the larger
community, has been reinforced by a national development strategy

Basket weavers, among the poorest in Sugao, face a bleak future.

For the grandsons of well-to-do farmers the future is brighter.

that encourages competition and private entrepreneurship, making for barren ground in which to sow the seeds of community spirit.

In Sugao, ties to caste and clan are much stronger than ties to the village. As a result, for example, Jadhavs will work readily at rebuilding the Jadhav meeting square, but they will show up to rebuild one side of the road to Wai only if the Yadavs turn up to do the other side. The artisans, lower castes, and other inhabitants of the village do not participate at all—reflecting their feeling that it is not really their village anyway. Villagers describe themselves as members of one or another of the village clans and claim to be Sugao people only when describing their affiliation to outsiders or when they are in Bombay.

If past experience is any indication, a collective shepherding of village resources based on group action appears to have a low probability of success. There has been little successful cooperative action in any sphere of village activity. Attempts at running jointly owned flour mills, cloth shops, and weavers' credit and materials-purchasing societies have all failed—often because individual members defaulted or embezzled the group's money. Currently there is no cooperative buying and selling of products except through the state-aided credit society, and this too is run for the benefit of the elites. The poor know that this is so. If cooperation is to work, people in the village need to learn, through successful participation, that cooperatives can be more beneficial to them in the long run than any short-term gains from embezzling or defaulting on a cooperative effort.

Caste has stratified Indian society into communal groups for many centuries; it has defined relative social status and economic power by controlling the distribution of productive assets. The case of Sugao illustrates how little this has changed in the last forty years, despite planned intervention by the government. In the old order the extended or joint family assured the mix of men, women, and children needed for subsistence farming and perpetuated an internal hierarchy defining each member's role and responsibilities. Thus caste governed the relationships between communal groups in the village, and the joint family controlled individuals and defined their social spheres (see figure 9).

The post-independence strategy of planned development, with its national, state, and local programs, affected this rural society in a variety of ways. These programs, the products of central or state governments staffed by urban elites, were based on an acquired sense of Western liberalism. They attempted to introduce concepts of equality into a society determinedly committed to hierarchy and inequality, institutionalized in the organization of caste. They reflected a concern for individual freedoms and rights in a society based on the joint family, an institution whose primary concern is perpetuating the kinship group and maintaining the hierarchical power relationships necessary for this within the family. The change unleashed by development programs, with their foreign ideas of egalitarianism and individual freedom, was thus a disequilibriating force challenging the old village order.

The ways in which this struggle has been played out between the old and the new has been described in the preceding pages. Since the significance of caste and family in the entrenched rural order was not fully acknowledged by the new programs, or if acknowledged was unsatisfactorily confronted, they enjoyed a mixed success. The attempts were piecemeal and unintegrated, and as a result their individual and collective impact was not dramatic. Sex, caste, and economic strata strongly determined the ways in which the various programs affected individual people's lives in the village, and determined the opportunities that became open to them. Some useful physical infrastructure in the village was developed, although here too the benefits were differentially distributed to the population. Planning efforts at various levels and on a broad front have sometimes helped to improve conditions for certain village groups or have enabled others to survive who otherwise might not have endured the changes that have occurred in rural society. Achievement of overall social change, however, has been much more modest. Despite the improved indices of development quoted by policy makers on the impact of planning on the countryside— literacy, communications, health, services, and so on—the overall reality of the village's daily life, the reality of sex roles, caste hierarchies, and access to development benefits, has changed only at the fringes, and more so for men than for women. The hold of family and caste remains firm, with little reduction of its control over rural society.

In Sugao two forces have been an exception to this. One is the increased dependence of the family on wages earned by a male worker in the city. Under the traditional joint-family farming mode, all productive assets and farm activities were shared, and individual family members had no reason to feel that they were doing an unfair portion of the work. Wages in the city, however, are paid to an individual holding a salaried job. The wage earner or his spouse begins to question why these earnings should be shared with the joint family. In Sugao, when this happens, there has been a tendency for joint families to break up into nuclear families. This is especially prevalent in cases where the family is land poor and there are fewer reasons for it to remain cohesive.

Another destabilizing force in the urban milieu has been an increased consciousness that transcends class in the organized trade unions. This phenomenon has acquired prominence since 1982 as a result of the strike of the textile workers. The impact of unions is not presently felt in Sugao, despite some attempts by urban groups to mobilize agricultural labor. Unionization and a loosening of the joint family system could allow for a fundamental change in the operation of the village community. Today, while the upper strata in the village have gained through development programs, women, small farmers, landless laborers, and untouchables have been denied many of the benefits. So far it has been inconceivable for members of these groups to cross lines of sex and caste and consolidate along lines of class and social status. They are locked into a have-not position in which, if there are no major shifts in the trends of development, they will always have inferior access to development benefits.

Anyone desiring new roles and responsibilities for these groups might try to consolidate their separately held resources, such as land, labor, animals, capital, and educational and technical skills. With increased political clout achieved from such consolidation, they

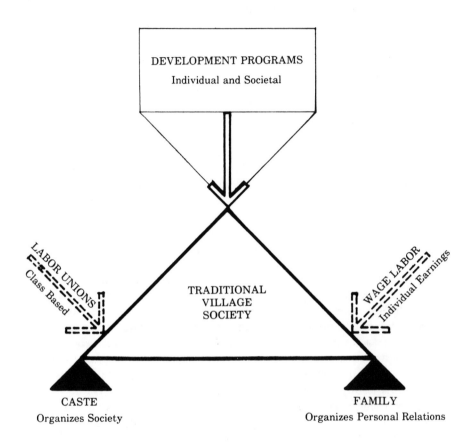

Figure 9: Traditional Village Society and Development Programs

might be able to reorganize the social system in more effective ways so that gains could accrue to the have-not groups within the village. But there are very few forces working to bring about such change. Given the current economics of the village, the existing system is very efficient, since the women and lower castes stay in their traditional roles and provide the labor needed for subsistence farming. These have-not groups in Indian rural society do feel hampered by their situation and by the rigid societal roles imposed upon them. Privately they voice a desire to gain control of their lives, to be less helpless in the village system, to be empowered to use their time and labor with some freedom. However, they do not possess the means with which to break the societal restrictions. Given this, it is unlikely that they will be able to reach beyond their family and peers in the village and make real changes in their lives.

This micro-study of Sugao has highlighted the fact that economic relationships in the village, which underlie power relationships, have undergone little change despite the greatly increased connections to urban areas like Bombay and the country at large. These economics will not change until the allocation of existing assets and power, now distributed by caste, family, and sex, undergoes a radical transformation. Until then, the lives of the poor and oppressed can only be marginally touched by programs intended to uplift them. Change can perhaps be initiated only by forces outside the closely knit village society and its power base. So far the urban migrants from Sugao have not provided this force. Unless this imperative to redistribute power and control of assets is clearly recognized and initiated by those outside the structure, the poor will remain helpless and unable to use their labor and energy to transform their lives. Those who wish to transform rural relationships must squarely face those structural characteristics of Indian society which make it difficult to tilt the balance in favor of the poor.

The human factors that contribute to social transformation and equity are perplexing and only partially understood. The personal, psychological motivations that hinder or aid mobilization for social change must first be understood and then accounted for, both at the scale of the individual and in the context of the social system, if development processes are to take root and flourish. Looking at the success stories of rural change internationally, it appears that there are three reasons why people in social groups cooperate for the societal good: (1) they have some shared utopian idea of the "good society" and are willing to expend the effort needed to actualize it; (2) they are coerced into submitting to societal rules; or (3) there is a crisis and they are cornered, with a choice between cooperating or not surviving at all. Since the first two conditions are unlikely to be fulfilled in any widespread fashion in the near future in India, for reasons that have been illustrated by the attitudes of people from Sugao, it may be that present trends will be radically altered only in the face of a crisis of insurmountable proportions.

CHAPTER 13

CONCLUSIONS

The dynamic of change in the day-to-day life of Sugao results both from the changes initiated by the macro-level development policies, priorities, and programs introduced in post-independence India, and from the internal socioeconomic structure of the village, rooted in historic tradition and culture. Friedmann's theory of polarized development (Friedmann 1973, 41–64), more popularly known as the core-periphery theory, helps to succinctly describe the dynamic of the changing relationship between the periphery (Sugao) and the core (Bombay), describing the nature of the shifting balance between the hinterland and its city. The theory postulates that innovation and transformation of the old order start at the core and diffuse to the periphery. In this process, the political, economic, and spatial dominance of the core is consolidated; in reaction, the peripheral regions form local elites. These elites are well adjusted to the newly evolving order, which is promoted by national policy and able to profit from it. They therefore lobby only for those changes in policy that will increase their share of and participation in the new economy; they are not concerned with promoting, and may even sabotage, policies that would be helpful to the non-elites in the village.

In Sugao, the local elite consists of well-to-do landowners whose families have historically dominated the village polity. This elite group is well adjusted to, and able to profit from, the more monetized economy promoted by macro-level national policy. Its children are educated and able to profit from development. Not surprisingly, therefore, development programs in India intended to promote equity have been largely unsuccessful; there is little commitment to them at either the center or the periphery if it is to be at the expense of the elite.

The dynamic of the development process at work in India, as documented in the microcosm of Sugao, is essentially dualistic. The macro forces operating nationally in India have brought Sugao to its present state. Conceptually one can categorize the villagers' work as of two kinds. The first, that of the fortunate few, is work in the protected, developing, modern sectors of the economy—the mills and industries of Bombay, where migrants work, and cash-crop farming in the village. The second type is work in the traditional sector—employment that is informal, small-scale, unprotected, and of low productivity; both urban and rural, this work includes the labor of landless and subsistence farmers in Sugao and of the hawkers, rag pickers, and domestic servants in the city.

As production in the protected sector has expanded during the development decades, it has captured the market for products in the unprotected sector and displaced jobs in it, producing cheap goods and services that compete with those of the unprotected sector. This has resulted in the gradual displacement of traditional artisans such as the blanket weavers, cobblers, and carpenters of Sugao, all of whom do not find alternate work in Bombay, and in the gradual displacement of small farmers who are unable either to enter into the new cash-crop economy or subsist on their village lands.

This released workforce has had to be absorbed largely by the informal sector, whether urban or rural. In Sugao this absorption has been in agriculture. More and more people, in absolute numbers and as a proportion of total village workers, are now occupied in subsistence agriculture. They try to continue living in the village by supplementing earnings from their land with wages from agricultural labor or by migrating to the city for work. This strategy of "one foot in the city, the other in the village" has proven to be the right one in the face of crises that threaten wage labor, such as the recent textile strike. One can always return to one's ancestral land and try to survive on it.

For most of the displaced there are more opportunities for work in the cities, so there has tended to be migration out of Sugao. This, however, has not prevented demographic growth from occurring in the village. Rural densities have increased mostly on poor land; the best holdings, including most of the irrigated land, are taken up by the larger cash-crop farms. This is clearly illustrated in Sugao, where a great proportion of village land is controlled by a few families and over half the farmers control only 16 percent of the land. The urban and rural protected sectors have continued to expand while the unprotected sectors, both rural and urban, have been impoverished.

If the current structural relationships in Indian society persist and priority in national planning continues to be given to industrial (or formal sector) activity in both urban and rural areas, it is reasonable to expect that the concentration of wealth in the hands of those in protected sectors will continue. The rural, traditional sector will go on absorbing more and more labor and supporting it less and less effectively. As in Sugao, the trickle-over in the form of remittances from formal-sector work might allow those in the traditional sector to survive, but only at a marginal standard of living. As evidenced by the fate of Sugao people, this existence becomes more precarious as formal-sector work becomes difficult to maintain. If rural development is to be achieved in any real egalitarian sense, the lives of the poor in the rural area itself must be improved. New structural relationships that allow for this must be devised, even if they require a dramatic shift in priorities at the national as well as regional and local levels.

Today the Indian economy is essentially capitalist, in which private enterprise and the individual good, not the collective society and collective good, are the governing concerns. Development plans have stressed aggregate growth, in the process of which the rich have gained disproportionately, often at the expense of the poor. Changing this would require tremendous ideological commitment by decision makers, from central-government politicians and planners all the way down to local elites. But, as this is a change detrimental to their immediate and perhaps their long-range interests, there are few compelling motivations for such a change.

Eventually the poor may become militant and demand a greater
share of development benefits. To date, however, the poor in India
have proven to be particularly stoic in accepting their inferior
socioeconomic position.

National and rural development policy in India continues to
foster a dualistic development pattern. Despite dissenting views
about the goals and approaches to development, national plans have
not really shifted emphasis or orientation. The tremendous
economic disparities and stresses created in the social fabric of the
country under the existing model of development become
increasingly obvious. The rich indulge in conspicuous consumption
in the cities and in more covert ways in the village, while the urban
and rural poor share a worsening poverty and misery. Urban living
conditions continue to deteriorate, public services are overloaded,
and rural living is not transformed in any dramatic fashion.
Perpetuating this trend for the next fifty years or more may lead to
an eventual confrontation between the rich and the poor or to mass
starvation (Lo, Salih, and Douglass 1977; International Labor
Organisation 1977; Griffen 1978).

In all fairness, it must be recognized that there are tremendous
forces in the international realm pressuring the national
government to make investments in industry and other corporate
sectors that promise rapid growth. The politics of international
relations mandates extensive investment in the most technically
advanced defense industry. And international development programs encourage greater involvement in the world's international,
capitalist, exchange markets. The programs of major institutions
such as the World Bank and the International Monetary Fund are
solidly entrenched in this concept of international exchange. Opting
out of this process to concentrate on such heretical programs as the
provision of basic needs and equal distribution of benefits, and on
development based on self-reliance and incremental advances in
appropriate, indigenous technology, is not encouraged by the world
order. The present Indian development process shows no inclination
toward making fundamental societal and structural changes that
would empower and mobilize the masses. Participation in and
commitment to the development process by the masses is essential

The economic gap between rich and poor is clearly reflected in housing.

Basic human needs must be met before the poor will be capable of participating in their own advancement.

if the country's urban and rural poor are to break out of their bondage.

It is my position that alternatives do exist: not easy ones that will result in instant development, but alternatives that would, given time, commitment, and political will (by both policy makers and the masses), result in a saner, more manageable world. The necessities for a full and fulfilling life would be produced for everyone, along with a greater mandate to share. The country's entire population, not just the privileged minority, would benefit and prosper from development, enabling all to lead more satisfactory lives.

To address this problem, development theory has suggested several possibilities for improving the lot of the poor through planned intervention. Three of these are worth noting. The first, and the only one implemented to date in India, is the trickle-down theory (Hirschman 1958; Rostow 1960). It advocates stimulating more rapid growth in formal sectors of the economy through urban industrialization and rural shifts to cash cropping. Globally this has tended to be accompanied by rapid outmigration from the informal, traditional, rural sector, which consists of the subsistence activity of the small farm. The effects of this approach were observed in Sugao and have been described. It was found that the urban-industrial sector has not grown rapidly enough to absorb all the potential migrants from the village. The real incomes of industrial workers who migrated and found jobs in Bombay have been falling, and more of the village workers have crowded onto village land trying to earn a living from agriculture. Stimulation of cash cropping and attempts at rural industrialization have not been successful in creating appreciably more employment for the people of Sugao. The rural economy appeared to be neither stimulated nor expanded through the spread effects of increased income. Few of the spread effects anticipated by the proponents of the trickle-down theory were observed in Sugao.

A second approach, which so far has not been emphasized in India, would be to stimulate growth of agricultural output in the informal, small-scale, unprotected, low-productivity, rural sector.

This could be achieved by improving the access of poorer landowning farmers to irrigation, and by emphasizing, in both agricultural research and extension, techniques of intensive farming for crops produced primarily for local consumption. The focus of agricultural research would shift from high-yield seed varieties that require large amounts of fertilizer and water (the so-called Green Revolution package) to increasing yields from small parcels of dry land. Such holdings are the predominant ones owned by the poor in Sugao. Agricultural research would work to increase yields by improving strains of indigenous varieties, which are hardy and better adapted to local conditions and do not disrupt the cropping pattern that has evolved through the years. Often the yield of these varieties can be increased by additional, more careful application of green manure and lower quantities of organic fertilizer and water than are required for high-yield varieties. Since more food would be produced for local consumption and less for exchange (which currently enables the villagers to buy goods and services from the outside), there would have to be a corresponding reduction of such outside purchases as chemical fertilizer. Use of fertilizer can be greatly reduced by development of the more appropriate seeds, and by introducing green manuring practices through scientific crop rotation and by the application of organic manure and treated night soil. A careful crop-rotation plan could be devised to maintain soil quality, and varieties that revitalize the soil, such as alfalfa or pulses, could be cultivated.

This alternative development strategy would help the rural landless and land poor in Sugao only to the extent that farm labor requirements would increase as cultivation became more intense on small farms. People could also be absorbed into nonagricultural, service-related activities or rural industries if higher farm incomes led to increased demand for goods and services produced at the local level. This seems unlikely if current industrial policy at the national level is not changed to favor rural areas. As was observed in Sugao, the present trend is for the rural demand for services and consumer goods to be met increasingly by urban industry.

The third alternative is to introduce a fundamental redistribution of assets and income from the rural rich to the rural poor and to change the development emphasis from the urban to the rural sectors of the economy. This is the most radical and dramatic of the three approaches, entailing on ongoing revolution that would result in programs similar to those now in place in China, Tanzania, Cuba, and Israel. The case of Sugao illustrates the need for fundamental structural change, both social and economic, if rural conditions are to be improved for the poor. In a primarily agrarian country like India, if a real commitment to a development policy aimed at the collective good is assumed (and this assumption itself is challenged by many), rural development must become the primary focus of national development policy. Budget allocations and fiscal priorities must reflect this, and the emphasis must shift from achieving industries-led aggregate growth to fulfilling the basic biological needs of all the people, increasing the self-sufficiency of rural areas, and restructuring the social organization so as to foster cooperation and participation. Among other things, this will involve choosing specific technologies to be adopted (with a view to increasing employment) and a careful meshing of the scale of activities chosen. Development schemes in urban areas and in rural towns and villages must be complementary, and not competitive as at present.

As outlined in the literature, the critical components of this new strategy are:

1. A political and economic commitment to rural development as the leading edge of national development.

2. A clear philosophical and ideological commitment to development for the collective good.

3. The formulation of strategies complementary at the national, regional, and local levels.

4. An effective effort to capture the national imagination and mobilize the population to bring about a dedicated restructuring of traditional society and the adoption of new values.

In this approach the emphasis shifts from industries-led aggregate growth and trade in the international marketplace to fulfilling the basic needs of the population while increasing the self-sufficiency of rural areas.

In this context a number of authors have written about the need to create local, autonomous, self-sufficient regions and subregions, consisting of appropriate numbers of villages and town centers functioning as viable economic entities able to meet most of the area's needs. There is a territorial, spatial foundation to this. A large body of literature deals with the theory of growth centers and with methods aimed at identifying the services and industries most needed to encourage more autonomous regions. In India, E. A. J. Johnson has been a particularly noted proponent of this strategy (Johnson 1970). There is growing international recognition of a self-reliant model of national development in which there is a concern for the quality of life, ecological balance, and cooperative and communal efforts, as well as an emphasis on rural development (Friedmann 1976; Friedmann and Weaver 1979; Streeton and Burki 1978).

A doctrine of self-reliant rural development is difficult to elaborate because at the action level it is a micro-scale concept, location specific and not definable in any universally accepted way. It is territorially based and grounded in local conditions, drawing on locally available assets, their quality and availability, and the sociocultural and historical conditions of a region. It entails different strategies for regions and subregions and is affected by the existing rural-urban relations of each. Despite this some general statements can be made.

If this sort of policy is adopted, a larger share of the national budget must be allocated to rural development. The emphasis of rural-development programs would have to be on production of goods and services meant primarily for local consumption, providing adequate food, shelter, and clothing for the whole population and enhancing the standard of living in rural areas. The goal is to increase self-sufficiency by encouraging the production of goods and services that have "use value" at the local level rather than exchange value in the national or global marketplace. A balance must be struck between production for local consumption and production for exchange within the region. Such a balance must be constantly redefined and modified in response to changing needs.

Today, the domestic Indian economy is relatively large, considering the level of its imports and exports, which accounted for only 4 to 5 percent of gross national product in 1980–81. It is therefore feasible in India to concentrate on development of the domestic economy, while acknowledging that some components of it must be geared toward production for export. An explicitly dualistic economy is implied: a small but technically sophisticated sector, catering to the demands of the international community of nations and producing for world trade and interaction; and a much larger sector oriented toward domestic concerns and the satisfactory provision of those goods and services required to meet the basic needs of the population. The main focus would be upon the domestic economy, on bringing about self-sufficiency, and on raising the standard of living of all people, but especially of the poor. In designing strategies, a major concern would be to evoke participation and mobilization of all strata of society because experience during the last four development decades indicates that self-sustained development cannot be attained without such commitments by the masses.

The formulation of a new direction for development is obviously a monumental task. It must be based on the belief that real development will occur only when people's priorities change and society itself is restructured. The welfare of the group must be considered as important as individual gain, if not more so. The struggle for personal wealth and material goods must give way to a struggle for better conditions for the entire population and for enhancing the quality of human existence in balance with the natural environment. This kind of development alternative has been criticized for being too "biological" in its emphasis and priorities. "What about," ask the critics, "the noble spirit of man? Who will address his intellect, his creativity, his imagination? These have no place in a monumental effort aimed solely at feeding and clothing an entire population." Such reservations are well founded. The basic-needs orientation does concentrate first and foremost on providing food, shelter, and clothing for those who are presently denied them. However, a basic-needs policy should be considered only a necessary first step. The goal is not to promote material acquisition in perpetuity, but to assure each human being freedom from starvation. People are better able to think and dream when their bellies are full and their children are clothed and sheltered. Before that is achieved, it is a mockery to urge upon them the refinements and dilemmas of the intellect.

There is growing evidence to support the belief that rising standards of living result in such changes as lower rates of population growth. This supports the theory that once basic biological needs are satisfied people begin to take control of their lives and make the changes necessary to achieve a more enlightened existence. An alternative, rural-based, self-reliant, development strategy for India is unabashedly suggested here with full confidence in the ability of the Indian people to move from the purely biological and material aspects of life to a creative level that will allow a full blossoming of the human potential.

EPILOGUE

My last visit with Sugao people began in Bombay on Christmas Day, 1984. Because of the holiday, traffic was lighter than normal, and my taxi driver made good time. Yet it seemed to me that overall traffic had worsened tremendously during the fifteen months since my last visit. I discovered to my surprise that it was now very difficult to cross even minor streets during the rush hour. A steady, noisy, variegated stream of vehicles blocked passage for all but the most fearless and experienced Bombay pedestrian.

Indeed, the overall quality of life in most Indian cities has not improved with the passage of time. For example, the level of ambient noise in even the smaller industrializing cities has become almost debilitating to an outsider, and must take its toll on the inhabitants as well. The high decible levels were brought home to me on this trip in a simple and nontechnical way. A musical teddy bear, a gift for a new nephew, had sounded cheerfully loud when I bought it in a toy store in Ann Arbor. It was practically inaudible in Bombay. When I took it to Nasik, an ancient Hindu city that has undergone tremendous expansion as a result of its designation as an industrial growth center, my nephew was charmed by the toy. But he had to hold the bear close to his ear in order to hear its song. I first suspected that American technology had failed me, but I was wrong. In the quiet of the Nasik night the stuffed bear's song was loud and clear once again.

The quality of life in the cities of many other developing countries has similarly deteriorated across a number of sectors.

289

Congestion and inadequate housing, expansion resulting in daily commutes of three to four hours, overextended water systems delivering increasingly polluted and inadequate supplies, lack of sanitary facilities, air pollution—all the conventional indicators show deterioration. The quality of life for most people has clearly not improved in the industrial cities of India.

In the aftermath of the long textile industry strike any "bright lights and glamour" that life in Bombay may have formerly represented for the Sugao migrant have faded. It was a very glum group with whom I tried to get reacquainted on Christmas Day. The strike had been debilitating, psychologically as well as economically, although most workers were not ready to say that it had failed. That would have meant admitting that the many months of economic hardship and personal struggle were wasted. But no one I spoke to from Sugao claimed that the strike had served them well. Only Pawar, the Sugao workers' leader and former mill jobber, continued to claim that the strike was not truly over. But despite his disclaimers, he too looked older and defeated. For the first time in all the years I have known him he sounded disillusioned with the Bombay dream. He was one of the few from Sugao who had claimed that they would live out the rest of their lives in the city. This time Pawar told me that he had reconsidered. The strike had soured the atmosphere around the mills for him. Bombay life was now tiring. He and his wife were building a house on the outskirts of Sugao and were going back to till their land and spend their last years in peace. Even for a relatively affluent worker like Pawar, the city had failed to become a permanent home.

After the strike, all the Sugao men were reemployed in the textile mills, except two who were suspected of being union activists. During the strike most had returned to Sugao to live. During that time many worked under a rather successful employment guarantee scheme introduced in Maharashtra State in 1978. The program was designed to provide guaranteed work at minimum wages for rural people. During the period of the strike it was instrumental in financing the labor to dig several wells in Sugao. Pawar claimed that twenty-seven new wells were dug while the textile workers were on strike. Consequently, he said, much more land in Sugao is now irrigated. In addition, he claimed that several piped water schemes had been developed to irrigate more land. This seems to confirm the claim of some that the growth of urban industry in India and its claim on the most able and productive men in the rural hinterland has been detrimental to the full flowering of rural development. The rural potential for growth and the creation of jobs have been stymied by the attention and resources lavished on urban, formal-sector growth and industrial development.

The Sugao migrants, in their conversations with me, have always expressed a preference for rural life and the village community. As jobs disappeared in Bombay they voted with their feet and returned to Sugao to eke out a living there. Factory wages keep them in Bombay, but, given the choice to earn equivalent wages in the village, most would prefer to live in the countryside. They have repeatedly told me that this is so.

Indian development policy has clung tenaciously to the concept of urban, industrial growth as the leading edge of development. Policies and budget allocations have reflected this bias. Investments in rural agriculture have been largely in support of the formal, cash-cropping cultivation dominated by the more affluent farmer. The disenfranchisement from the land of the poor and marginal farmers and their migration to the cities have been seen as necessary. So too has the consequent deterioration of city life. They are explained away as the price the nation pays on its way to a better tomorrow.

Recent events have raised doubts about the advisability of the policy: the leakage of poisonous gas from the Union Carbide pesticide plant in Bhopal that killed thousands of the city's inhabitants; the fragmentation and efforts to secede from the federal republic by such regions as the Punjab; the lagging behind of regions or people, such as native Assamese in Assam. All these have raised troubling questions about the long-range prospects for this model of development. The unevenness of development, the spatial maldistribution of benefits, and a widening in social stratification are all beginning to manifest themselves.

That rural development should and must occur, and that there need to be more opportunities for men to stay in their own villages, have been illustrated by the case of Sugao. This book has described the personal accommodations and psychological adjustments made by Sugao people. The cost of development has been high. It is by no means clear that the benefits have been commensurate with the pain; certainly they have not for people who were poor to begin with. A vast improvement in the quality of life, which is after all what the struggle to develop is all about, has not resulted. This book is one more call, among an increasing number, to take careful stock of what we have achieved and what we have not during the decades of development. The costs of predominantly industries-led development continue to outweigh the benefits. We must have the courage and boldness to find a new way.

Table 1: Caste Distribution of Sugao Population Inside and Outside the Village (percentages)

	1942		1958		1977	
	Inside	Outside	Inside	Outside	Inside	Outside
Marathas	67	57	68	59	70	64
Dhangars	10	8	8	10	7	9
Artisans	11	11	10	9	11	9
Neo-Buddhists	9	20	9	18	6	14
Others	3	4	5	4	6	4
Total	100	100	100	100	100	100
Number of persons	1621	271	2040	488	2583	737

Source: Full-census surveys of households in Sugao in 1942–43 and 1958–59 by the Gokhale Institute of Politics and Economics, Poona, and a similar survey of the village by the author in 1976–77.

Table 2: Family Type in Sugao and Adult Male Migration (percentages)

Family type	1942	1958	1977
1. Joint (all adult males living in Sugao)	19.3	14.1	13.2
2. Joint (at least one adult male living in Sugao)	26.0	26.7	33.1
3. Joint (all adult males outside Sugao)	6.7	6.2	6.3
Total joint families	**52.0**	**47.0**	**52.6**
4. Nuclear (one adult male in Sugao)	30.9	31.0	27.2
5. Nuclear (no adult male in Sugao)	8.9	13.1	13.4
Total nuclear families	**39.8**	**44.1**	**40.6**
6. Women alone, no male relative	7.7	6.9	6.1
7. Men alone	0.6	1.9	0.8
Total percent*	**100.1**	**99.9**	**100.1**
Total number of families	**327.0**	**419.0**	**493.0**
Percentage of families with no adult men in Sugao (nos. 3 + 5 + 6)	**23.3**	**26.2**	**25.8**

* Totals more or less than 100 due to rounding.

Source: Same as table 1.

Table 3: Sugao Migrant Workers in Bombay

Occupation	1942			1958			1977		
	M	F	Total	M	F	Total	M	F	Total
Textile mill worker	135	—	135	184	4	188	195	1	196
Percent			*67*			*58*			*41*
Factory worker	8	—	8	8	—	8	46	—	46
Percent			*4*			*2*			*10*
Police/military	2	—	2	12	—	12	51	1	52
Percent			*1*			*4*			*11*
Clerical and white-collar	1	—	1	9	1	10	45	4	49
Percent			*0*			*3*			*10*
Self-employed	3	3	6	10	3	13	13	1	14
Percent			*3*			*4*			*3*
Services: domestic, hotel, etc.	12	3	15	22	11	33	35	4	39
Percent			*7*			*10*			*8*
Other work	35	1	36	58	2	60	83	—	83
Percent			*18*			*19*			*17*
Total Earners	196	7	208	303	21	324	468	11	479
Percent			*100*			*100*			*100*

M = Male   F = Female

Source: Same as table 1.

Table 4A: Education by Sex of Residents of Sugao and Sugao Migrants

Education	1942			1958			1977		
	M	F	Ttl.	M	F	Ttl.	M	F	Ttl.

Number of Sugao Migrants of All Ages

Education	M	F	Ttl.	M	F	Ttl.	M	F	Ttl.
No formal educ.:									
Illiterate	106	36	142	99	67	166	42	51	93
Able to read	1	0	1	3	0	3	5	0	5
1st-3d grade	33	1	34	60	5	65	44	16	60
4th-7th grade	64	2	66	154	11	165	192	32	224
8th-10th grade	0	0	0	16	0	16	103	17	120
Secondary School Certificate	0	0	0	16	0	16	103	5	108
I.T.I., Teacher Diploma, etc.	0	0	0	2	1	3	23	2	25
Some college	0	0	0	0	0	0	14	0	14
College degree	0	0	0	0	0	0	15	1	16
Total persons	204	39	243	350	84	434	541	124	665

Percentage Distribution of Sugao Migrants of All Ages

Education	M	F	Ttl.	M	F	Ttl.	M	F	Ttl.
No formal educ.:									
Illiterate	52	92	58	28	80	38	8	41	14
Able to read	0	0	0	1	0	1	1	0	1
1st-3d grade	16	3	14	17	6	15	8	13	9
4th-7th grade	31	5	27	44	13	38	35	26	34
8th-10th grade	0	0	0	5	0	4	19	14	18
Secondary School Certificate	0	0	0	5	0	4	19	4	16
I.T.I., Teacher Diploma, etc.	0	0	0	0	0	1	4	2	4
Some college	0	0	0	0	0	0	3	0	2
College degree	0	0	0	0	0	0	3	0	2

Table 4B

Education	1942			1958			1977		
	M	F	Ttl.	M	F	Ttl.	M	F	Ttl.

Number of Sugao Residents Over Age 7

Education	M	F	Ttl.	M	F	Ttl.	M	F	Ttl.
No formal educ.:									
Illiterate	326	689	1015	247	712	959	183	623	806
Able to read	1	1	2	4	3	7	7	7	14
1st-3d grade	105	17	122	155	136	291	175	192	367
4th-7th grade	119	7	126	273	59	332	347	315	662
8th-10th grade	1	0	1	23	0	23	120	43	163
Secondary School Certificate	0	0	0	3	1	4	43	25	68
I.T.I., Teacher Diploma, etc.	0	0	0	3	1	4	9	3	12
Some college	0	0	0	0	0	0	13	4	17
College degree	0	0	0	0	0	0	13	3	16
Total persons	552	714	1266	708	912	1620	910	1215	2125

Percentage Distribution of Sugao Residents Over Age 7

Education	M	F	Ttl.	M	F	Ttl.	M	F	Ttl.
No formal educ.:									
Illiterate	59	96	80	35	78	59	20	51	38
Able to read	0	0	0	0	0	0	0	0	0
1st-3d grade	19	2	10	22	15	18	19	16	17
4th-7th grade	21	1	10	39	6	20	38	26	31
8th-10th grade	0	0	0	3	0	1	13	4	8
Secondary School Certificate	0	0	0	0	0	0	5	2	3
I.T.I., Teacher Diploma, etc.	0	0	0	0	0	0	1	0	1
Some college	0	0	0	0	0	0	1	0	1
College degree	0	0	0	0	0	0	1	0	1

M = Male   F = Female

Note: Percentages total more or less than 100 due to rounding.

Source: Same as table 1.

Table 5: Permanent Out-migration of Sugao Residents in 1958 and 1977

Place Migrated To	1958			1977		
	Male*	Female*	Total	Male†	Female†	Total
Bombay	2	1	3	26	21	47
Vele or Wai *taluka*	6	7	13	12	10	22
Satara District	2	—	2	6	2	8
Poona	—	—	—	4	2	6
Other	—	1	1	1	3	4
Father's house	—	11	11	—	15	15
Don't know	10	7	17	44	59	103
Total	20	27	47	93	112	205

* Between 1942 and 1958 male out-migration was 1.2% of total Sugao population in 1942 (1,621 persons), and female out-migration was 1.7% of the same.

† Between 1958 and 1977 male out-migration was 4.6% of total Sugao population in 1958 (2,040 persons), and female out-migration was 5.5% of the same.

Source: Same as table 1.

Table 6: Land Distribution in Sugao by Size of Farm

Land-holdings*	1942		1958		1977	
	No. of Families	Land Held†	No. of Families	Land Held	No. of Families	Land Held
1.0 or less	26	13.50	31	16.60	35	17.20
1.1 to 1.5	10	12.10	22	24.90	34	38.36
1.6 to 2.5	25	49.72	28	53.46	54	102.06
2.6 to 3.5	27	82.92	36	103.16	47	149.84
3.6 to 5.0	22	94.70	40	168.56	43	183.20
Subtotal	110	252.94	157	366.68	213	400.66
Percent	*37*	*9*	*44*	*12*	*53*	*16*
5.1 to 7.5	42	269.10	46	284.56	52	309.64
7.6 to 10.0	43	371.94	53	456.22	42	359.70
Subtotal	85	641.04	99	740.78	94	669.34
Percent	*28*	*22*	*28*	*24*	*24*	*21*
10.1 to 12.5	26	284.94	31	343.32	33	368.42
12.6 to 20.0	44	664.50	35	551.56	34	541.66
Subtotal	70	949.44	66	894.88	67	910.08
Percent	*23*	*33*	*18*	*29*	*17*	*29*
Over 20.0	36	1032.40	37	1119.86	25	1047.83
Percent	*12*	*36*	*10*	*36*	*6*	*34*
Total	301	2875.82	359	3122.20	399	3117.91
Percent	*100*	*100*	*100*	*100*	*100*	*100*
Landless	26	0	60	0	94	0

* Landholdings in adjusted acres. One acre of irrigated land equals four acres of nonirrigated land.

† Land held in acres.

Source: Same as table 1.

Table 7: Land Distribution in Sugao by Caste or Kin Group

Caste or Kin Group	Land Held in Acres with Percentages									
	1818-1876	%	1920	%	1942	%	1958	%	1977	%
Yadav	732.2	34	648.6	31	639.2	30	644.0	30	890.90	41
Jadhav	825.4	38	607.6	29	526.0	24	529.0	24	714.26	33
Kochale	78.7	4	97.9	4	107.0	5	110.7	5	116.31	5
Dhangar	14.0	—	42.6	2	65.4	3	62.5	3	65.66	3
Mahar	52.8	2	52.8	3	52.8	2	52.8	2	52.28	2
Pahune	—	—	106.6	5	176.5	8	189.8	9	186.40	9
Balutedar	—	—	112.7	5	101.9	5	97.0	5	102.90	5
Brahman	—	—	96.1	4	95.3	4	50.3	2	—	—
Rastes	274.8	13	363.7	17	363.7	17	362.5	17	—	—
Others	198.0	9	—	—	47.5	2	76.9	3	46.79	2
Total	2175.9	100	2128.6	100	2175.3	100	2175.5	100	2175.5	100

Source: Same as table 1; for 1920, District Office land records. Empty entries reflect unavailable data.

Table 8: Main Occupations of Sugao Workers

Occupation	Number of Earners								
	1942			1958			1977		
	M	F	Total	M	F	Total	M	F	Total
Cultivation	238	355	593	279	483	762	342	616	958
Percent		*60.0*	*76.5*		*63.0*	*75.7*		*64.0*	*73.4*
Agricultural labor	16	48	64	40	59	99	54	140	194
Percent		*75.0*	*9.5*		*60.0*	*11.3*		*72.0*	*16.6*
Cattle herding	11	3	14	8	1	9	4	4	8
Attached farm	2	–	2	5	–	5	5	–	5
Subtotal	267	406	673	332	543	875	405	760	1165
Percent		*60.0*	*86.0*		*62.0*	*87.0*		*65.0*	*90.0*
Production artisan	36	23	59	35	21	56	23	19	42
Service artisan	23	10	33	21	7	28	12	8	20
Trade	5	3	8	7	3	10	13	2	15
Construction	5	–	5	14	3	17	9	2	11
Services	3	–	3	14	1	15	28	4	32
Other	–	–	–	2	2	4	7	3	10
Subtotal	72	36	108	93	37	130	92	38	130
Percent			*14.0*			*13.0*			*10.0*
Total earners working in village	**339**	**442**	**781**	**425**	**580**	**1005**	**497**	**798**	**1295**
Earners working outside village	196	7	203	303	21	324	468	11	479
Outside male earners as percentage of total male earners	*37.0*	–	–	*42.0*	–	–	*48.0*	–	–

Source: Same as table 1.

Table 9: Crop Pattern in Sugao (percentages)

	Crop	1942	Ttl. %	1958	Ttl. %	1971	Ttl. %	1976	Ttl. %
Cash crops	Sugarcane	.71		2.11		4.76		4.71	
	Turmeric	.97		.97		.38		.24	
	Potato	3.09		2.74		1.43		1.41	
	Groundnut (peanuts)	3.13		4.21		5.87		5.64	
	Ghevada (broad beans)	.44	8	1.69	12	2.12	15	2.82	15
Food grains (cereals)	Paddy	.31		.42		.32		.47	
	Bajra (millet)	42.78		22.54		24.31		14.12	
	Kharif jowar† (millet)	1.55		1.48		1.42		9.41*	
								8.71	
	Rabi jowar (indigenous millet)	29.58		45.51		49.68		42.35	
	Wheat	2.65	77	1.69	71	.86	76	.94	76
Pulses	Gram	3.75		6.32		.57		.71	
	Other pulses	7.95	12	6.32	13	2.49	3	2.82	3
Others	Oilseed	2.21		3.16		4.50		4.24	
	Other crops	.88	3	.84	4	1.29	6	1.41	6
	Total	100.00	100	100.00	100	100.00	100	100.00	100
	Gross Cropped Area	2265.0		2373.0		2026.4		2125.0	

* *Ghasar matki*, which is an inferior *jowar*.
† Hybrid *jowar*, which is now predominantly a *kharif* crop.

Source: Government of Maharashtra, official crop records.

Table 10: Place of Residence of Sugao Individuals in 1942, 1958, and 1977

	In Sugao			Outside Sugao		
	Over 7 Years	Under 7 Years	Total All Ages	Over 7 Years	Total All Ages	Percentage Outside
1942						
Males	552	177	729	204		
Females	714	178	892	39		
Total	1266	355	1621	243	271	17%
1958						
Males	708	222	930	350		
Females	912	198	1110	84		
Total	1620	420	2040	434	488	24%
1977						
Males	910	250	1160	541		
Female	1215	208	1423	124		
Total	2125	458	2583	665	737	29%

Note: Male/female breakdown for migrants outside Sugao under seven years of age was not available.

Source: Same as table 1.

GLOSSARY

Ayurved. Indigenous system of medicine.

Bajra. A variety of millet; pearl millet.

Baluta. A system of personal arrangements in which village artisans render services to families of cultivators and to individuals in the village, in payment for which they receive a share of the farm product, usually cereals.

Balutedars. Traditional artisans in a *baluta* relationship. In Maharashtra a traditional, prosperous village would have twelve different artisans serving as *balutedars.*

Bhakari. A thick unleavened bread made from *jowar* or *bajra.*

Bidi. A cigarette in which the tobacco is rolled in leaves instead of paper. *Bidis* are cheap and smoked mostly by villagers and the urban poor.

Brahmin. Priestly caste; first of four Hindu *varnas*, or orders of society.

Caste. Originally from Portuguese, "caste" has been used to describe the prevailing social order in India and the component groups within that order.

Chambhar. A caste; cobbler.

Chappati. An unleavened bread made from wheat.

Chawl. Tenement structure.

Chula. Open stove made of brick or earth on which food is cooked over burning wood or dung patties.

Deshmukh. District collector or governor.

Deshpande. District accountant.

Gaon. Village.

Gaon Rahati. Literally "village life," a book featuring Sugao village.

Gaonthi. Produced, growing, or made in the country or in villages.

Ghasar matki. A type of millet that can be grown in poor soil.

Ghat. Literally "step"; used to refer to the coastal hills of southern India, e.g., Western Ghats.

Ghevada. Black bean, a variety of broad bean.

Gobar-gas. Bio-gas.

Gram-sevak. Village-level worker (VLW) in the government of India's Community Development Program.

Gur. Brown, unrefined, cane sugar.

Gurav. A caste; priest.

Hamal. A carrier of burdens, a porter, coolie.

Hamali work. Coolie work.

Inam. Gift.

Inam land. Land traditionally free of revenue assessment.

Janata. People.

Janata Housing Scheme. People's housing scheme, a government of India program to provide housing to the landless and land poor.

Jati. Originally referring to occupational categories, "*jati*" now describes various kinship and family forms in which families maintain endogamous relationships.

Jowar. A variety of millet.

Kaikadi. A caste; basket weaver.

Kali (mati). Black (soil), a term used to denote agricultural land.

Khan. A unit of measure, approximately five by ten feet, determined by the size of spanning beams and joists.

Khanawal. An establishment catering meals.

Khanawal bai. A woman who runs a *khanawal.*

Kharif season. The main growing season in winter following the monsoon rains.

Kulkerni. Hereditary office of village accountant.

Lakh. Ten thousand.

Mahar. A caste; village servant.

Mamlatdar. Subdistrict-level, revenue official.

Mandap. Ceremonial awnings and tents.

Mang. A caste; rope maker.

Mawal zone. A belt, twenty to thirty kilometers wide, immediately to the east of the Western Ghats, where rainfall is moderate but well distributed over the year, allowing reliable, rainfed cultivation of diverse crops during the *kharif* season.

Mhot. An irrigation device that lifts water using a leather bag.

Mulani. A caste; butcher.

Muslim. A follower of Islam, the religion founded by Mohammad.

Navi. A caste; barber.

Octroi. A tax on goods entering a village.

Pahndhri (mati). White (soil), a term usually applied to house sites.

Paisa. A coin. Under current coinage one hundred *naya*, or new *paisas*, are the equivalent of one *rupee.*

Panchayat. The coming together of five (*panch*) persons, all village elders, to arbitrate and mediate intervillage matters; the council of a village or caste group.

Panchayat Raj. People's rule.

Parith. A caste; washerman.

Patil. Village headman.

Police *patil.* Village headman who provides police protection at the village level.

Puja. A religious ceremony.

Rabi. Second dry-season, or winter, crop.

Ramoshi. A caste; night watchman.

Rupee. Basic unit of modern Indian currency.

Ryot. Peasant proprietor.

Ryotwari system. A system of individual peasant proprietors; a land tenure system wherein the individual pays taxes directly to the government without a landlord intermediary.

Sari. An unsewn garment worn by Indian women. In Maharashtra the nine-yard *sari* is traditional; the six-yard *sari* is considered "modern."

Sarpanch. Chairman of a *panchayat*.

Sonar. A caste; goldsmith.

Sutar. A caste; carpenter.

Talathi. Salaried village accountant and revenue collector.

Talim. A gymnasium, a place where men gather for exercise and recreation.

Taluka. An administrative division, a subdistrict.

Thal. Land attached to a village settlement.

Thalkaris. Joint proprietors of a village settlement and its attached land.

Toli. A work group or gang.

Vaidu. A caste group of medicine men, originally a nomadic tribe.

Watan. Duty or service.

Watan land. Land traditionally free of revenue assessment as payment for the provision of essential services to the village community.

Zamindar. Revenue collectors for the Moguls who were given outright, by the British administration, the land from which they once collected taxes. Their holdings were large and often cultivated by serfs or tenant farmers under oppressive conditions.

REFERENCES

Brahme, Sulabha
    1977 Role of Peasant Economy in Capitalist Development: Case Study of a Maharashtra Village. Unpublished. Copy at the Gokhale Institute of Politics and Economics, Poona.

Bureau of Economics and Statistics
    1960 *Handbook of Basic Statistics of Maharashtra State.* Bombay: Government of India.

    1974 *Handbook of Basic Statistics of Maharashtra State.* Bombay: Government of India.

    1977 *Handbook of Basic Statistics of Maharashtra State.* Bombay: Government of India.

Connell, John, Biplab Dasgupta, Roy Laishley, and Michael Lipton
    1976 *Migration from Rural Areas: The Evidence from Village Studies.* Delhi: Oxford University Press.

Dalvi, Jayant
    1974 *Chakra.* Bombay: Orient Longmans. English translation by Gauri Deshpande.

Dandekar, Hemalata
    1978 Rural Development: Lessons from a Village in Deccan Maharashtra, India. Ph.D. dissertation, UCLA.

Dandekar, Hemalata
    1980 Gobar-gas Plants: How Appropriate Are They? *Economic and Political Weekly* 15(20):887–93.

Dandekar, Hemalata
1981 Social and Spatial Constraints on Rural Women's Sexuality: Observations from an Indian Village. *Ekistics* 291(November/December):422–26.

Dandekar, Hemalata
1983A *Beyond Curry: Quick and Easy Indian Cooking Featuring Cuisine from Maharashtra State.* Ann Arbor: University of Michigan, Center for South and Southeast Asian Studies.

Dandekar, Hemalata
1983B The Impact of Bombay's Textile Industry on Work of Women from Sugao Village. *Third World Planning Review* 5(4):371–82.

Dandekar, Hemalata
1986 Rural Housing and Infrastructure: The Neglected Frontier in Developing Countries. *Central Papers on Architecture* (Winter):15–29.

Dandekar, Hemalata, and Sulabha Brahme
1979 The Role of Rural Industries in Rural Development. In *Rural Area Development*, edited by R.P. Misra and K.V. Sundaram, 122–43. New Delhi: Sterling Publishers.

Dandekar, Hemalata, and Allen Feldt
1984 Simulation/Gaming in Third World Development Planning. *Simulation and Games* 15(3):297–304.

Dandekar, V. M., and M. B. Jagtap
1959 *Maharashtrachi Grameen Samajrachana* [Social stucture in Maharashtra's villages]. Poona: Gokhale Institute of Politics and Economics.

Dandekar, V. M., and M. B. Jagtap
1966 *Gaon Rahati* [Village life]. In Marathi. Bombay: H. V. Mote Publications.

Desai, Neera
1957 *Women in Modern India.* Bombay: Vora and Co.

Desai, Sudha V.
  1980 *Social Life in Maharashtra under the Peshwas.* Bombay: Popular Prakashan.

Dumont, Louis
  1970 *Homo Hierarchicus.* London: Weidenfeld and Nicolson.

Friedmann, John
  1973 *Urbanization, Planning and National Development.* Beverly Hills and London: Sage Publications.

Friedmann, John
  1976 Two Doctrines of Development. Unpublished.

Friedmann, John, and Clyde Weaver
  1979 *Territory and Function: The Evolution of Regional Planning.* Berkeley and Los Angeles: University of California Press.

Gadgil, D. R.
  1971 *The Industrial Evolution of India in Recent Times, 1860–1939,* 5th ed. Bombay: Oxford University Press.

Government Central Press
  1963 *Gazetteer of the Bombay Presidency.* Rev. ed. Bombay: Government Central Press. Maharashtra State Gazetteers, Government of Maharashtra, Satara District. Revised edition of volume 19 of the original *Gazetteer of the Bombay Presidency* (1885), relating to Satara.

Griffin, Keith
  1978 *International Inequality and National Poverty.* London: MacMillan.

Harris, Nigel
  1978 *Economic Development, Cities and Planning: The Case of Bombay.* Bombay: Oxford University Press.

Heyneman, Stephen
  1979 Investment in Indian Education: Uneconomic? World Bank Staff Working Paper no. 327, May 1979. Washington, D.C.: The World Bank.

Hirschman, Albert O.
    1958 *The Strategy of Economic Development.* New Haven: Yale University Press.

International Labor Organisation
    1977 *Poverty and Landlessness in Rural Asia.* Geneva: International Labor Organisation.

International Labor Organisation
    1982 *Basic Needs in Danger: A Basic Needs Oriented Development Strategy for Tanzania.* Addis Ababa: ILO Job Skills Programme for Africa.

Jagtap, M. B.
    1974 Notes on the Mahars of "Sugao." In Marathi. Unpublished. Copy at the Gokhale Institute of Politics and Economics, Poona.

Jagtap, M. B.
    1975 Notes on the Dhangars (Weavers) of "Sugao." In Marathi. Unpublished. Copy at the Gokhale Institute of Politics and Economics, Poona.

Jagtap, M. B.
    1970 *Wai Talukyachya Poorva Bhagateel Sheti Vikasachi Watchal, 1937/38–1966/67* [The progress of agricultural development in the eastern part of Wai Taluka from 1937 to 1967]. In Marathi. Poona: Gokhale Institute of Politics and Economics.

Jain, Girilal (ed.)
    1983 *The Times of India Directory and Year Book.* Bombay: The Times of India Press.

Johnson, E. A. J.
    1970 *The Organization of Space in Developing Countries.* Cambridge: Harvard University Press.

Johnson, E. A. J.
    1972 The Integration of Agrarian, Commercial and Industrial Activities in Function Economic Areas. In *Market Towns and Spatial Development.* New Delhi: National Council of Applied Economic Research.

Kamat, A. R.
1968 *Progress of Education in Rural Maharashtra: Post-independence Period.* Bombay: Asia Publishing House.

Karve, Iravati
1965 *Kinship Organization in India.* Bombay: Asia Publishing House.

Korten, David
1980 Community Organization and Rural Development: A Learning Process Approach. New York: Ford Foundation. Reprinted from *Public Administration Review*, 1980.

Lewis, John P.
1964 *Quiet Crisis in India.* New York: Anchor Books. First published in 1962 by the Brookings Institution.

Lo Fu-chen, Kamal Salih, and Mike Douglass
1978 Uneven Development, Rural-Urban Transformation, and Regional Development Alternatives in Asia. Unpublished. Prepared for the United Nations Center for Regional Development, Nagoya.

Mandelbaum, David G.
1972 *Society in India*, vols. 1 and 2. Berkeley: University of California Press.

Mayer, Albert, and Associates
1958 *Pilot Project, India.* Berkeley: University of California Press.

Mazumdar, Dipak
1984 The Issue of Small vs. Large in Indian Textile Industry—An Analytical and Historical Survey. World Bank Staff Working Paper no. 645. Washington, D.C.: The World Bank.

Ministry of Information and Broadcasting
1975 *India 1975, A Reference Annual.* New Delhi: Publications Division, Ministry of Information and Broadcasting, Government of India.

Ministry of Information and Broadcasting
    1983 *India 1983.* New Delhi: Publications Division, Ministry
    of Information and Broadcasting, Government of India.

Moseley, Malcolm J.
    1974 *Growth Centers and Spatial Planning.* Oxford: Pergamon
    Press.

Mosher, A. T.
    1976 *Thinking About Rural Development.* New York: Agricul-
    tural Development Council.

Myrdal, Gunnar
    1968 *Asian Drama: An Inquiry into the Poverty of Nations,*
    vols. 1–3. New York: Random House.

Patel, Kunj
    1963 *Rural Labor in Industrial Bombay.* Bombay: Popular
    Prakashan.

Rodwin, L.
    1963 Choosing Regions for Development. In *Public Policy:
    Year Book of the Harvard University Graduate School of
    Public Administration,* vol. 12, edited by C.J. Friedrich
    and S.E. Harris. Cambridge: Harvard University Press.

Rostow, W. W.
    1960 *The Stages of Economic Growth: A Non-communist
    Manifesto.* Cambridge: Cambridge University Press.

Roy, Manish
    1972 *Bengali Women.* Chicago: The University of Chicago
    Press.

Selowsky, Marcel
    1979 *Balancing Trickle Down and Basic Needs Strategies:
    Income Distribution Issues in Large Middle-income
    Countries with Special Reference to Latin America.* World
    Bank Staff Working Paper no. 335, June 1979.
    Washington, D.C.: The World Bank.

Streeton, Paul, and Javed Burki
    1978 Basic Needs: Some Issues. *World Development* 6(3):411–
    21.

Streeton, Paul, with Shahid Javed Burki, Mahbub Ul Haq, Norman
    Hicks, and Frances Stewart
    1981 *First Things First: Meeting Basic Human Needs in the
    Developing Countries.* New York: Oxford University
    Press for the World Bank.

Waterston, Albert
    1965 *Development Planning: Lessons of Experience.* Baltimore:
    Johns Hopkins Press.

Wiser, William, and Charlotte Wiser
    1963 *Behind Mud Walls, 1930–1960.* Berkeley: University of
    California Press.

World Bank
    1983 *World Tables*, 3d ed. Washington, D.C.: The World
    Bank.

Zelliot, Eleanor
    1970 Learning the Use of Political Means: The Mahars of
    Maharashtra. In *Caste in Indian Politics*, edited by
    Rajni Kothari. New Delhi: Orient Longmans.

INDEX

Electricity, 6, 47, 82, 85, 149,
242
Elites, 21, 72, 242, 243, 254,
263, 267, 276, 277
Equity, 21, 22, 25, 27, 28, 32,
69, 138, 139, 234, 261, 266,
267, 271, 278

Family planning, 77, 79, 177
Family
hierarchy, 28, 108
significance, 104, 273
structure, 7, 8, 16, 30, 115,
116, 145, 146, 227, 231,
236, 242, 254, 270–72, 273
Farming, 144–46, 150–60, 261
Farm labor, 113, 122, 129, 147,
155
Farm size, 128, 130, 139, 156,
157, 261
Fertilizer, 20, 26, 151–53, 157,
267, 283
Field methods, 14, 15, 17, 18
Fieldwork, 12, 14, 17
Five Year Plans, 11, 24, 273
Food, 123, 129, 164–68, 200,
214, 226, 234, 238, 239,
256, 257, 268, 285
khanawal, 219, 220, 247, 250
staple, 110
typical meal, 151, 152
Fuel needs, 208, 210

Gandhi, Mahatma, 23, 25, 27
Goats, 198, 204–7
Gokhale Institute of Politics and
Economics, xvii, 16, 18, 19,
30, 132, 140, 145, 167
Goldsmiths, 183, 189

Grazing lands, 209, 210, 211,
263, 264
Green Revolution, 25, 26
Gur, 82, 157, 166, 183, 184

Hamals, 240–42, 288
Harvest, 129, 147, 154, 264
Headman, village, 15, 16, 66,
165
Health care, 24, 75–77, 79, 80,
83–85
Health expenditures, 80
High-yield crop varieties (HYV),
26, 283
Housing, 7, 13, 29, 102, 109,
161, 195, 201, 226, 228,
229, 237, 281
amenities, 6, 84, 110, 201
animal quarters, 196, 201,
205–7
appearance, 1, 5
availability, 16
construction, 180, 181, 190,
201, 239
government role, 32, 65, 68–
70, 238–40
layout, 7, 54, 55, 63, 64, 78,
84, 201
rents, 237, 238
staff housing, 243–46
talim, 233, 234
Hybrids, 268
jowar, 152, 268
lentils, 152
peanuts, 165
Hygiene, 6, 79, 201, 208, 290

Income, 262